T3-BNG-915

Data Warehousing and E-Commerce

Université d'Ottawa
BIBLOTHEQUES

LIBRARIES
University of Ottawa

WILLIAM J. LEWIS

ISBN 0-13-091154-2

90000

9 780130 911544

 Prentice Hall PTR
Upper Saddle River, NJ 07458
www.phptr.com

Library of Congress Cataloging-in-Publication Data

Lewis, William J.

    Data warehousing and e-commerce/William J.Lewis.

      p. cm.

    Includes index.

    ISBN 0-13-091154-2

      1.Data warehousing. 2.Electronic commerce. I.Title.

    QA76.9.D37 L48 2001

    658.8 4 —dc21

                                                    2001021680

Editorial/production supervision: *Vincent Janoski*

Acquisitions editor: *Mike Meehan*

Marketing manager: *Debby vanDijk*

Manufacturing manager: *Maura Zaldivar*

Cover design: *Anthony Gemmellaro*

Cover design director: *Jerry Votta*

© 2001 by Prentice Hall
Published by Prentice Hall PTR
Prentice-Hall, Inc.
Upper Saddle River, NJ 07458

Prentice Hall books are widely used by corporations and government agencies for training, marketing, and resale. The publisher offers discounts on this book when ordered in bulk quantities. For more information, contact: Corporate Sales Department, Phone: 800-382-3419; Fax: 201-236-7141; E-mail: corpsales@prenhall.com; or write: Prentice Hall PTR, Corp. Sales Dept., One Lake Street, Upper Saddle River, NJ 07458.

All products or services mentioned in this book are the trademarks or service marks of their respective companies or organizations. Screen shots reprinted by permission from Microsoft Corporation.

Quotations on page 2: *Building the Data Warehouse*, William Inmon, copyright © 1996 by John Wiley & Sons. Reprinted by permission John Wiley & Sons, Inc.; *The Data Warehouse Toolkit*, Ralph Kimball and Richard Merz, copyright © 2000 by John Wiley & Sons. Reprinted by permission John Wiley & Sons, Inc.; *The Electronic Commerce Dictionary*, Ted Haynes, copyright © 1995 by Ted Haynes. Reprinted with permission. Quotation on page 15: *Building the Data Warehouse*, William Inmon, copyright © 1996 by John Wiley & Sons. Reprinted by permission John Wiley & Sons, Inc. Quotation on page 57: "Ask Marilyn," *Parade*, April 27, 1997. Reprinted with permission from *Parade* and Marilyn vos Savant, copyright ©1997. Figure 4-3 is printed courtesy of Thunderstone Software. Figures 4-7 and 4-7 are printed courtesy of Crystal Decisions, formerly Seagate Software. Quotation on page 103: "The Technical Benefits of EJB and J2EE Technologies over COM+ and Windows DNA," Edward Roman and White Paper, The Middleware Company. Reprinted with permission. Quotation on page 129: Press release, September 25, 2000, announcing the merger of the Meta Data Coalition into the Object Management Group. Reprinted with permission of the Object Management Group.

All rights reserved. No part of this book may be reproduced, in any form or by any means, without permission in writing from the publisher.

Printed in the United States of America
10 9 8 7 6 5 4 3 2 1
ISBN 0-13-091154-2

Pearson Education LTD.
Pearson Education Australia PTY, Limited
Pearson Education Singapore, Pte. Ltd.
Pearson Education North Asia Ltd.
Pearson Education Canada, Ltd.
Pearson Educación de Mexico, S.A. de C.V.
Pearson Education—Japan
Pearson Education Malaysia, Pte. Ltd.
Pearson Education, Upper Saddle River, New Jersey

QA
76.9
.D37
L48
2001

To Becky—for getting me past that one
especially hard chapter…and other things
too numerous to mention

And to Eric and Jenny—the two absolutely
best kids in the entire universe

…you make it all worthwhile.

CONTENTS

FOREWORD

Bill Lewis kept erasing my disk drives. This memory is seared into my consciousness and I have yet to thank him for it. You see, several years ago, Bill and I worked together in the Data Resource Management department at a large regional bank in the Northeast. I was the DB2 DBA and he was the data administrator. We made a good team and I learned a lot from Bill—even though he erased my disk drives.

Bill has as keen a grasp on the business issues of data management as anyone I know. He always thinks about data within the context of its value to the business. Some folks may parrot the often-cited phrase: "We treat data as a corporate asset," but Bill lives and breathes it. As such, he is ideally suited to discuss the marriage of e-commerce to data warehousing. I've had the pleasure of reviewing this book as it was being developed and it offers some cogent insights into the business factors of merging bricks-and-clicks with data warehousing. This book describes in detail how data warehousing and e-business technologies complement and leverage one another. I learned a lot about channels, supply chains, and the impact of data warehousing and the new economy on both. I'm sure you will too.

Whether you are a strategist or technology manager such as a CIO, CTO, or corporate director; a technologist such as a DBA or an application developer; or a business line manager, this book will help you perform better on the job. After reading Bill's book, you'll be able to make better decisions about how to use your data to power your organization in the new economy. And believe me, you'll want to know how to do that! Even if you don't learn to thrive in the new economy, your competitors most surely will. The new economy is nothing if not highly competitive, with everyone looking for time-to-market advantages. If you read, understand, and implement what Bill is saying, you can gain a competitive advantage for your organization.

Now back to those disk drives. Bill didn't do anything as destructive as actually erasing data from real disk drives. Let me explain.

You see, as a DBA, whenever I talked about data, I did it within in the context of the physical database. So, Bill and I were at a design meeting, well before any physical database was to be implemented. I got up to the white board and started drawing my concept of the design. By natural habit, I started drawing the symbol for a disk drive for each new entity. Bill, the data bigot that he is, kept jumping up and erasing every darn disk drive I drew on that board, replacing it with a generic rectangle. His point was that I was jumping into physical issues before we had actually arrived at a conceptual design. That was an instructive lesson for me. And I want to thank Bill for teaching it to me. Now continue reading this book and let Bill teach you something too!

Craig S. Mullins
Houston, TX

INTRODUCTION

What does data warehousing have to do with e-commerce? Is this one book, or really two? Data warehousing is a means to an end; e-commerce is much more an end in itself. But with the ever-increasing importance of data in the digital economy, businesses more than ever need to do their very best in managing every last penny of value out of their digital resources—their *data*. Effective decision support requires effective data management. Data warehousing is an admittedly loosely defined set of techniques and technologies designed to manage data for effective decision support. These same technologies are quite adaptable to managing data assets for e-business.

Data has "come out of the closet." Prior to the widespread implementation of e-commerce, data management was "just" an internal challenge for businesses. Now the rush to the Internet is on, and businesses, in order to stake out a position in the digital marketplace, must expose the state of their data to customers, partners, and even competitors. Ready or not, this requires data integration, or at the very least, an *appearance* of data integration. Data warehousing technologies are fundamental enablers of data integration.

In some ways, this book is an information portal. Much of its content is available from other sources, but "content aggregation" is often a worthwhile task. Much content has been aggregated here with the hope that some value has been added along the chain from supplier to consumer. There are original thoughts here too, some of which have been simmering during a multi-decade journey through the sometimes fascinating landscape of commercial information technology. Then there are also opinions strewn about here and there . . . watch out and step carefully.

Tiosa Corporation Enters the Digital Economy

Tiosa Corporation is a fictional company that we will use as an ongoing example and case study throughout this book. Tiosa is a mid-size firm that provides financial services to the energy and utility industry. It is currently poised at the brink of the digital marketplace on several fronts at once. As various facets of data warehousing and e-commerce are covered in the text, we will visit the offices of Tiosa Corp. to observe how this company confronts these issues as a result of embarking on a "digital strategy."

And away we go . . .

Chapter 1

A Crash (or Collision) Course: A History of Data Warehousing

He who does not remember history is condemned to repeat it.
— George Santayana

The Current State of Data Warehousing and E-Commerce

The focus of individual and collective consciousness naturally tends to be drawn to the new and different, to the disadvantage of the old and familiar. It's not surprising, then, that most of the attention surrounding e-commerce is focused on the enabling hardware and software. In e-commerce, the world-wide network infrastructure, the Web browsers and Web servers, are the fundamentally newer components, therefore garnering the most continuous attention. However, without data, the increased sharing of which is, after all, the underlying basis for the Information Age, all this enabling infrastructure is but an empty frame.

This book will focus on the data aspects of e-commerce. There are of course countless other aspects of e-commerce, but in our admittedly simplistic, data-centric view of the digital economy, everything else that happens in e-commerce is just stuff that happens to data.

When it comes to the data, like *Alice in Wonderland's* Queen of Hearts, sometimes it seems as if we need to run as fast as we can to stay in one place. Here in the early 21st century, we're still trying to get our hands around all the data we accumulated in the late 20th century. As soon as a glimpse of light appears at the end of the tunnel, another IT revolution—client/server, the Web, and who knows what's next—confounds our best efforts, and it seems we are nearly back at square one. All the while, more data continues to accumulate, faster and faster, and in increasingly far-flung locations and disparate formats.

How best should we approach this dilemma, in order to assure our greatest chance of future success? By building on lessons learned from the successes of the past.

If sustained growth is an accurate indicator, data warehousing is by far one of the most successful information technology strategies in the history of commercial computing. For example, in a report by technology research firm IDC, worldwide revenue in the market for data warehouse tools is projected to "increase at a compound annual growth rate (CAGR) of 26 percent from $5 billion in 1999 to $17 billion in 2004."

As a first step in learning how to leverage our past successes for tomorrow's markets, let's take a look at the current state of data warehousing and e-commerce technologies, and how we got to where we are today. To get our bearings, here are some widely accepted definitions for both data warehousing and e-commerce. The most authoritative names in data warehousing define *data warehouse* as

> A collection of integrated, subject-oriented databases designed to support the DSS function, where each unit of data is specific to some moment of time. The data warehouse contains atomic data and lightly summarized data.
> —Bill Inmon, *Building the Data Warehouse*

> A copy of transaction data specifically structured for query and analysis.
> —Ralph Kimball, *The Data Warehouse Toolkit*

And from a similarly authoritative source on e-commerce:

> Electronic commerce is the buying and selling of goods and services, and the transfer of funds, through digital communications.
> —Ted Haynes, *The Electronic Commerce Dictionary*

In this book, we'll be focusing much more on *data warehousing* than on *data warehouses* per se. Data warehousing, in our context, refers to the process and the technologies (the "hows") used to build, maintain, and use data warehouses (the "whats"). Therefore, our objective is to learn *how to leverage our prior successes in the process and the technologies used to build, maintain, and use data warehouses to enhance our chances of success in the buying and selling of information, products, and services via computer networks.*

The market for data warehouses and data marts as autonomous, bundled sets of technologies has evolved and matured. No longer limited to early adopters, they have been deployed by many companies across the technology-adoption curve. Regardless of the success or failure of such efforts, the goals of data management architecture are expanding to encompass more than simply the construction of consolidated data sources. These goals now include the broader mission of making the greatest possible use of any and all available data assets.

Data requirements in today's electronic marketplace are challenging and will become even more so. E-commerce sites have been broadly categorized into business-to-consumer (B2C) and business-to-business (B2B). Many B2C Web sites are of course sales channels for retail businesses, where customers purchase goods sold by the business. Other common B2C sites are for financial services such as banking. These two types vary in their data content, and therefore data-integration requirements.

For example, the data content of a financial services site might include

- *Bank Accounts:* checking, credit, loans, mutual funds, brokerage
- *Products:* interest rates, terms, fees
- *Assets:* holdings in the accounts
- *Transactions:* bill payments, inquiries, account transfers

Financial companies also typically have multiple application systems (usually one per product line) that are the source or target, or both, of the data presented by the Web site's pages.

In contrast, the content of a retail business-to-consumer Web site typically includes the following types of data:

- *Product Catalog Items:* what is being sold
- *Inventory:* how much of each product is available (currently and projected)
- *Order:* how much of what has been ordered by whom, at what price
- *Credit:* how payment is to be transferred between buyer and seller
- *Shipping:* how the products are to be transferred between seller and buyer

- *Customer Profile:* everything the seller has been able to find out about the buyer

Often, these discrete types of data are stored and processed by a separate application system. Complicating matters further, only some—and potentially none—of these systems may be owned and operated by the retailer itself! Establishing and maintaining a reliable infrastructure enabling data to freely and reliably cross organizational and technological boundaries among multiple businesses often requires an unprecedented level of cooperation and coordination.

Existing heritage databases will not be replaced, but must be wired in and synchronized with the databases of multiple inbound and outbound channel applications. (More details on channels will be discussed in Chapter 2.) Data originating through inbound and customer-facing channels must be synchronized with back-office operational data. Orders coming in over the Web must be matched to inventory records, perhaps back-ordered with suppliers, then scheduled for delivery.

A prime example of this is amazon.com. This Web site enables a customer to not only establish an account and immediately begin placing orders, but also to track the status, including shipping information, of any order. A new Web-based business enterprise such as this has the luxury of near freedom from any stovepipe order-entry, inventory, and shipping applications. Such a business, *created* for the digital economy, may be able to enter the market armed and ready with an integrated value chain—and a cohesive data resource—by design. But on the downside, few of these new digital enterprises provide choices of channels beyond the internet...yet.

Such customer-facing Web sites continue to dramatically and irrevocably alter the expectations of their users. The external constituents (and not just customers, as we shall see) of an aspiring digital enterprise will not be content in an environment where the physical location or format of stored data is visible or of any consequence whatsoever. There is no doubt, however, that removing these barriers remains a major challenge confronted by digital business.

On the B2B side, the data challenges are at least as daunting as in B2C. Whereas B2C applications are characterized by large numbers of individual, small events taking place between humans and computers, a typical B2B application deals with fewer participants, and with events that involve larger dollar amounts, taking place in the context of computer-to-computer as well as human-to-computer interactions. In B2C e-commerce, the seller as a rule has control of the format of the data being exchanged. In B2B, the buyers, fewer in number but each with considerably more individual leverage over the seller than in B2C, may in many cases exercise as much or more control over

4

the format of the data being exchanged than does the seller. This state of affairs poses additional data-integration challenges for the seller and presents an opportunity for B2B exchanges, which we will explore in more detail later.

It's the Data, Stupid!
The Means to Many Ends

Data is, and will continue to be, the most stable, most slowly-evolving component of any company's information technology assets. It is the component most independent of the technology itself. It is also unique to each business enterprise—a significant source of its competitive differentiation—and, as such, an invaluable resource. Data is accumulating at accelerating rates, faster than software and hardware technology can address it; hence, hardware and software bottlenecks continue to constrain its usefulness. Not only is a history of facts being accumulated with the passage of time, but more and more replicated information is being created as a result of hardware and software bottlenecks. Software is required both to create the data records and to interpret the accumulated information, causing a need for more software and interfaces.

When computers were first applied to business use, the field of endeavor was named *data processing*. Now, of course, we know the field as *information technology*. But, as a way of getting back to basics, let's look at this thought problem.

A business has a choice of one, and only one, of the following disaster plans:

1. In the event of a disaster, all *hardware devices* and *software programs* in the company's IT inventory—*but no data*—are instantly duplicated at an alternate site, or
2. In the event of a disaster, all of the company's *data only* is instantly copied to an alternate site.

Which is the most prudent choice? Which will enable the business to continue functioning *at all?* Does it then follow that it makes sense to focus our priorities on the unique data resources of the business?

Another way of approaching the problem is from the view that a company's competitors could probably duplicate exactly its entire hardware inventory and the majority of its software inventory, *but its unique data cannot be duplicated* (at least not legally)!

The history of data warehousing is in many respects the story of the ongoing effort to get more value out of the data we have already accumulated, or, stated another way, to put large volumes of data resources to work. The goal is to transform data into action. This history is also characterized by *convergence*. As Figure 1–1 shows, over time many concepts and technologies have been introduced, and consequently influenced and converged with other concepts and technologies. In some cases, ideas may have been introduced before enabling technologies had matured, and when maturity did come, the enabling technology acted as a catalyst.

It's the contention of this book that with the convergence of data warehousing and e-commerce, data warehousing technologies have begun to act as catalysts for e-commerce—and that this catalysis will only intensify as the digital economy matures.

Figure 1–1 describes the progression of various trends in data warehousing technologies over the past 15 years, and how these trends have influenced, morphed into, merged into, or instigated other developments. We'll be discussing and interrelating many of these trends throughout this book.

Business Trends and the Use of Data

Electronic commerce predates the Internet and the explosion of the World Wide Web. Pre-Web e-commerce applications such as EDI (Electronic Data Interchange) were computer-to-computer data exchange; they were *purely* data-intensive. ("Have my computer call your computer.") Furthermore, these data-interchange applications were extremely structured—file layouts, semantics, and syntax were preestablished and rigidly controlled by standards organizations, suppliers, and service providers. Connections were one-to-one. Applications were stable for years at a time. Transfers of data usually took place only a few times daily, after business hours, not on weekends, and seldom crossed international borders.

The Web has brought e-commerce to the masses. Early commercial Web sites were far from data-intensive, being primarily *brochureware*—an electronic billboard, another channel for advertising. The databases were connected to Web sites in read-only mode.

As can be seen in Figure 1–1, from our data-oriented perspective, e-commerce is the latest in a long line of business initiatives that require a broad scope of data—a scope beyond that of a single application system. The most

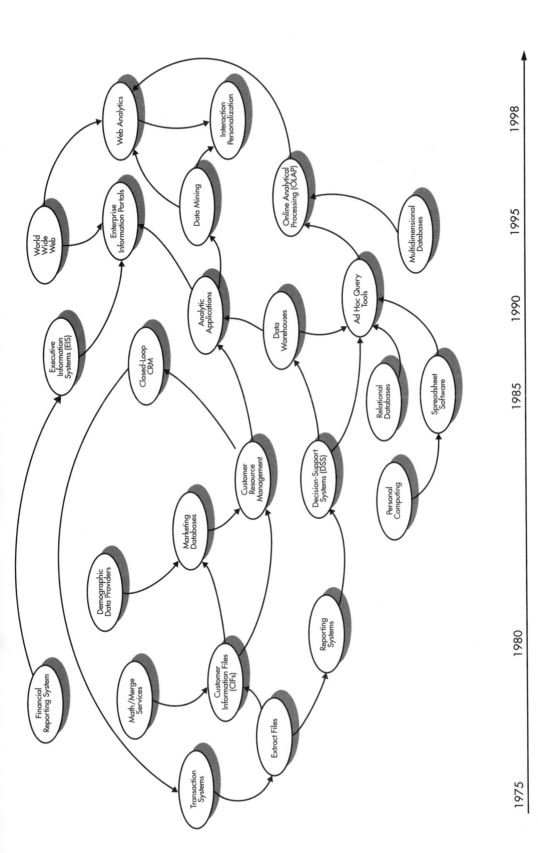

Figure 1-1
Trends and influences in data warehousing, 1975–2000.

common application of data warehousing processes and technologies in business are in support of these initiatives, many of which, as we shall see, are morphing into new forms integral to the world of e-commerce.

The majority of business application systems are built—*applied*—in support of specific business functions. Decision-making is of course a business function, but, in contrast to most other business functions, it creates little data on its own; it is a net *consumer* of data, rather than a *producer*. In the family of business applications, it's the parasitic brother-in-law who just won't leave. It commandeers the television, lays on the couch, raids the refrigerator, and consumes whatever resources it finds available. Luckily, as opposed to "real" resources like food and clothing, in the case of less tangible data resources, we do indeed have a replicator (remember the one in *Star Trek*?) available. We can create copies of data (as many as we need or want) from the applications that do the "real" work for the exclusive use of our decision-making needs.

Thirty or so years ago, under the cover of darkness, reporting systems began to leach data from transactional applications' files and create their own extracts, in formats more easily consumable by corporate decision makers. Impact printers banged out stacks of hardcopy "batch" reports on nightly, monthly, quarterly, and annual bases. Tape reels containing the extracted data were organized, labeled, and hung up in case a report was lost and needed to be rerun.

We'll now take a look in more detail at some of these trends in data-intensive business initiatives. Most of these initiatives came about due to the critical needs of companies to know and understand their finances, their customers, and "the big picture" of the company as a whole.

Know Your Finances

In many companies, the first department that made use of computer application systems was finance. And, predictably, the first business unit requesting reports and extracts for decision-making was the finance department.

Financial Reporting Systems

General ledger (GL) systems were the original decision-support systems: net consumers of data, existing almost exclusively to generate reports. GL systems create little data of their own and require a holistic view of all the financial comings and goings of a business. In many ways, a GL system does look much like a decision support system (DSS), but since the auditability of GL data is absolutely critical, support for alternative views—such as "what-if" analysis and cost and revenue projections—required construction of decision-support capabilities separate and isolated from the accounting system itself. Often, these included copies of the general ledger account files, perhaps organized or selected according to specified criteria (by product or organization, for example) and accessible to users without jeopardizing the source data itself.

Profitability Measurement: Customer, Product, Organization, and Channel

Profitability measurement also requires an enterprise-wide perspective on an organization's data assets. Profitability in general is the measurement of revenue relative to costs within a specific time period and a defined scope—commonly for individual or groups (segments) of customers, products, business units, and/or sales channels. Because of these multiple "dimensions" by which cost and revenue data needs to be viewed, this area has been a fertile one for the application of multidimensional databases and online analytical processing (OLAP) tools.

Continuous monitoring of costs, revenues, and profitability is required for a digital enterprise to remain responsive to changing market and competitive conditions. Monitoring and analysis of transaction activity for customers and products has been common in businesses for some time, but the evolution toward a multichannel interaction model by the digital enterprise mandates that costs, revenues, and profitability *across channels* also be monitored and analyzed. The goal is to both increase the profitability of the most active channels and concurrently increase the activity of the most profitable channels.

Many inbound channels capture data on literally every telephone button-push or mouse-click in every interaction of every customer. This data can be analyzed to determine, for example, how often customers decide to "zero out" to a human operator, rather than using menu options to finish their transaction. A high volume of zeroing-out indicates that menu options and structure may require changes, and also that the per-transaction costs have escalated due to increased involvement of customer service representatives (CSRs). CSRs require salaries, benefits, real estate, and safe working conditions; computer-based interaction units are much less expensive. If electronic channels are made more effective, human interactions are decreased, costs are driven down, and profits rise.

Activity-Based Costing

Activity-based costing (ABC) is closely related to profitability measurement, since capturing, allocating, and measuring costs is essential to calculating profitability. Numerous data-management challenges arise when attempting to define and track costs of activities within the organization. In order to be meaningful, a consistent activity cost measurement structure must be put in place across an entire company. Challenges include achieving all of the following, consistently, throughout the company:

- establishing the scope of what constitutes an "activity"
- capturing activities
- classifying and allocating activities against the production of revenue

If a company can achieve consistent data and process standards for cost accounting, they are far along the way to implementing ABC, and subsequently more meaningful profitability measurement.

Know Your Customer

Whereas transactional systems deal primarily with keeping the business running on a *daily* basis, a class of decision support systems known as *customer management systems* (CMSs) are concerned with optimizing the decision-making of sales and marketing organizations by taking a *long-term* view of the interactions between the business and its customers. The evolution of CMSs has primarily been an effort to steadily decrease the lag time between opportunities for outbound interactions with customers and prospects—from a few times annually to literally real-time.

First-generation marketing systems (mid-1970s to early 1980s) primarily supported intermittent marketing programs, such as direct-mail and mass-marketing campaigns. These programs were executed on a monthly (or less frequent) basis and as such were supported quite adequately with sequential extract files and batch processes. Early on in this generation, companies such as Harte-Hanks and Claritas appeared, from whom demographic data could be purchased for merging with and "enriching" a company's internal transaction data. The resulting increased awareness of geographic, affluence, and household data allowed marketing campaigns to be targeted to those prospects and customers having a potentially greater buying propensity, hence increasing the success rate and ROI of campaign efforts.

In the later 1980s, as marketing DSS evolved into a second generation, more emphasis was placed on increased and more frequent accessibility to extracted and consolidated data, often facilitated by the creation and population of a stand-alone relational database. At the same time, to remain competitive, many organizations attempted to change their fundamental strategy from "product-centric" to "customer-centric." Consolidating data into a single source from multiple transaction systems and attempting to derive customer data from transaction data exacerbated an already existing problem. For multiple sales transactions, the same customer information had often been solicited and recorded multiple times. Companies thus found themselves with "too much" customer information—often with duplicate or nearly duplicate records for the same customer—one for John Smith, another for John A. Smith, another for Jack Smith, and so forth.

An early attempt at solving this problem was the customer information file (CIF) concept. A CIF is closely related to a marketing database. The goal of building a CIF is usually to extract and de-duplicate ("de-dupe") multiple customer records, consolidating multiple redundant records into one, and also to relate to the consolidated customer record the *products* sold to each given customer. This CIF-building process was widely implemented in financial services organizations. Concurrently, other companies emerged that specialized in software and services for matching and merging customer records, as well as deriving "household" relationships from that data, based on matching last names, addresses, telephone numbers, and so forth.

The current, third generation of customer data management is widely referred to as customer relationship management (CRM). This generation has been strongly influenced by the increased control assumed by the customer made possible by the proliferation of delivery channels. This in turn has driven needs for "mass customization" techniques such as personalization and one-to-one marketing. Also coming into play in CRM is the requirement to "close the loop" between *front-office* (customer-facing) processes and *back-office* (internal operations) processes. In a closed-loop scenario, the results of analytical interactions are "fed" back into the information value chain at one or more points, either into the DSS system itself, or in the most advanced configurations, back into the operational systems. Figure 1–2 illustrates an example of a closed-loop scenario.

The World Wide Web affords businesses an additional "touch-point" for inbound and outbound interactions with customers and prospects. The extension of a company's presence to the Web offers the opportunity for the company to not only know their customers better, but also to capture information, from sparse to rich, on the interactions of *anyone* who "hits" their Web site. The sparsest of information is available on "anonymous" browsers; incrementally, more data can be captured as a function of the intimacy of the browser's interaction with the site—accepting cookies, registering for a logon ID, and through execution of transactions. More on this topic—Web analytics—is covered in Chapter 4.

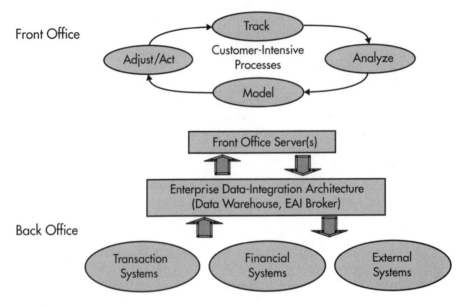

Figure 1-2
Closed-loop CRM.

Know Your Company

Truly "knowing the company" requires management to keep an eye on more than just the day-to-day financial details. The functioning of the company needs to be seen in a contextual perspective—requiring dynamic comparisons between current and past performance, projecting trends into the future, and benchmarking corporate metrics against the competition. Several techniques have been originated over the past decades to assist executives in keeping a finger on the corporate pulse.

Executive Information Systems (EIS)

The concept of the executive information system is an example of a wine being sold before its time. In the late 1980s, several vendors began offering what they dubbed executive information systems. EISs, essentially an output and data-visualization metaphor, purported to be an easy-to-read "dashboard" by which busy (and marginally computer-literate, to be honest) executives could monitor the overall "health" of their organization. EISs were positioned as decision-support systems that made decision-making information available "at a glance."

Most EIS implementations were dismal failures, precisely because the colossal behind-the-scenes data acquisition and integration issues were purposely ignored or downplayed by vendors. To be of any use, an EIS required data of enterprise scope. But at the time they were introduced, there were as yet no commercially available data-consolidation products, and the very few consolidation efforts that had been undertaken were confined to supporting decision-making of a more limited scope. When inquiries were made to internal information systems (IS) shops regarding the feasibility of acquiring and consolidating the data necessary to really "do" EIS, the response was overwhelmingly incredulous. There was no way for this integration effort to be accomplished within the time and cost ballpark represented to unsuspecting executive managers by many EIS vendors. IS was placed in a no-win situation.

However, the overall concept of the EIS as a 20,000-foot view of the entire company, after laying dormant for about a decade, was given new life by the ubiquity of Web browsers and data-consolidation architectures—and the result is now called Enterprise Information Portals, or EIPs.

Balanced Scorecard

The balanced scorecard concept was described by Robert S. Kaplan and David P. Norton in their book *The Balanced Scorecard: Translating Strategy into Action* (Harvard Business School Press, 1996). The scope of its data requirements is probably the broadest of all the DSS approaches discussed, encompassing data on financials, customers, costs, and more. It specifies four perspectives to be monitored on an ongoing basis by executive management:

- *Financial:* company financial resources
- *Customer:* how customers see the organization
- *Internal:* internal processes and activities
- *Learning and Growth:* continuous improvement capabilities

Balanced scorecard concepts complement EISs nicely as a pattern for classifying and presenting information within an EIS. Commercial applications have indeed built around this combination, including offerings from CorVu Corporation and Gentia Software.

Enterprise Information Portals

Enterprise Information Portals entered the scene in the late 1990s. The concept of an EIP is essentially that of an EIS for the masses. With an EIP, widespread employee access to a broad range of corporate data is enabled through the Web browser software on their desktops. However, EIPs, being front-ends like EISs, require the same back-end, data-consolidation plumbing as an EIS. Data warehousing and related data-management technologies, developed and widely implemented since the introduction of the EIS concept, have made EIPs more feasible than the EIS predecessors.

Now we've seen a number of common business applications that require access to a broad base of corporate data. In the next section, we'll dig deeper into the technologies that enable these "data warehousing-like" applications, and which can also give companies a running start into the e-commerce mêlée.

Technological Underpinnings

Throughout this book, we will discuss the technological underpinnings of data warehousing and e-commerce in terms of three broad areas, as follows:

1. *Output:* including analytic applications, business intelligence, user-data interaction models
2. *Storage:* software and hardware that is specialized for storage of data—including database management systems and high-performance servers
3. *Input:* including data movement, replication and transformation

In the remainder of this historical overview chapter, we will work our way from front to back—front office to back office—and briefly review the evolution of technologies in these three areas. In subsequent chapters, we'll discuss in detail how these areas fit into a company's e-commerce strategy. But first, a clarification of some terms may be in order.

Data Warehouses and Data Marts, Briefly

Bill Inmon is widely credited with popularizing the data warehouse concept and terminology; in fact, his Web site *(www.billinmon.com)* christens him the Father of Data Warehousing. Objectively, his 1992 book, *Building the Data Warehouse,* as well as numerous articles and presentations before and since, must be credited with propagating a common language around decision-support technologies—which in turn formed a catalyst for a great deal of successful software technology and human effort.

One of Inmon's definitions of a data warehouse was presented early in this chapter. Another, probably more widely quoted definition he has also offered is

> A (data) warehouse is a subject-oriented, integrated, time-variant
> and nonvolatile collection of data in support of management's
> decision-making process.
>
> —Bill Inmon

By way of additional explanation, Inmon provides these definitions:

- *Subject-oriented:* Data that gives information about a particular subject instead of about a company's ongoing operations.
- *Integrated:* Data that is gathered into the data warehouse from a variety of sources and merged into a coherent whole.
- *Time-variant:* All data in the data warehouse is identified with a particular time period.
- *Nonvolatile:* Data is stable in a data warehouse. More data is added, but data is never [never?] removed. This enables management to gain a consistent picture of the business.

Much has been written and spoken by Inmon, Ralph Kimball, and others comparing and contrasting *data warehouses* and *data marts*. For most intents and purposes, a data mart is a little data warehouse. Bill Inmon, Ralph Kimball, and Alan Simon are well-respected authorities in data warehousing and have written and spoken widely on the subject. Information on their recommended writings is available in the Bibliography.

Since the purpose of this book is not to investigate data warehouses themselves, we will not go into much more detail on these topics here. An abundance of books is available on planning, modeling, designing, building, managing, tuning, using, and just about any other thing anyone would possibly wish to do to or with a data warehouse. That said, however, one point fundamental to the premise of this book needs to be made here:

In any given e-commerce effort—regardless of whether or not the data within the scope of the effort meets any or all of the commonly stated criteria for a data

15

warehouse or data mart—the tools, techniques, and technologies commonly used to create, manage, and use data warehouses and data marts should be given serious consideration.

Output: From Reporting to Portals

All the behind-the-scenes data warehousing processing and technology—input and the storage—are means to an end: the output. The output is all about enabling more informed decision-making by the employees of an organization, and increasingly, for its customers as well.

When discussing output technologies, we're speaking about the human interface—the interactions between data and consumers of the data. A primary characteristic of the evolution of the DSS human interface has been the degree of *interactivity* afforded the end user by data-access software. Over the past three decades, data output technologies have changed dramatically. Throughout the 1970s, hardcopy reports were the norm; interactivity was limited to the visual, and perhaps extended to writing notes or highlighting on the reports. Today users have available highly–interactive, online, analytic processing and visualization tools, where selected data can be formatted, graphed, drilled, sliced, diced, mined, annotated, enhanced, exported, and distributed. The current culmination of this evolutionary path is the concept of *closed loop* business intelligence.

With early batch reporting systems, what the user saw—a specific set of "canned" reports—was what the user got. If any changes or additions to the reports were needed, a change request needed to be submitted and queued up with the IT shop. And since these systems were all customized, in-house creations, and the IT shop had the software firmly under its control, the turn-around rate for changes and enhancements was often slower than the user would have liked (an understatement, perhaps). An example of the type of technology available during this period is the programming language RPG (Report Program Generator), introduced by IBM in 1965. RPG was designed specifically to enable rapid development of batch reports.

During the late 1970s and early 1980s, both in-house development shops and newly established software vendors seized the opportunity to provide users with a greater degree of direct interactivity with their data. Software evolved that accepted input, in the form of parameters, by which the end user could select specific desired data and also specify the format in which the output appeared. No longer were separate reports needed for each sort sequence, selection criteria, field subset, and so on; the users were now able to specify what they wanted, when they wanted it.

Users' desires for this type of interactivity gave rise to a robust software industry that continues to this day. Trailblazers in the reporting software market were FOCUS (Information Builders, Inc.), Ramis (Computer Associates International, Inc.), and SAS (SAS Institute, Inc.). Each of these products originated during this period; each has grown and is going strong today, in its seventh or eighth major release.

Generally, in order for this type of software tool to function, any data to be analyzed needed to be copied and transformed into the specific format required by the tool, for example, into FOCUS databases or SAS files. This constraint actually pointed these vendors in the directions we know today as database middleware and extract-transform-load (ETL) tools.

The widespread availability of personal computers beginning in the mid-1980s presaged a significant change in the delivery and presentation of decision-making information. The most powerful change agents in PC software included, most significantly on the output side, spreadsheet programs such as VisiCalc, Lotus 1-2-3, and eventually, Microsoft Excel. These spreadsheet products gave users their first taste of "interacting with data."

The PC revolution, in putting graphical horsepower on knowledge workers' desks, moved end-user reporting tools such as SAS and FOCUS onto the desktop, as well as triggered the explosive growth of desktop reporting tools such as Brio.Enterprise, Cognos Impromptu, and Business Objects.

In the mid-1990s, users' ability to interact with data on their desktops took a huge leap forward, with the emergence of OLAP software products. OLAP enables a view of data based on the spreadsheet metaphor. Using an OLAP tool, a user can pretty much instantaneously alter the sorting, selection, intersection, and hierarchical arrangement of the data being observed. As we will see, OLAP functionality is critical in enabling access to the large amounts of data being generated through e-commerce interactions. In fact, most reporting-tool vendors have since expanded their offerings to support OLAP functionality.

Data mining software has also seen phenomenal growth in the last decade. Descended from artificial intelligence research and statistical modeling, data mining functions use large amounts of data to draw conclusions. Whereas query and even OLAP functions require human interaction to follow relationships through a data source, data mining programs are able to derive many of these relationships automatically by analyzing and "learning" from the data values contained in files and databases.

The concept of EIPs arose as a result of the Web-enabling of decision-support systems. Until the advent of the ubiquitous Web browser, in order to interface with a data warehouse, users typically needed to either have query software installed and configured on their workstation, or at the very least, had to be on the distribution list for—guess what—hardcopy printouts. This led inevitably to challenges in software cost, distribution, and maintenance, and to "killing more trees"—the elusive paperless office remained so. But with, in effect, a browser on every desktop in the workplace, Web-enabled query software extended the visibility of the data warehouse to potentially every authorized knowledge worker in an organization—and beyond.

Storage: Extract Files to Objects

In the 1960s, thanks to Herman Hollerith, we first codified the bulk of our business data in a digitally processable format: punched cards. Throughout the 1970s, precursors to "true" decision-support systems were constrained to reporting from punched cards or from the newer sequential media, tape reels. In the 1980s, we transferred most of our most dynamic data assets to the new, random-access disk drives, leaving the history on magnetic tape. Random access was a revolutionary development. In the last three decades of the 20th century, remarkable progress was made in data storage technologies. Now, as we begin a new millennium, we are reading data from smaller, faster, and cheaper...disk drives. When is the next revolution? Disks are being made faster and faster, more data is being packed into less space, but eventually, pure physics takes over. Only so much can be done with the current fundamental storage medium, iron oxide—rust. More on data storage media will be covered in Chapter 5.

The primary enabler for access to large amounts of data was what could be termed "the random-access revolution." Just as it is much easier and faster to select a particular song from a CD (or vinyl LP) than from a cassette tape, it's much easier and faster for a decision maker to select specific data from a revolving disk than from a tape. A disk is always "mounted" in place, whereas, even given advances in automated robotic tape silos, a tape must be located, taken to a reader, and mounted on the reader. Then, every record on the tape must be read up to the point where the required data is located—even if it is at the end. These days, of course, we take random-access disk storage for granted; we have gigabytes even on our laptops and home PCs. But back in the 20th century, random-access storage media fundamentally changed the relationship between data and its users. The most significant result of this was the rise of software systems specialized for managing the storage and retrieval of large, structured sets of data—databases. These products were dubbed database management systems, or DBMSs.

In the mid-1980s, decision-support data storage was dealt a double whammy: the almost simultaneous rise of personal computing and the productization of the relational database model. At nearly the same time that relational databases became available on mainframe and midrange computers, "personal" databases—relational and relational-like, such as Borland's Paradox and Ashton-Tate's dBase—began to grace the desktop PCs in homes and offices.

Relational databases achieved a level of user-friendliness unheard of in earlier hierarchical and network database management systems. The early 1990s saw the rise of relational databases such as Red Brick and Teradata, specialized or reengineered for mass updates and read-only, decision-support output. In the mid-1990s, multidimensional databases (MDDBs), most notably Essbase, appeared in response to the rigorous interactive performance requirements of OLAP applications. In the late 1990s, object database management systems (ODBMSs) made small inroads into mainstream applications.

Triggered by the growth of the World Wide Web, object DBMSs, such as Software AG's Tamino and eXcelon Corporation's Javlin, burst on the scene, optimized for storing and serving XML (eXtensible Markup Language) and for interacting with the object-oriented lingua franca of e-commerce, Java. Main-memory databases (MMDBs), such as TimesTen and Angara, entered the market as well—another solution offered for enhancing data-access performance.

The digital economy may speak new and unique languages while interacting with data stores, but most of the data it requests and receives remains quite recognizable, as that represented by the punched holes on our Hollerith's cards.

Input: From Extraction to Movement

Let's face it: Up to this point in time, data consolidation has pretty much come down to copying data from one place to another, with the goal of increasing the value, in terms of usability, of the data in the process. If the value of the data to the enterprise is not increased, the cost and effort of copying the data and storing the copy is not justified. Just the process of copying data from one place to another has a somewhat attention-grabbing (well, maybe not exactly spine-tingling) history.

Probably the most venerable example of moving data around between application systems is the GL system discussed earlier. To "feed" the GL monster, extract files are demanded from all application systems in which revenue or expense records can be found. Again under cover of darkness, the GL monster consumes these extracts, categorizing and summarizing the prior day's financial activities, then, at the end of its run, spitting out all manner of stacks of financial reports for internal management and external overseers. And the most venerated and critical of these financial management reports is, of course, the company's annual report.

A major variable in the evolution from this type of reporting system to more "authentic" decision-support applications is the breadth of the input, that is, the number of separate application sources and the diversity of the data that is consumed by the DSS. The GL systems in our prior example, while perhaps broad in the number of "feeder systems," are pretty much constrained in the types of data in which they are interested: revenues and expenses. CIFs and marketing databases (MDBs) were some of the earliest instances of extensive data consumers.

CIFs have been common in banking systems for decades. The IT landscape in banking is unique in the number of separate stovepipe applications that are typically necessary to run the business. Each banking product usually has its own specialized application. Customers typically have multiple banking products. If the supporting application systems are separate, how does a bank know that the John Doe in whose name a home equity loan is held is the same John Doe who has a checking account? Usually, the bank's CIF integrates such information.

CIFs and GL systems require periodic data feeds from multiple application systems to keep their data up to date. Early on, the computer programs required to ETL these data feeds were custom-coded by in-house IT shops. Concurrent with the growth of the data warehouse concept in the early 1990s, commercial software specialized for ETL processing began to appear. Prism Solutions was founded by Bill Inmon in 1991; Evolutionary Technologies, Inc. (ETI) was also founded in January 1991. Informatica, the current market leader, opened for business in 1993.

Data *consolidation* architectures, such as GL and CIF systems, data warehouses, and data marts, to this point had primarily followed a many-to-one model—where data from many sources is transformed and replicated into a single destination. This consolidation is typically done on a periodic, batch mode basis rather than on a synchronous real-time basis. The growth of the Web has resulted in another convergence, where transformation functionality—previously the exclusive domain of these batch-oriented ETL tools—has been combined with message brokering architectures, and from there subsumed into other families of e-commerce-focused software products: enterprise application integration (EAI) and application servers (or App Servers).

The integrated value chain (introduced in Chapter 2) required for contemporary e-commerce is likely to be supported by the same multiple, autono-

Table 1.1   Data Architecture Comparison

Property	Architecture	
	Data Warehouse Architecture	**Integrated Value Chain Data Architecture**
Synchronization frequency	Periodic (e.g., daily)	Real-time or near real-time
Source/destination model	Many-to-one	Many-to-many
Update mode	Batch	Transactional

mous transactional databases confronted by earlier data warehousing efforts. Transforming a pre-digital economy value chain into an *integrated* value chain requires data-movement, transformation, and replication technologies that provide real-time or near real-time synchronization of multiple sources with *multiple* targets—a real-time, many-to-many model. Table 1.1 compares and contrasts these two architecture types.

In response to the growing need for many-to-many, transactional, near real-time synchronization between data stores, the market for EAI software is exploding. Most EAI products bundle together several functions and technologies, including message brokering, workflow automation, and, most familiar to data warehousing technologists, data transformation and replication. EAI software products achieve data transformation and replication through message-broker middleware.

Say, for example, applications *A*, *B*, and *C* are found in various value links and channels across an enterprise. Say also that an update to the database in source application *A* must be replicated near real-time to target databases in applications *B* and *C*. EAI software enables *A* to transmit an update message containing the updated data to a central broker facility. The broker "hub" then performs any required transformations and routes update messages to applications *B* and *C*.

A class of software products labeled application servers has become highly visible since 1998. App servers, similar to EAI products, act as integration points, providing a single apparent source of data (as well as function and logic) to (usually) a Web site on the front end.

A historical overview of trends and influences in data input technologies, often referred to as *data-movement* technologies, is presented in Figure 1–3. These technologies are covered in more detail in Chapter 6.

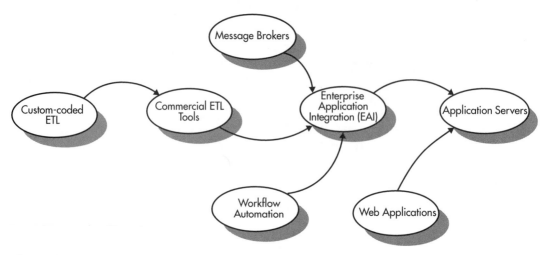

Figure 1–3
Trends and influences in data movement.

Data Warehousing and E-Commerce at Tiosa Corporation

On this, our first visit to Tiosa Corporation, we find T. Dan Roberts, Tiosa's chief information officer, up to his eyebrows in e-commerce initiatives. It seems that every business unit has already put up its own stand-alone Web site and now wants him to run it; those that haven't built their own sites are clamoring for Dan's staff to build one for them. On top of this, Collections is asking him if they should replace their electronic payment systems with XML (and what the heck is XML, anyway?), and Purchasing wants him to investigate Web-based procurement and B2B exchanges.

Dan is glad that at least the Y2K rush is over, and the various data warehouse and data mart initiatives of the past several years appear to be calming down a bit. Since he accepted the CIO position in 1995, it seems there has been one emergency after another.

Like most sizable companies, over the past three decades, Tiosa has an accumulated history of packaged and custom data warehouses, data marts, and decision-support systems. Some of the development efforts have been underwritten by technology units, some by business units; some have been successful and enduring, while others have fallen by the wayside. A proliferation of input, storage, and output technologies is the legacy of the IT decen-

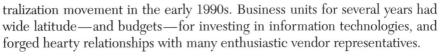

tralization movement in the early 1990s. Business units for several years had wide latitude—and budgets—for investing in information technologies, and forged hearty relationships with many enthusiastic vendor representatives.

Output technologies in use within various business units include those from Brio, Cognos and Business Objects. Databases, on multiple platforms, include IMS, DB2 for OS/390, Oracle and Microsoft SQL Server. ETL tools in use in various units include those from Informatica and ETI. In the mid-1990s, a valiant data-management effort led to the implementation of the Platinum Repository MVS; the product has now fallen into disuse.

As in many companies, Tiosa's finance and marketing departments have been trailblazers in marshalling their data assets in support of improved decision making. In the finance department, a multidimensional OLAP solution based on Hyperion Essbase is used for slicing and dicing revenue and expense data that's extracted on a monthly basis from the corporate chart of accounts in PeopleSoft Financials. The risk management department is experimenting with data mining products, attempting to get a handle on large customers with whom Tiosa may have greater-than-expected exposure, and to develop profiles of customers who are likely to default on loan payments.

In Marketing, an Oracle database is used as the basis for determining the profiles of the most profitable customer segments. Custom SQL scripts are used to load the database, and a team of analysts creates and maintains reports, primarily using Microsoft Access. A PhD statistician was recently hired to investigate data mining to predict customers' likely responses to various proposed marketing strategies.

Several revenue-generating lines of business have experimented with various decision-support applications, ranging from single-user PC databases used by several remote sales offices to a product-profitability SAS application on the corporate IBM mainframe by the cash management department. Other business units, such as Mortgages and Underwriting, have yet to embark on any ambitious data-management plans outside of their core mainframe and midrange package applications.

As discussions heat up with the various departments he supports, Dan is beginning to view his challenges as twofold. First, Dan's team needs to support the development of a "coherent interaction presence" (according to the new VP of e-commerce) in the digital marketplace for the company. Second, he needs to figure out how to integrate into this digital presence the considerable internal data assets under his and others' purview. The term *architecture* continues to turn up as a recurring theme in the early discussions of this integration.

"It seems we've spent the last decade or so consolidating and redistributing data in support of all these various flavors of decision-support applications," concludes Dan in a meeting with his direct reports. "Surely we can make use of the results of some of what we've accomplished to get data where it needs to be for these e-business projects."

Sounds like Dan may be on the right track. As we take a deeper look into the business and technical aspects of Dan's challenges, we will occasionally drop in for a status check on Tiosa's ambitious entry into the digital marketplace. Next, let's see if we can shed some light on the new VP's concept of a coherent interaction presence.

Chapter 2

THE NEW ECONOMY: WHAT IS IT, ANYWAY?

It is not the employer who pays wages—he only handles the money.
It is the product that pays wages.

—Henry Ford

New economy, digital economy, e-business, e-commerce, B2B, B2C, B2B2C
. . . the buzzword generator has been working overtime. In many respects, the
meaning of this brave new terminology is in the eye of the beholder, or vendor, or guru…or author. Often, terms are reiterated ad infinitum with little
shared meaning—leading to "freedom from content." The value of terminology is a function of its ability to clarify. Assigning some meaning (even dis-
putable) to these terms may provide clarification. Toward this end, most would
allow that fundamental first principles include data, of course, and—when it
comes to the economy, business, and commerce—channels, definitely.

Channels

Channels are the media through which a business interacts with other organizations and with individuals. They are the interfaces between a company's
internal activities and the external resources required for the successful completion of these activities. The most apparent channels are those connecting
the business with its customers, for delivery of products and services, and
with suppliers, for raw materials and resources. Less obvious channels exist

for interacting with *"partners"* of the business, such as subcontractors, investors, regulators, and associations such as buying and lobbying organizations.

Probably the most significant impact wrought by the advent of the *digital* economy (i.e., business transacted by digital means) is channel proliferation. Multiple digital channels have been heaped on top of existing multiple non-digital channels—the result can reasonably be designated the *new* economy.

Channels also can be broadly categorized into physical channels and information channels. Our focus here will obviously be on information channels; however, the two types are irrevocably intertwined. The appearance and growth of new information channels often contributes to the appearance and growth of physical channels, and vice versa. In addition, and predictably, physical-channel activity must be accompanied by parallel activity in a corresponding information channel. Complicating things further is the fact that in many cases the information is the product. So, as can be seen by these multiple interdependencies, the appearance of major new information channels, such as the Internet and the Web, is bound to initiate a ripple effect across most, if not all, other channels.

Companies initially staked their claim in the marketplace with channels of "bricks and mortar." As has been often observed, the bricks and mortar are not, and will not, be replaced; rather, new channels accrete to, rather than displace, existing channels. Early extensions of supply and delivery mechanisms into electronic channels were built on analog interactions: telephone call centers, interactive voice response (IVR), computer-telephony integration (CTI), and dial-up lines. Now, on top of these established channels are added the digital communication capabilities offered by the Internet: Web, email, chat, and Voice over Internet Protocol (VoIP). All of these interaction channels must be maintained, integrated to a greater or lesser extent, and actively managed. Customers and business partners expect the ability to choose the communication mechanisms most convenient to them.

The combination of the World Wide Web "window" and its Internet infrastructure is a major new channel for inbound and outbound interactions with all constituents with whom a business interacts. Few if any businesses utilize the Web or Internet as their exclusive interaction channel; for most, it is one of multiple channels.

The Value Chain

A useful planning tool for guiding the transformation of a company to a multi-channel business model is the widely accepted concept of the value chain, introduced in the 1985 book *Competitive Advantage* by Michael Porter of the Harvard Business School. A value chain is a high-level model of how a business functions by receiving raw materials as input, adding value to the raw materials through various processes, and selling a finished product to its customers. The generic value chain is illustrated in Figure 2–1.

The value chain is an abstract description of the processes within just about any type of business. As our investigation progresses, we will also present an abstract description of the types of data (a data model—dare we use the term?) utilized within most businesses, as well as an abstract group of data flows.

For any business enterprise, a critical prerequisite for success in the new economy is the implementation of an integrated value chain that extends throughout—and beyond—the enterprise.

> "Value chain integration can be defined as the process by which multiple enterprises within a shared market channel cooperatively plan, implement, and electronically, as well as physically, manage the flow of goods, services, and information...along the entire value chain, from point of origin to point of consumption...in a manner that increases customer-perceived value and optimizes the efficiency of the chain...creating competitive advantage for all stakeholders in the value chain."
> "Competition's New Battleground: The Integrated Value Chain" (Cambridge Technology Partners).

In this chapter we will take a front-to-back tour through the value chain. We'll investigate the data used and the technology challenges presented by the new economy within each link. Challenges we will be facing include

- Channel proliferation
- Cross-channel influences
- Process exposure
- Data exposure
- Hyper-competition
- Kano acceleration (customers expecting more, faster)

Figure 2-1
A generic value chain.

This investigation will position us to look in detail later on at the solutions data warehousing technologies offer in addressing these challenges, with the end goal of transforming a "pre-digital" value chain into an integrated value chain.

Value Activities

Value activities are the distinct activities a business organization performs. On the one hand, these activities must be delineated in order to be effective and manageable; on the other hand, this necessary delineation sets up boundaries that must be permeable, semitransparent—to enable the activities to function together toward common goals.

Marketing and Sales: eCRM

Although often grouped together in the same overall value chain activity, we will address marketing and sales separately for several reasons:

- They are most often performed by discrete units within a company.
- The activities typically have dissimilar goals and incentive structures.
- Most importantly, e-commerce has presented them with different problems and opportunities.

We'll address marketing—the attraction of qualified prospective buyers—first. For marketing, the digital economy is a classic case of "be careful what you wish for, you may get it." The Web, first and foremost, is a marketing tool—an electronic billboard. It has presented companies with a method to gain very inexpensive "face time" with orders-of-magnitude more prospects than before. Companies have invested much time, effort, and financial resources in developing and maintaining attractive Web sites, and attracting prospects to their sites. Challenges and opportunities presented to marketing by digital channels include

- What data, and how much data, is reasonable and valuable to collect from prospects and customers. In the eyes of marketing, existing customers are highly qualified prospects for additional sales, cross-sales, and up-sales. An additional attractive attribute of existing customers is that much more data is already available on them.
- How to deal with volumes of data: quality, sparsity, de-duplication, and summarization.
- Determining most fertile channels among many.

- How to best portray available products.
- How to gain best placement within search engine results.

The data of interest to marketing includes markets, products, channels, and of course customers.

To keep track of who does what to which data, we'll begin representing this by using a tool that has been around for many years, with the unfortunate designation of "*CRUD matrix*." "CRUD" stands for Create, Retrieve, Update, and Delete. For the purposes of this analysis, we will dispense with deleting—if an activity can create, we can assume it can also delete.

A note on particular considerations for the use of this technique is probably appropriate here. The intent is to give a *general* idea of the problems and opportunities for solutions, rather than to be absolutely precise. The assertions of how the data and activities are grouped, and who does what to which data, is obviously a generalization and approximation. Every company is different; that is why there are many companies and why marketplaces are competitive. There is no "one size fits all"—each company needs to undertake this exercise within its own circumstances and goals.

That said, Table 2.1 itemizes the proposed CRUD for marketing activities. The types of data required are listed in the first column. In the second column, the action(s) that the functions within the value chain activity can take on the type data in that row are listed. A brief description of the data required, from the perspective of those performing the activity, is listed in the third column.

In order to achieve shared goals, a great deal of data must be shared between marketing and sales. Sales must make data on customers and channels available to marketing; marketing must make data on markets and products available to sales. Sharing of data from creator to retriever results in a directional flow of data, or *data flow*. Identification and enhancement of data flows is critical for creating an integrated value chain and achieving competitive advantage. As we will see, data warehousing technologies can enable the creation and enhancement of data flows.

The data of interest to sales centers on transactions, customers, products, markets, and channels. The new economy poses opportunities and challenges to sales, including

- Transaction volumes
- Consolidating sales transaction data across multiple channels
- Dealing with multiple payment methods
- Preventing "disintermediation"; that is, continually proving the value added by sales personnel in the face of increasingly self-service delivery channels

Table 2.1 CRUD for Marketing Activities

Required Data	Marketing Action	Marketing-focused Description
Market	C	A set of prospective buyers with similar characteristics.
Product	C	Goods to be sold. Marketing does not actually "create" the products themselves, but creates product data for the consumption of prospects.
Channel	R	Specifically *sales* channels; media by which customers can indicate intent to purchase products.
Customer	CR	A purchaser of products.

Order-entry processes have shifted to the other side of the firewall, from internal personnel to the customers themselves. E-commerce enables customer *self-service* to a much greater extent than ever before. In order to facilitate self-service, customer interfaces such as Web pages must be compelling, intuitive, and easily navigable, with absolutely no training in a conventional sense required. The need to develop and maintain such interfaces has resulted in a tremendous premium on skills and experience in user-interface design. End-customers are a much more particular and less patient audience than time-honored, captive internal order-entry personnel.

Real-time "mining" of channel and customer data can drive automatic interaction personalization that includes customization of presentation and navigation, as well as tactful cross-sell suggestions. These are logical applications of the "actionable" output resulting from established decision-support techniques, including data consolidation, data aggregation, statistical functions, and predictive modeling. Many new and established software companies are concentrating on providing automated support for this type of analysis and its results.

As described earlier, effective data flows between sales and marketing are critical. In addition, effective and near-instantaneous flows of transaction and product data are required between sales and operations. See Table 2.2.

Customer Service and Support

Established "bricks-and-mortar" channels for customer service and support include stores/branches and remote, distributed, or centralized call centers. Increased accessibility to products and services has raised consumers' expec-

Table 2.2 CRUD for Sales Activities

Required Data	Sales Action	Sales-Focused Description
Account	U	A record of an aspect of the financial condition of the firm.
Customer	C	A buyer of the products of the firm.
Transaction	C	A purchase of the firm's products by a customer.
Market	R	A grouping of customers based on similar characteristics—geographic, type of business, or demographic, for example. In sales, primarily used for segregation of responsibility.
Product	R	Types of goods sold by the company.
Channel	R	The various media through which orders for products are received.

tation levels for the availability and quality of service and support. At the same time, full employment has resulted in both increased wage expenses and a trend toward lower quality service.

The primary competitive differentiator among e-commerce firms is (somewhat ironically) customer service. An excellent level of service remains the number one factor in customer retention. In order to achieve a competitive level of service, personnel who perform customer service activities must have immediate access to, and detailed knowledge of, all data on customers, products, channels, and transactions. If a customer service representative (CSR) receives a call from a customer, the CSR can be assured that the interaction is likely to be both an exception situation (automated means have failed) and a sales opportunity (the CSR can—when appropriate, and based on the situation—suggest additional products that may be attractive to the customer).

The growth of customer self-service enabled by digital buying channels has driven a corresponding hypergrowth in call center infrastructures and technologies.

Table 2.3 describes the data of critical interest to customer service and support. Accurate and timely sharing of data between sales and customer service is essential.

Outbound Logistics: Fulfillment

The digital economy makes it easy for marketing and order-taking to go global. But outbound logistics activities are responsible for actually delivering the finished products of the firm to its customers. These activities are where

Table 2.3 CRUD for Customer Service Activities

Required Data	Customer Service and Support Action	Customer Service-Focused Description
Customer	R	A buyer of the firm's products.
Transaction	CR	An inbound or outbound exchange of information between the company and a customer.
Product	R	An item purchased by a customer from the company.
Channel	R	A medium through which an inbound or outbound exchange of information takes place between the company and a customer.

the rubber literally meets the road, especially when it comes to the distinction between electronic and physical products. Fulfillment of orders for electronic products such as money, financial instruments, or information is most often more straightforward to consummate than the outbound logistics for physical goods. Physical product fulfillment is a completely different ballgame—much more labor-intensive (again, those pesky carbon-based life forms), with many more variables, allowing for less control by the company. Electronic information infrastructures, operating in parallel with physical logistical channels, enable integration of sales and inventory management into logistics activities.

The metrics by which outbound logistics activities are measured include primarily speed of fulfillment and cost control.

Outbound logistics processes care about data on customers, transactions, products, and (delivery) channels, described in Table 2.4.

Operations

Tasked with transforming resources—raw materials—into products as rapidly and cost-effectively as possible, operational activities of course require data about products, transactions, and resources. Turnover, velocity, and through-put—these are the goals and metrics of operations. Product development, manufacturing, and inventory management are the typical operational activities.

Operational activities are where the "value add" happens, where the raw material is assembled and polished into the finished product. This is the "back office," where, depending on the line of business, the PCs are assembled, the pizza is baked, or the stock trades are executed. The new economy allows—and requires—data to be shared and understood between operational activi-

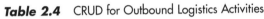

Table 2.4 CRUD for Outbound Logistics Activities

Required Data	Outbound Logistics Action	Outbound Logistics-Focused Description
Customer	R	A person or organization to whom one or more products must be delivered.
Transaction	CR	An order for products that must be delivered.
Product	R	The content of a delivery.
Channel	R	The means by which an order transaction is fulfilled.

ties at the maximum speed of the network connections among the internal and external partners executing the value-adding processes.

The goal of operations is just in time (JIT), precisely matching production to sales. To do so, operational activities require timely and accurate information on sales transactions and must provide timely and accurate information on resource requirements to procurement and inbound logistics.

In the area of product development, the digital economy has facilitated the growth of *collaborative development*—the specification, design, and creation of products by a firm in partnership with suppliers and consumers. Collaborative development requires the near real-time sharing of product specification data among not only the product-development areas within a company, but also across the "extended enterprise" formed by a company and its partners—customers, suppliers, consultants—with whom it may jointly conceive, design, and manufacture its products. See Table 2.5.

Inbound Logistics: The Supply Chain

Inbound logistics processes manage the actual receipt, storage and management of resources—inputs—for which procurement has secured agreements from suppliers. In e-commerce, factors impacting *inbound* logistics are predictably similar to those affecting *outbound* logistics—determined in large part by the distinction between, and correlation of, physical and electronic resources.

The purchasing company's inbound logistics activities interface with the selling company's outbound logistics activities. Physical inbound logistics are much more labor-intensive, with many more variables, allowing for less control by the company. Electronic information infrastructures, operating in par-

Table 2.5 CRUD for Operations Activities

Required Data	Operations Action	Operations-Focused Description
Resource	R	Raw material used directly or indirectly in the making of products.
Transaction	R	An order for products that must be created.
Product	CR	An item created by the company from its resources. Operations actually creates the instances of products, based on specifications.

allel with physical logistical channels, enable integration of sales and inventory management into logistics activities. Electronic channels allow companies and their suppliers to remain constantly online and in touch, connecting them into networks of collaborative planning, forecasting, and replenishment (CPFR) relationships.

Inbound logistics activities require data on suppliers, transactions, and resources, as described in Table 2.6. They must share this data quickly and effectively with procurement and operations.

Support Activities

The activities related to the value-creation activities of the enterprise, rather than directly creating value themselves, are designated *support activities*. These include staff functions such as financial and executive management, procurement, and human resources. Support activities generate no revenue on their own, so their primary metrics are cost control.

Executive Management

Managing corporate performance in a digital enterprise requires the consolidation and analysis of cost and revenue data from multiple channels and value chain links, on a real-time or near real-time basis. Analytic applications tap the data that accumulates during the course of doing business, add value by summarizing and analyzing the raw data, then deliver the results through dissemination services—such as information portals.

Continuous monitoring of costs, revenues, and profitability is required for a digital enterprise to remain responsive to changing market and competitive

Table 2.6 CRUD for Inbound Logistics Activities

Data Required	Inbound Logistics Action	Inbound Logistics-Focused Description
Supplier	R	Organizations from whom raw material is obtained.
Transaction	RU	Receipt of resources into the company.
Resource	R	Raw material used directly or indirectly in the making of products.

conditions. Monitoring and analysis of transaction activity for customers and products has been common in businesses for some time. But the evolution toward a multichannel interaction model by the digital enterprise mandates that costs, revenues, and profitability *across channels* also be monitored and analyzed. The goal is to both increase the profitability of the most active channels and concurrently increase the activity of the most profitable channels.

In order to achieve this goal, executive management requires daily, if not up-to-the-minute, highly summarized data from across all channels and value chain activities, as described in Table 2.7.

Financial Management

The responsibilities of financial management include keeping the "books," or accounts, from which the performance of the organization can be derived. Asset management is included within financial management because real assets of a company are viewed and handled as investments.

The viewpoint of financial management is a subset of executive management's highly-summarized view, focused on the monetary results of the firm's activities. See Table 2.8.

Procurement

Procurement activities are responsible for purchasing—at terms most beneficial to the company—the resources necessary for both the creation of products and the supporting activities of product creation. Creating the most beneficial sourcing arrangements with suppliers requires that procurement have access to as much external market information as possible. Data on supplier performance as well as pricing is critical in order to achieve the greatest leverage relating to current and potential suppliers.

Procurement is the primary activity of business-to-business (B2B) e-

Table 2.7   CRUD for Executive Management Activities

Required Data	Executive Management Action	Executive Management-Focused Description
Account	R	A classification of the assets, liabilities, revenue, and expenses of the company.
Customer	R	A purchaser or potential purchaser of the company's products.
Employee	R	Critical resources of the company—that keep it running.
Transaction	R	The lifeblood of the company. Raw material for summarized information necessary to understand the current and future direction of the firm.
Organization	CR	Mobilization of employees for action.
Market	R	The playing field in which the company operates.
Asset	R	Tangible and intangible resources owned by the business for its benefit.
Resource	R	Input consumed in the process of creating the firm's products.
Product	R	Goods and services the company offers to its market—that must be more attractive than its competitors'.
Supplier	R	Specialized partners of the company.
Channel	R	The connections of the company into its markets.

commerce: *e-procurement*. Multiple new trading models have been enabled by increased use of the Web and Internet, including auctions, reverse auctions, and exchanges. These new models are changing the relationships between suppliers and purchasers, in many cases greatly increasing the advantage of purchasing organizations over their suppliers.

In the new economy, a business must have the ability to exchange data with its suppliers quickly and easily. Procurement activities must recognize and understand data originating outside the enterprise, and also replicate and transform it for use by internal and external downstream processes: inbound logistics and operations. See Table 2.9.

Table 2.8 CRUD for Financial Management Activities

Required Data	Financial Management Action	Financial Management-Focused Description
Account	CR	A classification of the assets, liabilities, revenue, and expenses of the company.
Organization	R	A categorization of responsibility for the assets, liabilities, revenue, and expenses of the company.
Asset	R	Revenue-producing investments which must be carefully managed.

Table 2.9 CRUD for Procurement Activities

Required Data	Procurement Action	Procurement-Focused Description
Supplier	CR	An organization from which resources can be purchased.
Resource	CR	Items necessary for both the creation of products, and the supporting activities of product creation

Technology

There's no way around it: Technology is, after all, what is driving all the changes wrought by the new economy. Establishing a presence in the digital economy requires that a company, new or old, make large investments in technology—humans, functions, hardware, software, and data—in order to survive.

Existing companies have a pre-established technology infrastructure—good news and bad news. Much of the existing infrastructure can be expanded and enhanced to support a company's entry into new electronic channels; however, a significant amount of coordinated effort is required to accomplish this while simultaneously ramping up direct support required for new digital channels. The scope of critical information needed for technology-expansion efforts, perhaps surprisingly, is closely aligned to those of executive management. However, rather than summarizations of actual instance data, as is the case for executive management activities, in order to accomplish their mission,

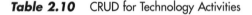

Table 2.10 CRUD for Technology Activities

Required Data	Technology Action	Description
Account	R	How should e-transactions be accounted for?
Customer	R	Who are the new and existing customers?
Employee	R	What are the staff and skill requirements?
Transaction	R	What type of activities are to be supported? How often, how many, and from where to where?
Organization	R	IT resources used and required by internal and external organizations.
Market	R	The IT marketplace: products, vendors, trends.
Asset	R	IT assets: hardware, software, and data.
Resource	R	What information technology resources—hardware, software, and data—are required, and what existing resources can be mobilized?
Product	R	What will be sold through new channels?
Supplier	R	From whom can required new IT resources be obtained?
Channel	R	What are the new channels to be deployed—and when?

technology activities need *meta-data*—data *about* the data across the organization. This meta-data includes volumes, frequencies, data types, service level requirements (undoubtedly 24/7—no downtime acceptable), response time, security requirements, and geographical distribution. See Table 2.10.

Information technology is a key component in building an effective and competitive value chain. In addition to optimizing the information available *within* value chain activities, IT plays an even more critical role in increasing the flow of information *across linkages* among value chain activities of all types.

Human Resources

As it does for all other activities in the value chain, the new economy poses new challenges and opportunities for the human resources (HR) department. Most serious among these are

- Keeping current on new, changing skill set requirements.
- Responding rapidly to needs of all areas for new skill sets.

- Developing and maintaining competitive, innovative compensation packages in order to compete effectively for scarce skill sets in a seller's market.

- Developing convincing justification for costly compensation packages.

- Developing and implementing effective tactics for the capture, retention, and distribution of corporate knowledge—especially critical in a high-turnover environment.

- Developing, justifying, and implementing effective employee retention strategies.

- Effectively procuring and managing temporary and contract staff as required.

- Managing outplacement processes made necessary by buyouts, acquisitions and reorganizations.

The list could undoubtedly go on. A key component to dealing effectively with these and other challenges is, yep, you guessed it…data—as much data as can be acquired and managed, on skills, prospects, other companies competing for the same scarce prospects, and employee compensation. For our purposes here (with the reader's agreement) we can group this data under the general heading of Employee data.

Looking back to the CRUD matrices in earlier sections, we can see that each value chain activity has responsibility for creating and retrieving data relating to (current and required) employees. Employee skill and experience requirements must be quickly and effectively communicated from across the firm to HR in order for requirements to be met in a timely fashion. All areas must be responsible for capturing and persisting as much employee knowledge as possible to shield the firm from "brain drain" resulting from high turnover rates.

Profitability per employee is a key metric that can be employed to track—and clarify for executive management—the cost of skills required for the company to remain competitive. This can be calculated by comparing total employee-related expenses, including compensation and benefits, to revenue over the same time period. See Table 2.11.

Data and the Value Chain

Table 2.12 summarizes the value chain activities we've covered and the data that each is primarily interested in and responsible for. As a company considers its course of action toward engaging in the new economy, it must quickly plan and undertake steps to strengthen the cohesiveness—integration—of

Table 2.11 CRUD for Human Resources Activities

Required Data	HR Activity	HR-Focused Description
Customer	R	Organizations the company may not wish to hire from.
Employee	CR	Persons directly or indirectly compensated for activities performed on behalf of the company.

Table 2.12 CRUD for the Entire Enterprise

Data/Activity	Marketing	Sales	Customer Service	Outbound Logistics	Operations	Inbound Logistics	Executive Management	Financial Management	Procurement	Technology	Human Resources
Account		U					R	CR		R	
Customer	CR	C	R	R			R			R	
Employee	CR	CR	CR	CR	CR	CR	CR	CR	CR	CR	CR
Transaction		C	CR	CR	R	RU	R			R	
Organization							CR	R		R	
Market	C	R					R			R	
Asset							R	R		R	
Resource					CR	R	R		R	R	
Product	C	R	R	R	CR		R			R	
Supplier						R	R		CR	R	
Channel	R	R	R	R			R			R	

the data resources under its management. As can be seen from the chart, this is a tall order, but one which is both necessary and a valuable investment in the future of the enterprise.

The meta-data collected in this matrix should be used to develop a map of critical data flows among value chain activities and channels. This is a valuable tool for plotting our strategy for competing in a multichannel marketplace that includes e-commerce and bricks-and-mortar channels.

We'll look more closely at data integration after discussing the impact of channel proliferation on the value chain.

Channels and the Value Chain

Prior to the advent of the Web, the set of channels through which various value activities interacted with the "outside world" were long-standing and well-established. Since the mid- to late-1990s, the growth of e-commerce has required businesses to establish new channels, digital and otherwise, into many value chain activities. And with every new channel comes the requirement to integrate the information flows of this channel with established channels.

B2C Channels: Press 0 for a Carbon-Based Life-Form

Early (mid-1990s) B2C sites were limited to *brochureware*—read-only presentations of product-marketing collateral. Most consumer-oriented sites have now moved, or are furiously moving, beyond this to supporting actual business (money) transactions on their sites. As companies move to "real" e-commerce, they have quickly learned that consumers are not content to be limited to electronic interactions. The human touch of the conventional call center has not been eliminated by the Web; on the contrary, B2C e-commerce sites are a prime example of the rise of new channels deeply impacting other, pre-existing channels. In fostering an increased level of interactivity with customers, B2C e-commerce has given rise to "blended media" call centers, where CSRs (human beings) are available by phone, email, chat, or VoIP—a means of transmitting voice communication over the Internet. Figure 2–2 shows the progression of B2C high-level models since the advent of Web-based e-commerce.

The primary B2C delivery channels include (but are not limited to) the following:

- Branches (bricks-and-mortar)
- Kiosks/ATMs/Video
- Call Centers, utilizing
  - computer-telephony integration (CTI)
  - VoIP

- Web chat
- Web
- email

When developing a cohesive multichannel B2C strategy, it is critical to consider the following dimensions of data to be collected, stored, distributed, and presented:

- Channel-specific data (e.g., Web site, call center)
  - visits/calls
  - page-hits/button-pushes
  - customer behavior (trajectory)
  - consummated sales
  - lost opportunities (abandoned carts, hang-ups)
- Cross-channel comparative data
- sales and profitability, by
  - channel
  - customer/category
  - product/category
  - geography
  - time/date/season

In order to support a comprehensive view of sales activity, consolidation of data from multiple databases and application systems—across channels and value chain activities—is an absolute necessity.

Figure 2-2
B2C channel trends.

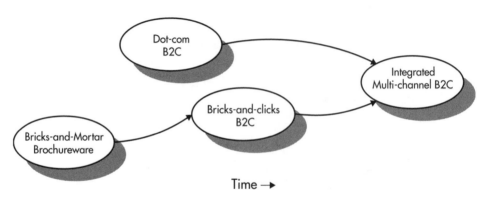

B2B Channels

Business-to-business e-commerce is far from a new phenomenon; businesses have been doing back-office electronic business for over a decade. The prime example of pre-Internet B2B is electronic data interchange (EDI). EDI is a set of standards for business data interchange that encompasses both layered transaction-record formats and layered network transport protocols.

What *is* different about the new B2B economy is that while EDI enabled a limited number of large businesses to do business interactively, the proliferation of a low-cost, ubiquitous network—the Internet—essentially levels the playing field for companies of all sizes.

An important determination that must be made by any company considering B2B is to what extent they may already be doing B2B—what volume, with what technologies, and with what partners. There is definitely a consideration of "if it ain't broke, don't fix it"; for example, if EDI suffices quite well, why abandon it and leap whole hog to new format standards such as eXtensible Markup Language (XML)? (XML is covered in more detail in Chapter 6.) Whereas B2C is more of the nature of "build it and they will come," in order to even be feasible, B2B requires active participation of trading partners— suppliers and (yes) consumers, which must be planned for and coordinated in advance of taking the plunge. Trading agreements must be established, connectivity options must be investigated, transaction frequency and volumes must be anticipated, and, last but definitely not least, common data formats and semantics must be agreed upon.

EDI has a head start of many years in developing and promulgating standard formats and semantics for business transaction data. Several groups have more recently been established specifically to facilitate the agreement on formats and semantics for B2B transactions expressed in XML. Development of XML B2B schema (formats) can be tracked in at least two Web sites, *www.XML.org* and *www.biztalk.org*. These are *schema repositories* at which schemas are registered (stored). There is also a significant amount of activity around mapping the older format standards, such as EDI, Federal Internet Exchange (FIX), and Interactive Financial Exchange (IFX) in the finance industry, to XML schemas.

The primary B2B physical and electronic channels include the following:

- Branches, distribution centers (bricks-and-mortar)
- Geographic distribution and receiving networks
- Web
- EDI/XML

43

- Internet
- Email

When developing a cohesive multichannel B2B strategy, the following data dimensions must be collected, stored, distributed and presented:

- Channel-specific data
  - transaction volumes
  - per-shipment costs
- Cross-channel comparative data
- Supply costs, timeliness, risk exposure, by
  - channel
  - supplier/category
  - resource/category
  - geography
  - time/date/season

Integration

The term *integration* indicates the process of combining multiple *different* things—data, processes, and goals, specifically—into a single thing, or at least into what *appears* to be a single thing.

Companies of significant size are likely to be comprised of constituent units with divergent (if not conflicting) data, processes, and goals. Trends quite often exist that optimize the performance of individual units at the expense of overall organizational performance. For example, marketing personnel may be measured by numbers of leads generated; sales may be measured by total sales volume. Neither of these is directly related to product profitability, against which product development may be measured. If departments are not measured against common metrics, they are not likely to be motivated to work toward common goals through adopting common processes and data.

For decades, companies have approached data and process integration in fits and starts (in a *dis*integrated fashion!). The reason that integration is an issue at all is, of course, the existence of dissimilar data and processes that, on occasion, an organization might prefer to have behave, or at least to appear, in a similar fashion. Prior to the advent of the digital economy, with a *limited* number of interaction channels, most companies had been able to persuade the limited data and processes exposed to the outside world to jump through somewhat the same hoops and to present a unified face. But with the double whammy of channel proliferation combined with the transparency of value activities demanded by the new economy, data and process integration becomes at the same time more challenging and a critical prerequisite to a company's viability in the marketplace.

Data integration, rather than goal or process integration, is of course the topic of this book. But since goals are dependent on process, and process is dependent on data, data integration is a fundamental enabler of an integration effort of any type.

In the value chain concept, integration points—interfaces—between activities in the value chain, are known as *linkages. Coordination* and *optimization* of these integration points are necessary to achieve sustainable competitive advantage. Data warehousing technologies are important tools in enabling the coordination and optimization of value chain linkages.

Companies participating in electronic commerce have been categorized into two broad types (as I pointed out earlier, the buzzword generator is working overtime), described in Table 2.13.

As the new economy emerged, conventional wisdom held that the weight of the bricks and mortar legacy back-office functions, systems, and data would prevent more established companies from being nimble enough to effectively compete in the new channels. Now that multichannel marketplaces are beginning to transition from explosive growth to maturation, many "pure" dotcoms are falling prey to consolidation, if not to outright failure.

A new Web-based business enterprise—a dotcom—has the luxury of near-freedom from any stovepipe order-entry, inventory, and shipping applications. Such a business, *created* for the digital economy, may be able to enter the market armed and ready with an integrated value chain. But on the downside, this requires starting from square one, with no "bricks" to mortar together, and even if this can be done, few of these new digital enterprises can also provide their customers choices of extra-digital channels.

Table 2.13 Types of E-Businesses

Business Type	Description	Example
"Dotcoms"	Those doing business exclusively, or nearly so, through digital channels.	Amazon.com
"Clicks and Mortar" or "Bricks and Clicks"	Those with an established physical, in addition to digital, presence.	Barnes and Noble

The availability of an established value chain is now coming to be viewed as an important asset—*if effectively leveraged*—in ensuring the durability of a digital marketplace participant. Effectively leveraging an established value chain requires that it be transformed into an integrated value chain. An integrated value chain must be supported by the same multiple, autonomous applications and databases confronted by earlier data warehousing efforts.

An integrated data architecture can be developed, using data warehousing principles, to wire together a firm's constituent value chain activities, and also to combine the newer and older interaction channels of the newly digital enterprise.

Next, we'll pay another visit to our friends at Tiosa Corporation and examine the impact that the growth of e-commerce, in combination with recent business changes, is having on their inbound and outbound channels.

Tiosa Corporation's Value Chain and Channels

Since its inception in 1960, Tiosa Corporation has served the financial needs of the energy and utility industry. Tiosa's role has been primarily in providing lending services to help finance the development and enhancement of major facilities of their customers—production facilities such as wells and generating plants, as well as transmission and distribution facilities. It can be concluded from this that historically, the relationship between Tiosa and its customers has been B2B. In addition, since their products are primarily financial (money), in the past three decades, the company's value chain has developed around the provision of electronic, rather than physical, products. Figure 2–3 illustrates Tiosa's original channels and constituents.

With the widespread deregulation of the energy and utility industry begun in the mid-1990s, Tiosa found its customer base changing radically. Many customers have found it necessary to divest themselves of expensive producing and transmission facilities in order to remain competitive in their regional retail distribution markets. These customers' facilities (and their associated debt) have been spun off into independent companies, or have been sold off either to large concerns specializing in facilities management or to larger competitors. A good portion of Tiosa's loan portfolio has thus changed hands, or been paid off entirely. The company, as a result, has seen steadily decreasing revenue from their traditional products.

In response to these changing market conditions, Tiosa's management

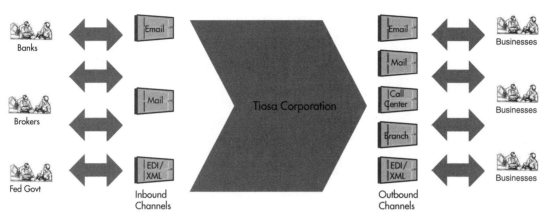

Figure 2-3
Tiosa's original channels and constituents.

recently made a decision to move aggressively into what they saw as a unique opportunity in the retail utility business. As a result, Tiosa acquired a smaller retail business, Gasomatic, Inc., which specializes in providing natural gas-related products and services to consumers. Gasomatic sells household natural gas appliances, such as stoves, dryers, grills, and lamps, and also offers financing gas-line insurance services. Gasomatic does not manufacture products, but has a well-established value chain of its own, including inbound and outbound logistics as well as a network of inventory and distribution centers.

Tiosa's management saw Gasomatic's product line as complementary to its traditional products, as well as providing a solid entry enabling the company to follow its long-time customers into the consumer marketplace. Figure 2–4 illustrates Gasomatic's original channels and constituents.

As we can see, in one fell swoop, Tiosa has expanded both its products and channels tangentially to where they have previously focused. They have expanded from an exclusively electronic-product, B2B firm to become, in addition, a physical-product B2C firm. This will seriously impact Tiosa's value chain and channels, requiring the identification and consolidation of overlaps.

Upon legal consummation of the acquisition, the combined company will do business as Tiosa Group, Inc. Figure 2–5 describes the proposed value chain/channel configuration the combined entity.

The announcement of the intended acquisition has come somewhat as a surprise to Dan, the Tiosa CIO. He and his team had begun making progress on a strategy for moving Tiosa forward based on its original channels and constituents, leveraging its existing IT infrastructure and data-management archi-

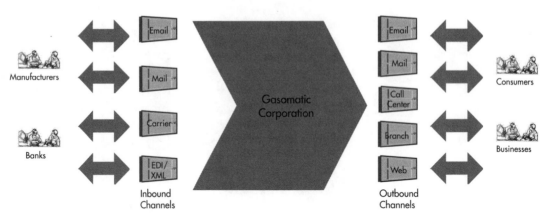

Figure 2-4
Gasomatic's original channels and constituents.

tecture. Now the roadmap has suddenly become significantly more complicated, so the e-commerce team will need to take a step back, assimilate some new members (the Gasomatic e-commerce team), inventory the resources of the combined new organization, and recast its e-commerce strategy to support the new organization.

Dan began to prepare for the combined strategy group meetings by first developing the overview diagrams shown in Figures 2-3, 2-4, and 2-5. His next step was to textually summarize the channels with which the new organization will interact with its constituents, the value chain activities utilizing each channel, and some likely directions for each channel/activity combination:

- **EDI/XML:** Tiosa's investment management and cash management departments (inbound logistics and operations) have operated B2B e-commerce for several years, via EDI connections with banks, the Federal Reserve, and brokerages. Customers also have had the option to submit payments through EDI to the loan servicing department (operations). Gasomatic's purchasing department (inbound logistics) has used B2B EDI to submit orders to manufacturers and also to make payments to manufacturers.

- **Email:** The customer service departments of both organizations have begun using email extensively to communicate with their customers. Gasomatic's marketing department has begun to investigate "permission marketing."

- **Carrier and Wireless:** Delivery of Gasomatic's physical products must of course be done by carrier—but many opportunities exist to

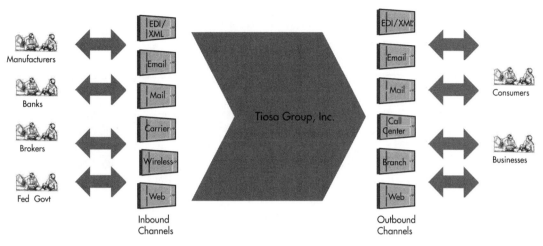

Figure 2-5
Tiosa Group's proposed combined channels and constituents.

optimize this channel through disseminating information through wireless channels.

- **Mail:** Many smaller Tiosa customers who cannot justify the cost of an EDI infrastructure continue to send in their loan payments through the mail. Nearly one year ago, Gasomatic implemented a pay-by-Web mechanism by which its retail customers can make regular payments on financed purchases of its products. Tiosa Group may want to consider expanding this mechanism to offer a less disruptive payment alternative for its smaller utility customers. An XML-based solution may be feasible for consolidating both Web-based and EDI-based transactional activity.

- **Call Centers and Branches:** Both Tiosa and Gasomatic have well-established branch networks and call centers, which provide and maintain a high level of customer service. Management of the combined company is likely to consider consolidating branches and call centers, but will not want to compromise the competitive level of customer support provided. In any case, when Tiosa Group becomes a reality, all CSRs will need
  - basic knowledge in the company's diverse product base
  - access to all information on customer activities—across all channels— necessary to provide timely, excellent response to customer requests.

- **Web:** Since Tiosa's traditional customer base has been energy utility companies, its public Web site has, to date, been a channel for marketing rather than sales or transactional activity. With the acquisition of the Gasomatic consumer constituency and its full-fledged Web-based order-entry and payment channel, Tiosa Group has an opportunity to develop a combined Web strategy to leverage its digital presence across its combined direct and indirect customer base.

Tiosa fully intends to use the Web to market Gasomatic's products and services to its corporate utility clients. Tiosa Group will offer to utilities the opportunity to sell Gasomatic's products and services under the utility client's name ("private labeling") or under the Tiosa brand—a win-win situation with many revenue-sharing opportunities…and potential challenges for Dan and his newly expanded technical staff.

Chapter 3

ENTERPRISE IT ARCHITECTURE
FOR THE DIGITAL ECONOMY

Variety of uniformities makes complete beauty.
—Sir Christopher Wren

Up to this point, we have looked at what data warehousing is, and was, and at the effects that the advent of e-commerce is having on data usage across value chain activities and channels. In order to begin to make the connections between data warehousing and e-commerce, in this chapter we will take one step back (and hopefully not fall off the cliff in the process), and assume a perspective from which we can look at both of these topics within the context of an even broader one: information technology (IT) architecture.

Actually, this book is not about *just* data warehousing and e-commerce; in a broader sense it is about *data management for* e-commerce, within the context of IT architecture. It just so happens that, because of its history and the enormous, sustained attention data warehousing has received, its various facets comprise what is pretty darn close to the "state of the practice" when it comes to data management in an architectural context.

Entire books, indeed, entire enterprises and careers, have been devoted to the pursuit of IT architecture. We will constrain ourselves here to a single chapter, and focus on just the subset of IT architecture concepts that are relevant for clarifying what data warehousing means to e-commerce. We will propose some definitions for both IT architecture itself and a set of constituent components. Then, we'll discuss ways to develop and use IT architecture, focusing on data warehousing and e-commerce. Finally, we'll again visit our friends at Tiosa Group and see what progress they may be making in applying data warehousing to e-commerce, within the context of their overall IT architecture.

Why Do IT Architecture?

In the 1966 motion picture *The Flight of the Phoenix,* an airplane carrying a group of men crashes in the middle of a desert. One of the surviving passengers, Heinrich Dorfmann, convinces the rest of the stranded survivors that he can design a new airplane using components of the wreckage of the old. Just before the maiden flight of this new (downsized) flying machine, *The Phoenix,* it is discovered that Dorfmann has never designed a real airplane, only toy model airplanes. But lo and behold, *The Phoenix* does indeed fly, and carries the exhausted and dehydrated survivors back to civilization.

Is there a moral of the story that can be applied to IT architecture? Are we crash-landed and stranded in a desert, with nothing but wreckage from which to construct our salvation? Hopefully not, but…a model—an *architecture,* if you will—that uses existing components should indeed enable the construction of a truly workable result from an assortment of disjointed pieces and parts. In the field of computers in business, models have had a checkered history, a highly qualified success. Why yet another model? Because this model comes with *all* the pages of the assembly manual, and can truly enable the construction of a Phoenix.

Before going any farther, we should probably address the question of why any company, given typical priorities, backlogs, and time pressures, presumes to undertake yet another effort, such as developing an IT Architecture. Any company utilizing information technology to any extent is doing (and redoing) IT Architecture already—on an ad hoc basis; on a project-by-project basis; perhaps also at an enterprise "conceptual" level…and never the twain shall meet.

With e-commerce channels constantly amassing on top of and beside established channels, companies more than ever need to find and stake out the technological high ground from which they can assess and advance their competitive position. They need to achieve *maximum maneuverability* to effectively respond to existing and future opportunities and threats, which are appearing and transforming at an accelerating rate. To do this, companies need to identify and manage to their benefit the technological *variables and constants,* and their interdependencies. IT architecture is a tool with which constants and variables can be identified, constants can be stabilized, and variables can be optimized and managed to the benefit of the enterprise. Applying a *comprehensive, calculated, disciplined* architectural approach will enhance the probability of success and enable the measurement of success.

As we've done with data warehousing and e-commerce, let's take a brief look at the landscape surrounding the concept of IT Architecture.

Who's Doing IT Architecture?

Significant early work in articulating and proselytizing architectural approaches for information technology was done by James Martin and groups within IBM and dates back to the 1970s. More recently, much credit must be given to John Zachman, and his Zachman Framework, for almost single-handedly creating and sustaining most of the ongoing popular interest in IT architecture. Bernard Boar of AT&T has published several excellent books describing various facets of IT Architecture, primarily within the context of IT strategy. Larry DeBovier has written and spoken on what he has termed *adaptive architectures* for information technology. Steven Spewak has also written and presented extensively on IT Architecture techniques. (Published works by these authors are listed in the bibliography.)

Many companies have undertaken IT Architecture projects within the past 20 years. The lack of success of most of these efforts is due primarily to these factors:

1. Lack of clear steps and methods for applying the results of architecture efforts to real-world projects.

2. Failure to generate a "critical mass" of organizational will sufficient to sustain the effort through to complete implementation.

3. Failure to articulate persuasive metrics for demonstrating success.

Your company is likely to have undertaken and abandoned one (or more) of these efforts. The approach described in part here offers a good possibility of success, due to

1. Its ability to unite past, current, and future IT projects—including e-commerce efforts.

2. Its inclusion of, and emphasis on, interfaces and transformations—a critical emphasis hitherto lacking.

What *Is* an IT Architecture, Anyway?

> One of the principal objects of theoretical research in any department of knowledge is to find the point of view from which the subject appears in its greatest simplicity.
>
> —J. W. Gibbs

Fields of endeavor other than information technology speak of architecture, but discussions in few if any other disciplines focus with such frequency and reverence around one or another exposition of *an* architecture—as a thing in and of itself. *An* architecture, in IT terms, is more precisely a model.

Similar to C. J. Date's suggestion that a database is simply a large, structured variable, a model such as an IT architecture is also simply a large, structured variable (or more precisely, a set of variables) that forms one side of an equation. An equation is a mathematical statement that says that two things are equal. In our IT equation, on the left of the equal sign is the model (architecture); on the right is either the existing state or some desired state. For example,

$$IT\ Architecture = Model = (\Sigma(resources) + \Sigma(interfaces) + \Sigma(transformations)) = f(desired\ state).$$

The desired state is that ideal state of IT usage allowing for, at the least possible cost, the best continuous informing (*informing* being the removal of uncertainty) of the business it supports.

For the purposes of this discussion, let me propose these definitions:

- An IT architecture is the representation and implementation of a strategy.
- A strategy is simply a plan for moving from *where you are* to *where you want to be*.
- An IT strategy is an actionable description of how *best* to apply IT resources for competitive advantage.
- An IT architecture, therefore, is the representation and implementation of a plan for applying IT resources to move your competitive advantage from where it is to where you want it to be.

In order to do this, an IT architecture needs to include

- A *representation* of where you are—what your IT resources are and how they are currently deployed.

54

- A *representation* of where you want to be—what you want your IT resources to be and how they are to be deployed.
- The *implementation* of where you want to be—you'll have it when you get there!
- A series of *effective actions* for getting from here to there.

An IT architecture worth its salt is *not* just stagnant shelfware or binders. Above all else, an architecture must offer a mechanism for managing change —which has become the single most critical activity in the application of IT in business. It should define comprehensively all the IT "things" about which decisions must be made in order to move from a current state to a future state. If the model is indeed valid for implementing cost-effective change, then it should aid in achieving changes required to move from a pre-architected state to an architected state. The model should assist its users in recognizing "force multipliers," levers, and synergy among the pieces and parts of the architecture model. It should identify interrelated areas where nonoptimal decisions can result in diminishing returns, but more importantly, it should identify those areas where optimal decisions offer increasing returns.

To be of value, an IT architecture should be verifiable by testing and observation, and useful for making accurate predictions. It should be relevant for an entire enterprise of any scope, as well as any subset of an enterprise, down to and including a given application system or even parts within an application system.

Components of an IT Architecture

The IT architecture described in this section can assist organizations in avoiding some of the pitfalls described earlier. The architecture model is comprised of resources, interfaces, perspectives, and transformations. But…the *whole* is greater than the sum of the parts!

Resources

In this unique approach to IT architecture, the resource types shown in Figure 3–1 are the fundamental building blocks of the architecture—an inventory of humans, functions, data, hardware, and software. If we are trying to gain competitive advantage by applying an IT architecture, we should try to gain differentiation in those components that are not easily duplicated by our

Figure 3-1
IT architecture resources.

competitors—those component types that are not commodities. Hardware is a commodity; software is *increasingly* so over time. Some functions can be differentiating—those that are done in some unique, high-quality and/or low-cost way; customer service is a prime example of this in the new economy. Humans, while certainly not commodities (but this is not a philosophy or human rights dissertation), have *skills and experience* that to a great extent are interchangeable and seem to be interchanged more frequently from one company to another as time goes on. This leaves us with the least duplicable type of resource—you guessed it—data. Data about *your* company's business plans, customers, products, relationships, markets, and channels is the most unique, least interchangeable asset in your IT arsenal.

Discussion of how applying a comprehensive IT architecture approach can assist in moving a company into the new economy is well beyond the scope of this book. However, focusing exclusively on the data resource type and its related components should shed considerable light on how best to apply data warehousing to the challenges and opportunities of the new economy.

Interfaces

One goal of our architectural viewpoint is to endeavor to truly conceive and manage each resource type strictly as a *type*. In object-oriented terms, a type is a set of objects with a common specification *and common interface*. If we conceive the building blocks of an IT architecture in this manner (see Figure 3–2), we can then begin to manage *resource types* by managing their interfaces.

Each resource type interfaces with itself and with each of the other resource types. A more complex diagram showing all of these interfaces could be presented, but since we are concentrating on data (you may have gotten this idea by now), we'll focus in on the interfaces to the *data* resource type. The diagram shown in Figure 3–2 shows blocks depicting the data resource type and each of its interface types. From now on, we will focus exclusively on the data resource type and its related architectural components.

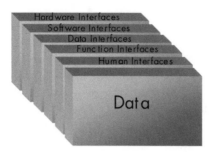

Figure 3-2
The data resource and its interfaces.

An interface is a common boundary. A standard interface is a common boundary implemented widely enough to enable nondisruptive replacement of components—effectively, a commodity interface. We will define for our purposes the term *framework,* widely used and accepted in discussions of IT architectures, as specifically the set of interfaces within the IT architecture. One can conceive of this architecture model as a honeycomb, with the framework of interfaces being the comb, and components "snapping in and out of" the cells in the comb.

> In the great civilizations, a higher and higher standard of living
> requires more and more standardization, which produces both brilliant
> and beautiful improvements.
>
> —Marilyn vos Savant

Supposing we can indeed accomplish this, we will find that solving for, or standardizing, the component types in the equation is, believe it or not, only half the job—and the lesser half, at that. The more important half of the job is determining and standardizing (i.e., rendering as *constants*) the interfaces in the architecture. While this may appear to make our intimidating job even more complicated, accomplishing the standardization of interfaces is even more powerful than standardizing component types. Standardizing interfaces allows components of the same type to be fungible; that is, interchangeable.

Interfaces enable the encapsulation of resource types. Interfaces, by being abstract enough to deal with whatever nature their resource types' contents may assume, render as inconsequential any distinctions between any two instances of a given component type. The most significant result of this is that the "contents" of the resource "black box" may be completely replaced, if required, with absolutely no effect on the functioning of its interfaces, or on any resource instances with which it interfaces. The resulting implications for change management are enormous.

Perspectives

A perspective, in the visual arts, and for our purposes in IT architecture, is simply a point of view. In solving a problem (such as a business or technological challenge or opportunity), adopting a different perspective as more information is revealed assists in moving toward a solution to the problem. Figure 3–3 illustrates the interfaces and perspectives of the data resource.

Perspectives in this IT architecture include

- *Conceptualization:* A description of the problem. Having a clear understanding of a challenge or opportunity greatly increases the likelihood of successfully conceiving effective potential means (solutions) for addressing the challenge or opportunity.
- *Specification:* A description of a solution. Having a clear and precise understanding of one or more solutions greatly increases the likelihood of successfully implementing an effective solution.
- *Realization:* An implementation of a solution. This may sound like the end of the story; however, as anyone who has implemented a system understands, the implementation of a solution, if at all successful, leads to additional challenges and opportunities to be addressed...which leads us to transformation.

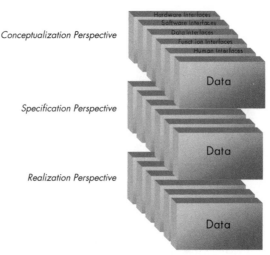

Figure 3–3
The data resource with its interfaces and perspectives.

Transformations

A transformation is a set of actions which, over time, converts one perspective into another, as follows:

A description of a problem (a conceptualization) is transformed into...a description of a solution (a specification), which is transformed into...an implementation of a solution (a realization). Then, humans being fallible and scopes of efforts necessarily being constrained in order to be manageable, an implementation of a solution (a realization) is transformed into . . . a description of a problem (a conceptualization)!!

And, as in the words of The King of Siam, "Et Cetera, et cetera, et cetera!" Figure 3–4 shows the continuous loop of IT architecture transformations. Figure 3–5 illustrates the interfaces, perspectives, and transformations of the resource data.

Therefore, in order to be completely effective, an IT architecture must accommodate *resources* and *interfaces* from multiple *perspectives* undergoing a recurring cycle of *transformations*.

An example of working our way through one cycle of this architecture, *specifically focused on the data resource and its interfaces*, would progress somewhat like this:

1. Opportunities, which are likely to also have an impact on one or more of its interfaces, arise within the current data resource. A simple but topical example is, *Our competitors have enabled customers to order their products on their Web site. Our Web site is not currently enabled for customer order entry.*

2. The opportunities are conceptualized—transformed into a conceptualization perspective, a description of the opportunities. In our example, *In order to enable our customers to enter order data over the Web, people, functions, software and hardware, and additional, different data are required.*

3. The conceptualization perspective is transformed into a specification perspective—the description of one or more potential solutions. This description details specific people, functions, software, hardware, and additional data, as well as the methods with which these interface with the required data.

4. One or more specification perspectives are transformed into a realization perspective—the solution(s) are implemented. The required people, functions, software, hardware, and additional data are devel-

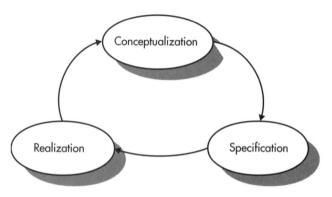

Figure 3-4
IT transformations loop.

Figure 3-5
The data resource with interfaces, perspectives, and transformations.

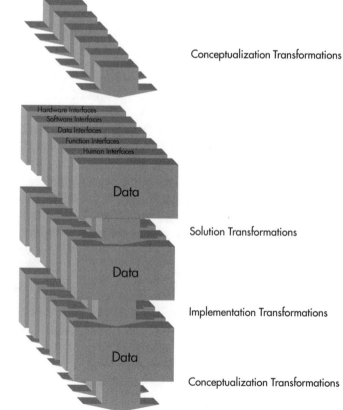

oped or procured, and deployed, enabling the acquisition of order data from customers.

5. An opportunity is identified to increase Web sales by targeted discount campaigns, enabled by permission marketing. Data is required from customers, indicating their consent to email marketing—then, back to step 1.

This recurring cycle of transformations is a fundamental difference between IT architecture and IT *projects*. A project has an end; an architecture is never complete (this always causes difficulties in funding such an effort). An IT architecture is a context within which IT projects—such as data warehousing or e-commerce efforts—are coordinated with common, standard means (especially interfaces!) towards a common end: the enhanced competitiveness of the enterprise.

Over the past two decades, data warehousing has created a sustained emphasis on the criticality of data resources and interfaces. An architectural approach can be applied to fuse this data emphasis into e-commerce efforts.

Developing and Using a Data Architecture for E-Commerce

Now we'll discuss the subset of an IT architecture, which we'll call *data architecture*, and how a company can apply data architecture management concepts to enhance its competitive position in the world of e-commerce. In subsequent chapters, we'll look at more short-term, project-focused applications of data warehouse technologies to e-commerce.

The process for establishing an IT architecture can begin at any point in the cycle. The common steps, regardless of the resource(s) to be focused on, are as follows:

1. Set up the support structure by educating a critical mass of analysis and development resources in the architecture and mobilizing and committing to the success of those resources.

2. Determine the point in the cycle that is the end goal of the initial effort—a synch point at which success can be measured. *Begin with the end in mind*.

3. Determine your *entry* point into the structure—the point providing greatest leverage toward reaching the goal.

4. Determine all dependencies within the scope—interfaces and transformations.

5. Determine risk factors and tradeoffs—which dependencies, if any, can be compromised.

6. Based on all the above, determine *scope* and *trajectory* within the structure.

If an IT architecture cycle for optimization of data resources were to be initiated by a company, it would typically fall within the responsibility of a data resource management, data administration, or data warehouse administration group—or, in a smaller organization, a group with a relatively wider scope performing these functions. The goals of these groups are challenging enough, but the demands on providing quality data for e-commerce value chain activities and channels raises important issues above and beyond successful management of the data *resource* alone. Even in cases where data management groups make important progress in enhancing the value of the data resources of an enterprise, these improvements are likely to be limited by *constraints on the interfaces of the data component*. IT architecture provides a means for confronting and dealing with these constraints.

Let's use the term *data architecture* to designate the subset of the IT architecture, including specifically the data resource *along with its interfaces and transformations*. The function of managing the data architecture (mobilizing the architectural transformations), including *data resource management* plus *data interface management,* can be called *data architecture management.*

With regard to perspectives, the conceptualization perspective of the data architecture includes what is often termed *business meta-data,* that is, a description of the data and data interfaces required by the business currently and in the future. (Note that the noun form *meta-data* is carefully chosen. The prefix meta-, meaning "above" something else—e.g., metaphysics, metacarpals—indicates a perspective in this case higher in abstraction than the perspectives below it. There is no independent noun *meta.*) The specification perspective of the data architecture is comprised of what is often termed *technical meta-data;* that is, a description of a solution to the business data and data-interface requirements.

Data warehousing to date is the discipline most closely aligned with, and comprehensive of, data architecture management, because of the historical inclusion in its scope of not only the data resource, but also all the *interfaces, perspectives, and transformations* dealing with the data resource.

Data warehousing disciplines have dealt with the data-human interface as it applies to business intelligence. They address the data-function interface through understanding of decision-support functions as well as, by necessity, those functions that create the data consumed by those functions. Many data-modeling and database-design professionals have gravitated to data warehousing as a result of their knowledge of, and career-long fascination with, data-data interfaces. And no data warehouse or data mart can be built and maintained without quality data-software and data-hardware interfaces.

The data warehousing lifecycle addresses all architectural perspectives and transformations of the data resource and its interfaces.

Concurrent with supporting ongoing projects, e-commerce-related and otherwise, data warehouse administration, d/b/a (doing business as) data architecture management, needs to investigate and implement whatever techniques are available to help promote the benefits of an architectural approach. These benefits are more important than ever to mobilize the necessary transformations within the enterprise to confront the challenges and opportunities posed by e-commerce.

One compelling such technique is the *theory of constraints* (TOC) developed by Eliyahu M. Goldratt. TOC suggests that in order to achieve the greatest improvements in a given system (such as a budding data architecture), we should focus on its weakest links, or *constraints*. Data architecture management can put the data architecture transformations into action by focusing on the constraints on each data interface, using these TOC "focusing" steps:

- *Identify the constraints:* So far, we have explicitly labeled and described *resources* and *interfaces*, which is prerequisite to identifying the constraints on the resources and interfaces. Next, performance measurements should be identified for each that are realistic and meaningful in judging the impact of any changes.

- *Exploit the constraints:* Exploit means to get the most out of existing resources and interfaces. This is the domain of the "quick fix." In general, this means optimizing the performance of available technologies to the extent feasible within the current fiscal period's constraints. Optimization is measured by changes in the values of the relevant measurement units.

- *Elevate the constraints:* Elevate means to apply additional resources to the constraint. This requires investigating, planning for, and acquiring new and expanded techniques and technologies for optimizing interfaces to the greatest extent possible within the *next* fiscal period's constraints and beyond. Sustainable, ongoing optimization is made possible through the implementation of durable and sustainable technical and technological *standards*.

The level of success enjoyed by data warehousing can be attributed to its success in *elevating* the constraints on data interfaces, the *third* of the TOC focusing steps. Significant opportunities for *identifying* and *exploiting* constraints on data interfaces remain to be explored, especially with regard to their application to e-business.

The following sections describe how the data-related interface components of the IT architecture—those components typically addressed with data warehousing technologies—can be optimized for the goals of e-commerce efforts. From time to time, examples of applying the TOC focusing steps for architectural transformations of these interfaces will be given. Architectural optimization of the data resource itself will be covered in Chapter 5.

The recent explosion of e-commerce development has brought two areas of discipline into especially sharp focus, primarily in the area of business-to-consumer e-commerce Web sites. The critical impact that these disciplines are having on data interfaces is not yet widely realized. These disciplines are user interface management—also known variously as human-computer interaction, cognitive and creative, or user experience—and content management. Personnel with skills and experience in these areas continue to be rare and in high demand, which gives rise to many challenges in their practical application. As we investigate the management of data interfaces, we'll give special attention to the interaction that data architecture management needs to have with these disciplines.

The E-Commerce Data-Human Interface: B2C Channels

The data-human interface is the common boundary between an organization's data resource and the human producers and consumers of that resource.

The emphasis of information technology in the 1970s and 1980s was in capturing and accumulating data resources. During the heyday of data warehousing in the 1990s, this emphasis turned to making use of data already captured, broadening the focus of data-management technology from input optimization to output optimization. B2C e-commerce has once again shifted the emphasis to the accumulation of data—now just as likely to be produced by customers as by employees—precipitating a return to emphasis on input optimization.

Design of Web sites has expanded from pure presentation of graphical and document-based information to include a much greater capability for users— again, most often customers—to interact with data. The discipline of human-computer interaction (HCI) is receiving increased attention due to the expansion of B2C e-commerce. A subdiscipline, human information processing, within HCI deals with how humans interact with data, including of course both input and output functions.

Information results from the presentation, within an appropriate context, of facts that are relevant to, but not yet known by, the user. This is where the value of data output originates. The output side of the data-human interface is what results in the transformation of data into information, it is content plus context.

Returning to our data-architectural focus directs us to compile the realization perspective of the data-human interface by identifying the nature, extent, *and constraints* of the current human-computer interactions of the enterprise.

Transforming the realization perspective to the conceptualization perspective begins with the understanding that the value of the data resource of course depends on the humans by whom it is created and interpreted. The data-human interface assists or hinders input quality. Conceptualization of where the enterprise needs to go dictates constant improvement of the quality of data input and output.

To exploit and elevate constraints on this interface, data architecture management works to increase the level of knowledge transfer, cross-training, and communication between data providers and data consumers—internal business users, external business users, and customers—and between these groups and data architecture management. A durable and effective data-stewardship program should be initiated, with appropriate links to job performance measurement. Many valuable resources are available on data stewardship and data quality. Publications and presentations on these subjects by Larry English and Robert S. Seiner are especially recommended. Please see the Bibliography for details.

The capacity of the Internet to make more data available to more people—within and especially outside a business enterprise—has greatly intensified the issues surrounding ownership of data, especially data on and about customers. Much activity has sprung up in many quarters to address customer data privacy issues, including activity within the United States Congress and the World Wide Web Consortium (W3C). Data architecture management should become a primary participant in assessing and applying such efforts as customer information privacy policies within its enterprise.

Data architecture management, working in conjunction with data providers and data consumers in business areas, can optimize available data-capture and interpretation technologies to the extent feasible within the current fiscal period's constraints.

Data architecture management, in conjunction with data providers and consumers, then transforms its conceptualization perspective of the data-human interface into a specification perspective. Data architecture management should ideally provide guidance and context in developing durable and sustainable standards for data-capture and data-presentation technologies to the work of available cognitive-and-creative specialists in HCI. The high demand, short supply, and compressed working timeframes of HCI-skilled personnel typically causes significant challenges in attempting to offer a data-architectural point of view to data-human interface development. The time-to-market-critical nature of e-commerce participation being what it is, often the best an enterprise can hope for is a gradual evolution toward mutual accommodation of project and architectural interests.

The data-human interface specification perspective is transformed into the next-generation realization perspective by investigating, planning for, and directing the acquisition of innovative data-capture and data-presentation and technologies—by wireless devices, for example—to optimize this interface to the extent possible within the next fiscal period's constraints and beyond.

Goldratt advises that effectively dealing with constraints requires identifying and managing to a set of realistic measurements. The primary measurement unit of data-function interface effectiveness can be designated the *data inventory turnover ratio*—a measurement of the amount of data use and reuse by functions occurring within a specified time period, relative to the amount of data in storage. The turnover of a segment of the data resource—say, a file or database table—could be measured as a comparison of "hits" (read accesses) and updates, over a period of time, relative to the size of the data store, perhaps in bytes. A data resource with more read accesses, relative to the number of updates, over a similar time period, would have a higher turnover ratio than a resource of similar size with fewer reads per update. The data inventory turnover concept is covered in more detail in Chapter 7.

The evolution of the data-function interface driven by e-commerce expansion is multifaceted. Much more data is being created by customers, who are performing both new functions and functions off-loaded from internal order-entry personnel. At the same time, due to the nature of e-commerce software and available data-hardware technologies, more and more copies of existing data are proliferating—product catalog, banking or brokerage account balances, and inventory data being typical examples. The developing area of Web analytics, covered in more detail in Chapter 4, is offering opportunities for increased usage of this newly accumulating data and will likely result in a trend toward higher data inventory turnover ratios in the near future.

The E-Commerce Data-Function Interface: B2B Channels and the Integrated Value Chain

The realization perspective of the data-function interface is the current usage of data by business functions. E-commerce is adapting existing functions into new channels, and in some cases creating entirely new functions. Each shift in technology support for an existing function creates new data-software interfaces; each creation of new functionality creates new data-function interfaces. Any company which has successfully embarked down the road of data architecture management will have a head start in identifying and applying new and existing data resources to these functions.

The important role of the data-function interface in strengthening the linkages among value chain activities (functions), as Porter points out in *Competitive Advantage*, becomes even more critical in B2B e-commerce. As competitive threats and opportunities arise in a company's marketplace, the company must have the infrastructure in place—through all architectural perspectives—to rapidly modify and enhance its business processes and reposition itself. In B2B e-commerce, all new and enhanced functions are sure to be highly data-dependent, making this interface a powerful enabler or constraint.

Many B2B e-commerce opportunities, such as e-marketplaces, e-procurement, and collaborative planning, forecasting, and replenishment (CPFR), require the exposure of a company's data to computerized functions performed by other organizations. This exposure greatly expands the scope and significance of the data-function interface of the e-commerce-enabled organization. As with other data interfaces, the involvement of a skilled and experienced data architecture management function is critical to comprehensive and high-quality administration of this interface.

The E-Commerce Data-Software Interface: Supporting Integrated Channels and Value Chain

The e-commerce technology area of content management (CM) was introduced briefly earlier. Looking first at the conceptualization and specification perspectives, we begin to see the impact of the CM discipline in e-commerce technology through its impact on the data-software interface. The end goal of CM is to assure that data of various types is effectively and efficiently presented to e-commerce software.

CM is primarily concerned with providing a structured approach for administering the content of a Web site through a series of what are essentially perspectives and transformations. This approach draws on precedents in both software change management and workflow management.

CM is in a state of evolution that parallels the expansion of the types of data that comprise the content of a typical Web site. Early (mid-1990s) Web sites were comprised almost exclusively of visual, "unstructured" data types—images, text, and documents—and it is these types of data that CM techniques and technologies have typically been focused on managing. But with the expansion of Web site content into more structured data—data stored in databases—challenges arise for integrating the disparate, specialized disciplines of CM and conventional database management. These challenges are exacerbated by issues similar to those of HCI. CM-skilled resources are rare and in demand (consequently tending to be transient—but these will stabilize), and the need for speed in e-commerce development tends to relegate architectural concerns behind the priority of getting sites up and running.

Causing a widespread impact of e-commerce on the data-software interface is the advent of specialized e-commerce application server software. E-commerce application server products, such as Broadvision or Blue Martini, focus on managing the data-human interface for Web-based B2C channels. This type of product typically requires a dedicated copy (database) of data within its scope in order to properly function, in turn necessitating the creation and maintenance of additional data-software and data-data interfaces, effectively identical to a data warehousing extract-transform-load (ETL) scenario. More on this technology will be covered in later chapters.

The E-Commerce Data-Data Interfaces: Semantic, Technological, and Transformational

Data-data interfaces—common boundaries and relationships between data and other data—have always been rich and multifaceted. The opportunities offered by e-commerce conspire to make these common boundaries even more complex and wide-ranging. Data-data interfaces typically are semantic, technological, or transformational in nature.

Data-data interfaces at the conceptualization and specification perspectives of the data architecture include primarily semantic, business-level ("entity-relationship") data *relationships*—a customer can have many orders. The realization perspective of the e-commerce data-data interface includes proliferating instances of *replication* interfaces. Examples of e-commerce replication interfaces include

- The duplication of order items from a B2C Web application server database to a back-office inventory or fulfillment application.
- Redundant database instances required to assure 24/7 Web site availability.

E-commerce is driving a proliferation of replication interfaces due to the critical data-hardware interface bottleneck and the requirement for implementing stand-alone, yet interfaced, application package software in order to meet razor-thin time-to-market windows.

Current Check-Outs summary for Chhabra,
     Thu Dec 13 17:25:30 EST 2018

BARCODE: 39003022773054
TITLE: Data warehousing and e-commerce /
DUE DATE: 2019 Apr 16

:es can be conceived as either *vertical* or
span perspectives; they deal with trans-
o another, such as implementing a con-
le specification. Horizontal transforma-
data into another unit within the same
rformed by data warehousing ETL tools
ional data interfaces are increasingly im-
allations, often implemented under the
ration (EAI) architectures. Transforma-
lly important in B2B e-commerce appli-
ist be transformed from one company's

there are no better-equipped personnel
agement functions required for identify-
ese data-data interfaces than data ware-
g, database design, data replication, and
data warehousing professional's toolbox.
chitecture management function should
rfaces, let's look again at the concept of
terfaces. The performance level of any
ata structure) is dependent on, and con-
ical, and transformational interfaces to
rspective and within other perspectives.
iould measure, exploit, and elevate con-
straints on these interfaces. Example data-data interface measurement units
include counts of identified and implemented semantic, technological, and
transformational interfaces across the data resource. Data architecture management must facilitate communication among data providers, data consumers, and itself, with the goal of developing durable and sustainable standards
for the identification, development, implementation, and reuse of semantic,
technological, and transformational data-data interfaces. Demonstrable business value should be attributable to these interfaces. Typical examples with
demonstrable e-business value are elimination of redundant data through cus-
tomer-record matching and deriving family units through a "householding"
process—discussed in more detail in Chapter 9.

The E-Commerce Data-Hardware Interface

Data-hardware interfaces relate to computer memory, external storage, and
network connections. These interfaces allow data to both move and rest. Constraints on this interface are not at all difficult to identify. In the world of e-

commerce, in the words of Neil Young, "Rust Never Sleeps." Iron-oxide based storage technologies remain a critical data-hardware interface bottleneck in IT inventories. Performance and availability constraints on these interfaces are exacerbated due to increasing volumes of data. Will increasing processor and network line speed ever overtake the accelerating increase in data volumes? Will primary storage ever become cost-effective enough to enable persistent stores large enough to break the bottleneck? We can write "IBM" in atoms, but still need to be concerned with "seek time"—the time a read-write head takes to find data on a disk. Long-term hope rests in the development of alternative storage materials enabling holographic, molecular, and silicon-based data storage (more on this in Chapter 5).

The only hope of a short-term fix for the hardware-data bottleneck seems to be staging of data—that is, creating multiple copies of data, in multiple media, in order to serve multiple uses. The combination of data staging, dedicated processors (e.g., parallel query) and software *mediators* (translator/interpreters) could alleviate the bottleneck somewhat in the near term.

The hardware resource within the IT architecture is a critical component in supporting a company's e-commerce channels. Planning, designing, configuring, building, and maintaining the networks, servers, and routers is another area of discipline in which skilled personnel are scarce, in demand, and tend to be transient. The hardware resources of an organization comprise the fundamental conduit for reliably containing data and moving it to where it is needed by functions and human beings. To optimize the interface of data to hardware, it is critical that data architecture management work closely with staff that is charged with maintaining an organization's hardware resources.

The performance of data depends on hardware—the installed and available external storage, memory cache, and data transmission technologies. Therefore, the data-hardware interface is a constraint on the use of the data resource. Examples of data-hardware interface measurement units include bandwidth, seek time, transfer rate, and storage density.

Knowledge transfer, cross-training, and communication should be initiated and maintained between data architecture management and the storage technology staff, especially those supporting e-commerce efforts. Storage technology, data architecture management, and e-commerce staff must work together to optimize available data-hardware technologies—to the extent feasible—within the current fiscal period's constraints. Durable and sustainable standards for data-hardware interface technologies need to be investigated, and their implementation begun. The groups then must work together to investigate, plan, acquire, and expand data-hardware technologies to optimize this interface to the extent possible within the next fiscal period's constraints, and beyond.

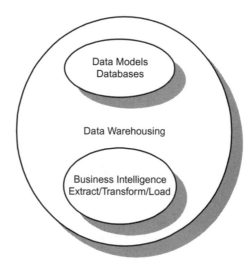

Figure 3-6
Pre-data architecture data warehousing.

Figure 3-7
Data warehousing redeployed as data architecture management for e-commerce.

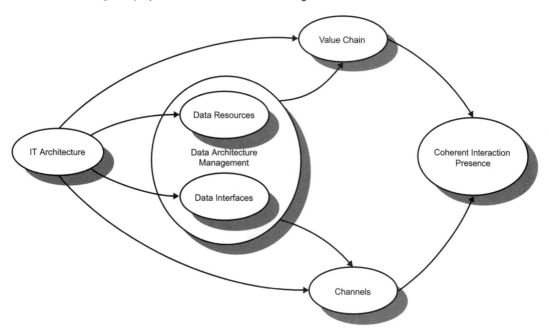

By way of summarization, Figure 3–6 and Figure 3–7 depict a scenario of "redeployment" of data warehousing technologies into a data architecture management configuration. This will result in more effective leveraging of data resources and interfaces in support of the types of e-business enablement we'll begin to discuss in Chapter 4.

Tiosa Group Initiates Data Architecture Management

Tiosa Group CIO Dan has read a good bit on IT architecture and heard John Zachman speak at two different conferences. He's contemplated for some time the possibility of initiating some sort of architecture effort, but up to this point he has hesitated to proceed. He had concluded that it was necessary to start such an effort on a large, all-or-nothing scale—a "big bang" or "grand design" effort—rather than with a smaller "skunk works" project, using limited available resources. He knew it would be a near impossibility to get funding approval for a big bang, all-or-nothing, grand design architecture proposal.

Dan now believes that beginning with a focus on data architecture management will enable Tiosa to get a foothold on IT architecture. He realizes that Tiosa's data is its most differentiating and proprietary IT resource, and that identifying, elevating, and exploiting any and all constraints on its interfaces will begin to give Tiosa an important competitive advantage in the data-driven world of e-commerce. And because a data architecture management focus, rather than being totally isolated, includes all related data interfaces, the initial effort will not be cut off from the rest of an expanding architectural framework. The results of the efforts of a data architecture management group will be plugged in to work surrounding the other architectural components and their interfaces, once these other initiatives are able to kick off.

Dan calls together his staff, whose functions relate directly to the care and feeding of Tiosa's data resource: database administration, data administration, and the various data warehouse and data mart administrators across the company. Most are enthusiastic about pursuing Dan's ideas. Since most of the personnel concerned with data management are well aware of the fundamental value of data in e-commerce and elsewhere, to a large extent Dan finds himself in this session preaching to the choir.

His next step is to identify and enlist those groups responsible for the care and feeding of the various data interfaces, specifically within the various planned and ongoing e-commerce efforts in the Tiosa and Gasomatic subsidiaries. This is where organizational politics must be finessed, since e-commerce projects, corporate-wide or business unit-focused, often tend of necessity to be self-contained, "damn-the-torpedoes," and target-date driven. But by carefully managing his requests for their time, Dan is able to convince the managers responsible for these efforts to sit together and consider his proposals for involving data architecture management personnel in their projects. Many internal Tiosa IT personnel have already been more or less leveraged across several of these projects on a part-time or full-time basis. Dan has been able to propose a convincing offer to the e-commerce managers that these resources bring a valuable enterprise-wide perspective and should work closely in the e-commerce projects with the internal and contracted CM, user interface design, and Web application server resources. The results will benefit each current e-commerce project as well as those in the planning stage.

The data architecture management team will work closely with the e-commerce teams—within the necessary e-business time constraints, of course —and act as a catalyst to begin to identify, standardize, and optimize data interfaces to the greatest extent possible. Interface standardization will allow the encapsulation of data resources, fostering their greatest flexibility and reuse. It will minimize variables and maximize constants, and will form the basis of a stable IT architectural framework, giving Tiosa Group a strong point of leverage from which it can convey a coherent, competitive e-commerce interaction presence.

A prime example of Dan's redeployment of Tiosa's data interface management skills and experience for e-commerce is in the area of electronic payments. Tiosa has for some time encouraged its corporate customers to submit their loan payments via EDI channels such as automated clearinghouse (ACH). With the acquisition of Gasomatic, it wants to continue to offer financing of gas appliance purchases to qualified buyers and to accept submission of electronic payments on these loans as well.

As part of achieving potential economies of scale resulting from the Tiosa/Gasomatic merger, Dan has also been asked to assess the feasibility of consolidating the processing of both corporate and consumer loan payments into a single loan accounting system. An existing interface built for the Tiosa loan processing system is able to convert EDI payment transactions into its own proprietary transaction format for processing. However, many smaller financial institutions, with which many of Gasomatic's consumer customers hold accounts and generate loan payments, have begun to actively research the use of eXtensible Markup Language (XML) as a more economical and flexible alternative to EDI.

Dan needs to investigate publicly available mappings for transforming EDI transactions into equivalent XML transactions. He finds that he can now call on the data transformation (data-data interface) specialists, redeployed to data architecture management from the erstwhile data warehousing units, to take responsibility for investigating and implementing industry-standard EDI/XML transformations. When available, these transformations—standard data-data interfaces—can be expediently implemented and can avoid any impact on the EDI data-software interface to the existing loan processing system.

Chapter 4

OUTPUT: TURNING DATA INTO INFORMATION

Knowledge is of two kinds. We know a subject ourselves,
or we know where we can find information upon it.

—Samuel Johnson

We proposed earlier that data warehousing can be broadly categorized into input, storage, and output functions. Output functions operate on data that has already been collected and stored. Stored data can of course be output for use by either humans or computers. In this chapter, we will deal with the output aspects of both the human and software interfaces, respectively.

In data architecture terms, information output is a subset of both the data-human interface and the data-software interface. Within the domain of data warehousing, various output technologies are often grouped under the term *business intelligence,* or BI.

When it comes to e-commerce BI, or e-BI, some variables have remained relatively stable, while other factors are changing rapidly. The majority of the information that is output in support of decision-making functions continues to be concentrated within the domain of sales, marketing, and finance. The most radical change is the accelerating pace of data accumulation, which is a challenge not only for storage technologies, but also for output technologies—technologies specialized for data retrieval and presentation.

As a result of its impact on channels and value chains, the expansion of e-commerce has increased the criticality of existing decision-support applications and, at the same time, created a need for entirely new types of BI applications. These applications include internal applications, B2C e-commerce, and B2B e-commerce, as well as what has been termed *Web farming.*

Successively Broader Scopes of Data

BI, decision support, analytical capability—it's all about attempting to predict and influence the future. In general, the more data about the past and present that's available to decision-makers, the greater the probability they have of accurately predicting the future. The challenge, of course, is making these volumes of data available in a comprehensible format.

Probably the greatest challenge posed on data warehousing technologies by e-commerce is the increasing volume and diversity of data available for analysis. Any type of e-businesses is confronted with these challenges, but they are likely to arise from different directions and according to a different timetable, depending on the type of e-business model on which an enterprise is based.

E-businesses typically fall into one or the other of the following:

- Single-channel—"pure-play" e-businesses, or dotcoms
- Clicks and mortar—companies with prior established channels outside their e-business initiatives

Which of these types a given enterprise falls into typically determines its stage of e-business "maturity" at a given point in time. A typical pure-play e-business enterprise probably entered the digital marketplace earlier than its more conservative bricks-and-mortar competition, and is therefore likely to be farther along in the e-business maturity cycle. However, bricks-and-clicks multichannel organizations are quickly overtaking the pure-plays. Bricks-and-clicks are discovering that what was previously thought to be a disadvantage—the existence of legacy data assets—is in actuality an advantage. A time-tested technical infrastructure is likely to constitute another considerable advantage of established businesses.

Pure-play e-commerce businesses, in order to grasp the range of data necessary compete with more established competition, must span vertical channels to partners' data. Clicks-and-bricks e-businesses need "only" reach out across their own value chains to acquire the necessary scope of data assets.

Either position has apparent advantages and disadvantages relative to the other, as described in Table 4.1.

As the scope of available analytical data expands, so naturally does the cost of obtaining and compiling the data, as well as the potential value of actionable information produced (see Figure 4–1).

Table 4.1 E-Commerce Business Model Comparison

Business Model	Advantages	Disadvantages
Dotcom "pure play"	• "First-mover" • No legacy IT "albatross"	• No established brand • No established alternative channels • No legacy data assets on customers and transactions
Bricks-and-clicks	• Established brand • Alternative channels • Legacy data assets on customers and transactions • Established technical infrastructure	• Effort required to integrate legacy data assets

Figure 4–1
Comparative scope of e-BI data (not to scale!).

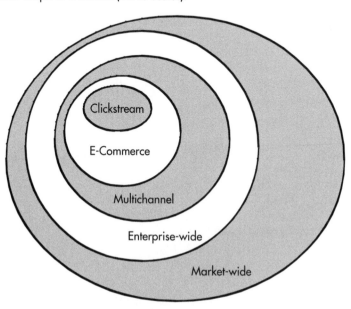

Clickstream Business Intelligence

The primary vehicle for B2C e-commerce is of course the World Wide Web. The largely standardized software architecture of the Web and the architecture of commercially available B2C e-commerce server software influence to a great extent the basic types and content of the data created by Web B2C interactions. It will be helpful to examine these types of data before discussing the types of decision-support output that can be generated from B2C e-commerce data.

The primary data entities involved in Web-based e-commerce include

- End-user gestures, or "clicks"
- Customers
- Products
- Orders

The last three entities are of course part and parcel of the business of selling, regardless of what channel is utilized for the selling activity. *Clickstreams* are an entirely new source of customer-behavior data made possible by the Web, and are indeed part of the very fabric of this new channel.

Essentially, a clickstream is a record of the *path* that a given Web site user takes through the e-commerce channel exposed to him or her by the selling enterprise. This path record provides considerably more detailed behavioral data than that made available by any other selling channel. A company's Web-based e-commerce site is in many ways analogous to a published product catalog and order form. Imagine if an equivalent amount and detail of behavioral data was available on a customer's interaction with this more traditional channel:

1. Customer receives catalog in mail
2. Catalog stacked in pile of mail
3. Catalog retrieved from mail pile
4. Catalog opened to index
5. Pages turned to hiking outerwear
6. Pages turned to clearance items
7. Pages turned to order form
8. Pages turned back to clearance items...

And so forth—with the hope of terminating in the mailing of a completed order form. This is exactly the volume and level of detail of the data collected in Web server logs. It is easy to see why we are becoming increasingly dependent on intermediate software to categorize, summarize, and derive conclusions from data of this nature.

Both types of e-businesses can acquire and maintain clickstream data with equal effort. User clickstreams can be compiled, summarized, and analyzed to determine trends in customer behavior—most importantly, what behavior most typically leads to a successful sale and results in the generation of revenue for the enterprise. The results of such analysis can be fed back into personalization, cross-selling, and even pricing rules invoked in subsequent customer visits.

E-Commerce Business Intelligence

Companies progress at varying rates from initial Web storefronts to adding the "real" functionality required for true Web e-commerce. Real functionality requires the capability for visitors to input data—registering as buying customers, providing credit card information to enable payment, selecting products and placing orders, and viewing account status and balances.

Log files generated by Web servers are specific to clickstreams coming from Web pages. To begin to provide e-BI, explicit data relationships must be established among diverse data collected in Web logs, e-commerce, and legacy operational and financial systems. Examples of such valuable data relationships include, among many others,

- Web purchase transactions connected to the clickstream leading to the purchase
- Geographies of visitors compared to that of purchasers
- Busiest Web traffic volume compared to highest purchase days and times

Integration of overall e-commerce data—including digital channels above and beyond B2C clickstreams—gives a company a correspondingly broader analytical perspective on its relationships within the overall digital marketplace. Other typical digital channels include email, Voiceover IP (VoIP), chat, XML, and EDI.

Multichannel Business Intelligence

Integrating analytic information from all channels—non-digital, such as physical branches and distribution centers, as well as digital—gives a company the broadest possible view not only of cost- and revenue-generating activities, but more importantly, of its customers.

Within the past decade, an influential business trend with considerable impact on data warehousing has been the drive for businesses to become increasingly "customer-centric," or customer-oriented. Customer-centricity entails a shift in enterprise focus from one of selling products to one of pleasing customers—a focus often summed up in the phrase "Know thy customer." This perspective continues to evolve, expanding from just knowing the customers' current characteristics and past behaviors to attempting to predict what their future behavior will be, in order to anticipate and proactively fulfill their wants and needs.

From a data perspective, customer-centricity requires that any available customer-related data be consolidated, cross-referenced, analyzed, and internally disseminated to the greatest extent possible. This requires integration of data on customer characteristics, transactions, and all other activities, gathered from across all channels with which the company's customers interact.

Widely adopted applications for this data include closed-loop CRM and personalization. In addition, increased depth and breadth of knowledge on customers enables increased capability to anticipate and/or detect fraudulent activity.

Closed loop customer information management consists of four major function groups connected into a closed loop by data flowing between the function groups. This flow is shown in Figure 4–2.

1. *Track:* Internally available customer-related data (transactions, click-streams, call center logs, etc.) are merged with customer demographic data available from external providers. The most common storage implementation for this merged data is a single database such as a data warehouse. However, in some cases a middleware connectivity infra-

Figure 4–2
Closed-loop customer information management.

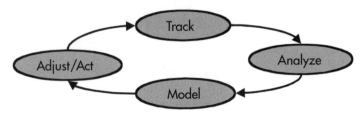

80

structure can allow multiple stand-alone databases to be accessed as a single data source. Each approach has benefits and drawbacks.

2. *Analyze:* Calculations based on user-defined metrics are performed using the integrated data as input. Profitability scores are assigned to individual customers and/or groups of customers.

3. *Model:* Campaigns and promotions are devised and targeted to groups of customers *(clusters)* with similar profitability scores and/or behavior characteristics.

4. *Adjust/Act:* Campaigns and promotions—cross-selling, up-selling, discounts, permission marketing, etc.—are invoked within customer-facing processes (browsing, shopping, order entry, phone contacts), through multiple channels, in an effort to promote and reward profitable customer responses.

Responses from customer interactions—positive, negative, and neutral—are fed back into the integrated data store to be used in determining subsequent promotional activities. This loop enables customer-interaction processes to "learn" from the success or failure of previous profitability-enhancement efforts, with a resulting increase in success rate and overall profitability, over time.

Enterprise-Wide Business Intelligence

A wider analytical perspective is made possible through integration of enterprise-wide data across all channels and value chain linkages. Revenue as well as cost information across all channels and value chain activities can be juxtaposed and interrelated for the benefit of timely and informed decision-making.

Enterprise Information Portals (EIPs) can be said to span whatever gap there may be between the ambiguously bounded realms of BI and knowledge management (KM). EIPs have appeared as a means by which a "standard" user interface (i.e., data-human interface) can be imposed on diverse data sources and formats as a method of coercing such various data sources into an appearance of integration. Often, such a veneer is all that is called for. Conversely, in many cases the last step of cross-relating the various pieces and parts is left up to the end user.

Three converging phenomena—widespread adoption of the Java language, e-commerce pressures, and hungry software vendors—have induced a rapid evolution in information delivery for decision support—from query-and-reporting facilities, through online analytics, to what can fairly be termed business intelligence *applications*. Applications of this type are typically designated EIPs, or *digital dashboards*. Microsoft uses the term digital dashboard in reference to EIP applications built using its software products—specifically Office 2000, Outlook 2000, and Exchange Server.

How is an EIP distinguished from a simple Web reporting application? In a nutshell, an EIP usually

- Contains multiple windows within a single screen
- Contains diverse information, often represented in different presentation metaphors—charts, spreadsheets, images, videos, graphics, tickers, etc., presenting information from multiple sources both inside *and outside* the company.
- Combines decision-support information with operational information such as email and transaction processing
- Has typically been constructed using a "component-based approach," that is, pulling together diverse, smaller "pieces and parts" of software—such as Java applets—and data.

Marketwide Business Intelligence

Combining a company's internal data with discerning observations about its marketplace—competition, prospective customers, historical trends, and so on—adds a significant level of analytical capabilities to its arsenal. The more a company can discover, retroactively and proactively, about where it stands relative to its current and future competitive marketplace, the more astute and advantageous can be its responses to the marketplace.

A representative concept leading to enablement of marketwide data availability and analysis is that of Web farming. Originated and promoted by Richard Hackathorn, Web farming describes techniques for searching, compiling, linking, and analyzing data from across the World Wide Web, with the objective of gaining and maintaining a clear understanding of the activities of a company's marketplace. Such marketplace data—detailed and summary information on the company's competitors and partners—is freely available in the content of Web documents such as annual reports, news releases, and stock market reports.

A challenge above and beyond merely acquiring such data is the ability to integrate and interrelate this data with internal data within the four scopes previously described. Data warehousing disciplines and tools in data mapping, reconcilement, and transformation can be applied to make significant progress in connecting these types of disparate data sources and formats.

Current Check-Outs summary for Chhabra,
Thu Apr 18 14:38:54 EDT 2019

BARCODE: 39003022773054
TITLE: Data warehousing and e-commerce /
DUE DATE: 2019 Sep 24

Interactive and Exploratory Data Analysis

Because of the accelerating accumulation of data, businesses are increasingly dependent on software to take a first shot at analyzing these large volumes of data and extracting actionable information. Businesses depend on software to deliver useful conclusions to human users, rather than dump the whole nine yards on desktops for users to sift through. Two classes of data warehousing software tools experiencing increased applicability in the world of e-commerce are those that support interactive and exploratory data analysis: online analytical processing (OLAP) and data mining, respectively.

Online Analytical Processing

Classifying and generalizing is an instinctive human reaction to the complexity of existence. Computer software has proven quite capable, if given sufficient input, of being productively applied to classification tasks. OLAP is a widely-used platform for classifying and generalizing.

OLAP software products allow *interactive* analysis of large amounts of detailed data (transaction records, for example). OLAP reporting is distinguished from conventional hardcopy, canned, and even ad hoc reporting by its support for interactive (in OLAP terms, *on-the-fly* or *speed of thought*), flexible, and extensive *aggregation* and *classification* of detailed data. Detailed, transaction-level data can be classified and summarized into as many hierarchical groups as the analyst has the ability to comprehend. Some examples of OLAP output are shown on page 98, "Multichannel Business Intelligence."

During the course of an OLAP analysis session, a single data set may be accessed multiple times and quickly presented at various higher or lower levels of detail, as well as grouped by various classifications at various levels. This activity is known in OLAP terminology as *slicing and dicing*. An OLAP data set is sometimes envisioned as a "cube," or "hypercube," with one dimension (classification) per side and data values envisioned in each "cell" of the cube.

OLAP analysis has been widely applied in business areas where data classification is integral to the function, namely, sales, marketing, and finance. OLAP analysis can help increase revenue by promoting customer acquisition and retention, as well as helping to control costs.

A "best of all possible worlds" application is one where the classifications of customer segments to be used in OLAP analysis can be built *automatically*.

Clustering algorithms, available with some types of machine-learning software, make this capability possible.

Machine Learning and Predictive Modeling

As we've seen, the increasing volume and detail of data generated by a multi-channel enterprise creates the necessity for generalizing, classifying, and summarizing this data. Whereas OLAP requires relatively labor-intensive, manual creation of generalizations and classifications, data mining techniques offer automated capabilities for accomplishing these classification tasks—or, at the very least, offer ideas for potential classifications and groupings of detailed data.

Machine-learning applications come into play when the data-software output interface acts as a proxy for the data-human output interface.

Offline Machine Learning: Data Mining

Data mining originated from efforts in artificial intelligence research to enable computer software with the human-like ability to draw conclusions, modify its own instructions, and take appropriate action, based on data presented to them. One term applied to this ability is *machine learning*. It has been concluded from these studies that the greater the volume of (relevant) data that is presented to a machine learning program, the greater its accuracy in drawing appropriate and successful conclusions based on that data. This is definitely one instance where such computer programs do closely model human behavior—the more anyone knows about a type of situation ahead of time, the more likely they will respond to similar situations to their benefit in the future.

A very common application of data mining is the attempted prediction of the behavior of customers and prospects. A *predictive model* is a set of rules, usually implemented as a computer program, which can be used to predict the behavior (i.e., *dependent variables*) of one or more customers or prospects, based on some set of their attributes (i.e., *independent* or *predictive variables*). Each record studied and predicted for—a customer, typically—is termed a *case*. The behavior that such a case exhibits over time—either historically or predicted into the future—is termed a *time series*. Advanced predictive models can forecast not only *what* behavior a case will exhibit in the future, but *when* the behavior will happen. In general, the farther into the past the available time-series data extends, the farther into the future behavior can be predicted.

Predictive models can be created by *data mining tools* (software programs), based on relationships found by the tool software among potentially predictive and dependent variables in a large set of *historical* behavioral data. A complete predictive cycle comprises *building* a predictive model and *executing* the predictive model.

Building of models takes place on a periodic basis, offline to the marketing and customer-contact functions themselves. Executing of models can take place both on a periodic basis, offline (in batch) mode and in a real-time mode, embedded in (called by) marketing and customer-contact functions.

Execution of a model results in the output of dependent variables, which usually take the form of either

- numbers or percentages (i.e., *scores*)
- classifier codes (e.g., high-net-worth, senior-citizen, etc.)

For customers on which a significant amount of predictive data is already stored, model execution can be done in batch mode. In batch model execution, the results of the execution, such as scores and classifications, are then stored with customer record(s). Scores and classifications can be later retrieved by marketing and customer-contact functions in both human (customer service representative, or CSR) and electronic channels. Campaign lists and next-likely-product-purchase lists may also be created based on these scores and classifications.

The past decade has seen much effort and progress in improving the usability of machine-learning programs in commercial data analysis applications. One of the toughest challenges for such applications has been in the sourcing and preparation of data prior to presenting the data to machine learning programs. Lessons learned by data warehousing efforts have been especially fruitful in helping to evolve a previously arcane, academic, and, from a data-management perspective, sometimes tedious set of disciplines into a set of capabilities poised at the forefront of the digital economy.

Even just a few years ago, data mining software products were in general very particular and unforgiving about the types and formats of data structures that they could consume and learn from. Commercial applications of machine learning and predictive modeling pretty much required input data to be presented to the mining software in flat, or sequential files, formatted specifically for the case or time series to be studied and predicted for. However, in just the last four to five years, driven by the significant revenue opportunities represented by e-commerce—and particularly B2C e-commerce—vendors have modified their products to accept as input the same types of data structures common to human decision-support functions, including relational database tables and OLAP cubes. With the data mining components of SQL Server 2000's Analysis Services, Microsoft has stretched the application of relational concepts in data mining to a perhaps extreme, but nevertheless compelling, extent—by actually instantiating data mining models as rows in relational tables.

An understanding of the content and meaning of the data available, whatever its physical format, is an essential prerequisite to any data mining effort. (An accessible and comprehensive inventory of an organization's data assets—assembled, perhaps, as part of a data architecture initiative—is a resource of considerable value to such data mining efforts.) Such efforts in sourcing, analyzing, cleansing if necessary, and transforming data from widespread, diverse legacy data sources are essentially the same as those necessary to construct and maintain a decision-support database such as a data warehouse or data mart; the processes and techniques are quite familiar to data warehousing professionals. The means are very similar, the ends somewhat different. Data prepared for data mining is input directly to more software; data prepared for human decision-support applications is stored for later use.

Even just a few years ago, after the historical/transactional data required for a "mining run" was located, studied, and understood, it would likely need to be "massaged"—transformed—into structures that strictly defined the cases and time series that needed to be predicted. Due to the widespread growth of relational databases, such as DB2, Oracle, and Microsoft SQL Server, today the required data is more likely to be both more accessible and logically organized. In addition, these structures can be input directly into data mining tools rather than having to be reformatted. Data mining efforts are becoming faster to implement, and with quicker turnaround in model construction and testing, more accurate models can be built within the same competitively driven timeframes. Data mining is moving out of the realm of Ph.D.'s, into the world of DBAs, and eventually to end users themselves.

Online Machine Learning: Personalization, Permission Marketing, and 1-to-1 Campaigns

In cases of prospective customers where no data is yet available on file, model execution needs to take place in real time, embedded in customer-contact processes—such as Web site interaction. Predictive variables must be obtained from the prospect and input to the model in order to enable model execution and subsequent scoring and/or classification. Rules must be created in advance, either manually or through machine learning, or both.

All major B2C e-commerce server products include robust facilities for assembling and reacting to *personalization rules,* based on comparison of a customer's historical buying habits, or resemblance to a human- or software-constructed "profile," or generalization, of customer traits and/or behaviors.

The most common results of such personalization of a customer's browsing experience are suggestions of products to which the software has concluded that a customer of that particular type is most likely to positively respond.

Grouping customers into such types, or profiles, is a task for which clustering algorithms, another type of machine-learning program, are an excellent tool. Clustering enables the automatic analysis of many variables in a set of data to determine those whose values appear to naturally occur together. The famous "diapers and beer" story—men who bought diapers before the weekend were found to often also buy beer at the same time—is a result of the output of a clustering algorithm. As we pointed out earlier, human-computer interaction is especially effective when the results of such a clustering algorithm can be cycled into an interactive analytic environment such as OLAP for further action by human analysts and decision-makers.

Meta-data for E-Commerce and Beyond

The hypercompetitive and multichannel business environment of the upcoming decades will demand an increased reliance on meta-data—data about data, or, in short, data documentation. Users will need to know the meaning, source, and appropriate disposition of an increasing diversity and volume of data emanating from this environment at an accelerating rate. Several trends are likely to arise as a result of this increased dependency.

- Integration of data and meta-data within the data-human interface
- Widespread implementation of enterprise-wide business information directories
- Increasing importance of data classification taxonomies and the appearance of automated "meta-data miners" and classification agents
- Growth of user-managed meta-data

The primary driver of all these trends will again be the proliferation of data in many forms, from many sources. Business users will be confronted, on an increasingly frequent basis, with the need to respond in a competitive way to these new forms and sources. This will result not only from more conventional upheavals such as mergers, acquisitions, and reorganizations, but also from constantly shifting and reconfiguring internal value chain linkages, as well as linkages through multiple new and existing channels with customers, partners, and even competitors.

Data-Meta-data Integration

The underlying value proposition of data warehousing is that of making the diverse data resources of an organization appear to be physically integrated in a single location. This being the case, what sense does it make to allow the meta-data about this integrated resource appear to be "somewhere else," separate and apart from the data it describes? Like the illuminations enhancing the text of documents from the Middle Ages, or the melodic text coloration in Baroque and Classic vocal music, meta-data, to be of most value, must be part and parcel of the decision-maker's user experience. As data proliferation accelerates, it will be less and less acceptable to require users to search for data documentation after completing a perhaps demanding search for the data itself.

Currently, meta-data integration may extend to developers and data administrators, but by the time the data reaches its intended audience, any explicit linkage between the data and its documentation has usually fallen by the wayside.

End-user reports, commonly distributed in hypertext format, can contain links from headings or from data fields themselves, to their associated meta-data documentation—including source, meaning, variants, disposition, derivation formulas, and where-used and other cross-references. These links can be accessed as click-throughs or fly-overs.

Business Information Directories

Meta-data provides an important tool for enabling decision-makers to define and locate the data they need. Organizing the mass of data with which a typical business organization is confronted is a critical prerequisite to mobilizing and leveraging this data in support of rapid, nimble, and accurate business decisions.

Data classification taxonomies will assume increasing importance. A taxonomy is a hierarchical classification scheme, such as that used in biology. A data classification taxonomy is useful for consecutively narrowing a search for data required for decision-making activities. A taxonomy familiar to most Web users is that which underlies Yahoo!® (an example of taxonomy is shown in Figure 4–3). The creation and maintenance of the Yahoo! taxonomy is a manual, labor-intensive process. Although the amount of data within the scope of interest of a typical corporation is likely to be less than that which some Websites such as Yahoo! attempt to address, any business is likely to benefit from the establishment of a standardized classification of its data resources. An intuitive,

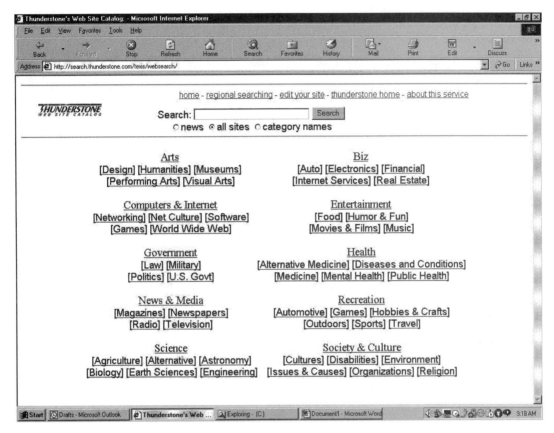

Figure 4-3
An information catalog on the Web. (Courtesy Thunderstone Software.)

comprehensive data taxonomy can be of immense value in guiding users to the data required to support decision-making activities.

Pioneering software tools that support a taxonomic approach to meta-data include IBM's DataGuide and Data Shopper from PLATINUM Technology, Inc. (now Computer Associates). Tools of this type support the creation of visual data-classification hierarchies—similar to Windows or UNIX file-folder tree structures—which enable users to click through more and more specific levels of the hierarchy until the desired data is reached. Physical data assets—files, tables, documents, spreadsheets—can be directly linked to the meta-data objects at the appropriate level for click-through access by users. Descriptive and associative meta-data can be linked to any and all levels of the taxonomy as well.

Establishing and maintaining data classification schemes is typically somewhat tedious and labor-intensive. The growth of XML-formatted data resources may allow the appearance of automated meta-data miners and classification agents, which can automatically build, maintain, grow, and disseminate data taxonomies. An XML-formatted data source, in addition to its actual data "payload," typically contains both descriptive labels for its constituent data elements, as well as an implicit tree structure, which classifies its data elements hierarchically within its own domain. These characteristics allow a software agent, working in conjunction with an XML parser, to locate or extract a meta-data description (a *schema*) of the XML data resource for immediate or offline display, along with the data itself, to interested users.

If XML data-element labeling is rigorously based on a well-constructed, standard taxonomic scheme, such as the Universal Data Element Framework (UDEF), the content of any new XML structure being presented to an organization could be automatically linked into an existing taxonomy based on that scheme. This would support rapid assimilation of new data resources by the software and human consumers within the organization—in turn enabling a high level of responsiveness to competitive threats and opportunities to which this new data may be applied.

UDEF is a tool for identifying and resolving *semantic equivalence*, multiple names meaning the same thing. It therefore resolves synonyms and prevents homonyms. More information on UDEF is available at *www.udef.com* and *www.intelligententerprise.com/000428/supplychain.shtml*.

Org Chart Directories and LDAP

A very common type of computer-based information directory is one that represents the hierarchical structure of individuals and organizations within a business enterprise. This type of directory is widely used to control access to data resources within the business by these individuals and organizations. The growth of Internet-based e-commerce, and the consequential obscuring of organizational data boundaries, has resulted in a movement away from earlier, more platform-specific authentication technologies (e.g., RACF, ACF2) toward Internet-based, platform-independent standards, most notably the Lightweight Directory Access Protocol (LDAP). LDAP specifies standard formats and processes for defining and accessing hierarchical data structures. Many products are available that implement LDAP standards, including Microsoft's Active Directory, IBM's SecureWay, and Novell's NDS e-Directory.

Such an org chart, or authentication directory, is a special type of database optimized for fast read access and representation of hierarchical relationships. Most implementations, such as those utilizing the products listed above, require a stand-alone, dedicated storage structure to contain the representation of individuals, organization units, relationships, and authorizations. In many situations, this type of data is already contained in digital format (e.g., in a personnel database). Products are available (e.g., the Virtual Directory Server from Radiant Logic, Inc.) that can provide a "virtual directory" layer above relational database storage and present this data in an LDAP-compliant interface. This type of functionality can eliminate redundant data storage and the consequential need for periodic synchronization between the directory data store and other data sources.

User-Managed Meta-data

The current status quo in meta-data creation is a labor-intensive, offline and semi-isolated process, primarily initiated and performed by IT specialists— data administrators and data analysts. The acceleration of change in business will render unacceptable the current latency between the appearance of new data types and formats and their classification and interpretation by such meta-data specialists. As a result of the combination of this trend and the increasingly close linkage between data and its documentation, management of meta-data will be more and more frequently assumed by the creators and consumers of the data.

An important prerequisite to the success of a user-managed meta-data environment will be providing adequate incentive for data creators (content providers) to take the steps necessary to facilitate the classification and indexing of data under their control. (More on this in Chapter 6.) A model for this process can be found in the Web e-commerce world, where Web site managers strive diligently for better placement with search engines, such as Yahoo! and Alta Vista. By conforming to the rules by which the search engines find and categorize Web page content, site managers can assure that their sites can be found and can achieve higher rankings—being displayed at or near the top of search results lists—within the search engines.

Web e-commerce sites are obviously motivated by potential revenues to make content easily discoverable by consumers. User-managed meta-data will require that businesses establish similar incentives for optimizing creator-consumer communications internally.

The Business Intelligence Dissemination Lifecycle

The results of decision-support processing need to be delivered to more recipients than ever before. The paperless office may still be a receding goal, but email and Web dissemination of BI has become an absolute necessity. Vendors of BI software have universally responded by providing Web-based dissemination facilities for their existing products.

The lifecycle of BI data (see Figure 4–4) is an example of a cycle through the perspectives and transformations of the data-human interface component of the data architecture—specific to data *output*.

Conceptualization Transformation and Perspective

Decision-makers first determine the parameters of the data-human interface required for supporting successful choice among alternative directions toward which the business can be taken. These parameters typically need to include data content, format, frequency, and audience. The requirements are documented and communicated, more often than not quite informally, to data technologists, who may or may not in turn compile a specification perspective for validation.

Solution Transformation and Specification Perspective

Prior establishment of a formal data architecture results in significant enhancements to this process and to the following attributes of the data resource, in turn enabling this process to take place quickly and completely within the scope of control of the decision-maker(s).

- transparency
- accessibility
- comprehensibility
- reusability
- integrity
- accuracy
- relate-ability

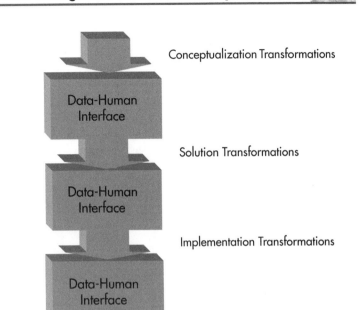

Conceptualization Transformations

Conceptualization Perspective

Data-Human Interface

Solution Transformations

Specification Perspective

Data-Human Interface

Implementation Transformations

Realization Perspective

Data-Human Interface

Conceptualization Transformations

Figure 4–4
IT architecture transformations in the data-human interface.

The requirements, as stated by information consumers, are translated into technical specifications with which the various data requirements can be met. Components of this specification include

- Security constraints and authorizations
- Database connection requirements
- Data-data interfaces (e.g., joins, classifications, data-meta-data linkages)
- Determination of subscribers, triggers, and channels

Implementation Transformation and Realization Perspective

During implementation transformation, developers convert specification perspective components into implementable technology artifacts—queries, reports, spreadsheets, multidimensional database representations, execution and distribution schedules, and even EIPs. Data formatting, sorting, selection, parameterization, and groupings are described to the development environment (tool) by data and tool specialists, then tested and turned over to production.

To realize the new data-human interfaces, output artifacts are chosen and runtime parameter values are specified. The results are published and delivered to identified subscribers. Subscribers take delivery of the resulting information and use the results to make decisions and to conceive of new and extended requirements...and the loop begins once again.

BI Data-Hardware and Data-Software Interfaces: E-Commerce Impacts

The rapid expansion of e-commerce has caused a number of ripple effects in the presentation of decision-making information. As a result of data sources and formats proliferating, challenges arise in presenting a comprehensive, yet comprehensible, picture of the state of a business enterprise, both historically and as of a point in time. The increased complexity of the available information—*information overload*—gives rise once again to the perennial dichotomy of simplicity versus flexibility.

The increased volumes of available data, exacerbated by the rapidly expanding numbers of information-hungry users—more and more often across multiple corporate and even household sites—challenge the performance capabilities of our existing output mechanisms. How much data can be presented to how many users at one time, within acceptable response times?

On top of these pressures, demands for increased timeliness of data allows for less and less flexibility in extracting, staging, and isolating decision-support data from the operational "line of fire." Solutions to these problems are being introduced by vendors of data-storage software and hardware (more on this in Chapter 5), as well as by vendors of BI products.

One common technique for handling increased decision-support output scalability and performance requirements is to separate onto dedicated platforms the runtime technical components necessary to get "raw" data resources into the data-human interface. These components can, for example, be separated out into query processing, output formatting, and output distribution.

Query processing is the most resource-consuming process by far. It is the only process that must have direct physical access to the data within the scope of the decision-making activity. Its performance will be significantly constrained by the available data-hardware interfaces—the speed, capacity, and number of storage and processing devices. Therefore, dedicating more, bigger, and faster hardware specifically to query processing is currently the most effective method for grappling with increased volumes of data required for decision-making.

Output formatting and distribution is relatively light on resource requirements compared to query processing. Techniques for scaling of output formatting and distribution include centralized storage of distribution lists, schedules, and widely shared output format templates and—to allow for information presentation chiefly on an on-demand basis where possible—a "pull" rather than a "push" scenario.

First-generation batch reporting applications generated reams of paper, multiple copies of the same voluminous reports, a significant number of which would inevitably be consigned to the round file. Second-generation decision-support relied on a two-tiered client-server architecture where much of the heavy lifting remained on the client workstation. Current multitier architectures with a browser-based "thin client," coupled with a pull, or on–demand, scenario enable more efficient use of hardware and software resources (minimizing data-hardware and data-software interface bottlenecks) by putting the heavy computing power where it can be shared and allowing assembly and output only when requested. An example configuration of such resources is shown in Figure 4–5.

Figure 4–5

Example scalable business intelligence architecture.

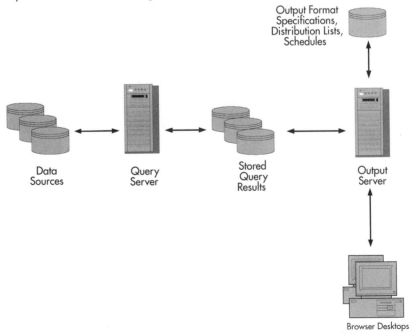

E-Business Intelligence at Tiosa Group

It will now be more challenging than ever for Tiosa to assemble a comprehensive, yet comprehensible, current and historical view of its performance within its marketplace. The company's management—and its shareholders—are very interested in keeping track of revenues and costs across the newly merged organization. Data about its broad base of financial, service, and consumer appliance products, sold through both digital and traditional bricks-and-mortar channels, will need to be assembled, related, analyzed, formatted, and distributed.

One consequence of the merger of Tiosa Corp. and Gasomatic was the creation of a combined e-business task force, which was given a one-month timeframe to complete and report on the following:

1. Assessing the current state of Tiosa Group's overall e-business presence.

2. Assessing the current state of its competitors' e-business presence, as well as the competition's future plans for doing business online.

3. Developing a "gap analysis" comparing Tiosa Group's position relative to its competition.

4. Developing a detailed set of recommendations and a plan for implementing the recommendations.

CIO Dan, as a member of the task force, provided valuable input on technical feasibility and resource requirements as the task force developed its recommendations. Now that the task force has completed its study, presented its recommendations, and gained approval of its plan from the executive committee, Dan will need to dig down into the next level of detail on how to get the plan into action from an IT architecture perspective.

Management of data architecture-related aspects of this aggressive e-business plan are, of course, only a part of the overall picture. Dan's responsibility is to carefully consider, plan for, and integrate all changes required to all components of IT architecture—including hardware, software, process, and humans (i.e., employees and external parties)—in order to assure the success of his company's e-commerce initiative. Dan wants to be sure that the initiative effectively leverages existing and future data resources and interfaces. To make sure this happens, he assigns responsibility for this to the data architecture group.

Table 4.2 Tiosa Group's E-Business Implementation Plan

E-Commerce Capability	Former Company	Target Date
Online Catalog—Consumer Products and Services	Gasomatic	Current (Year0)
Online Catalog—Corporate Services	Tiosa Corp.	1QY1
Online Transactions—Consumer Services	Gasomatic	3QY1
Online Transactions—Consumer Products	Gasomatic	1QY2
Online Transactions—Corporate Services	Tiosa Corp.	3QY2

One means by which the data architecture team approaches the assignment is by looking at successively broader scopes of data that will need to be addressed within the e-commerce initiative. The team members carefully study the e-commerce initiative plan to determine during what timeframe each data scope is planned to be available—and will be subsequently needed for business intelligence.

The current implementation plan for Tiosa Group e-business enablement is described in Table 4.2.

A smaller group, designated the DA-BI group, is formed within the data architecture team to look ahead to transformations that will be required for business intelligence—data-human and data-software (output) interfaces—as the plan goes forward. Overlapping groups are formed to manage transformations of other data architecture components; we will look at their efforts in later chapters.

Since the best place to start is at the beginning, the DA-BI group begins with the existing e-commerce BI data: that generated from Gasomatic's current Web site.

Clickstream Business Intelligence

Prior to its Web site first going online, the Gasomatic Web team had reached a decision to implement a Web log-reading product in order to track and analyze traffic and clickstreams on the site. They have used the reports generated from this product to track basic site visit information over time, such as

- numbers of hits per page
- most-visited pages

- numbers of visitors
- top referring pages

When Tiosa Corp.'s initial brochureware Web site is brought up, displaying its products and services for corporate customers, it will be relatively easy to merge Tiosa's Web site activity data with Gasomatic's. This will provide decision-makers a consolidated—and comparative—view of the entire Tiosa Group's Web presence from that point in time forward.

E-Commerce Business Intelligence

Gasomatic's initial Web site was primarily a marketing tool and an online catalog. According to the e-commerce initiative's plan, after rolling out a similar capability targeted toward corporate services, a significant project will be launched to add functionality to the site. The functionality will enable visitors to register as buying customers, provide credit card information to enable payment, and select and place orders for Gasomatic's consumer products on the Web site.

Since up to this point the Web site's log-reading product will track and report only on data that shows up in the log files generated by the Web servers, the only information generated will be specific to clickstreams—Web pages. The DA-BI team advises Dan that in order to provide e-commerce BI—comprehensively monitoring and understanding visitors' and customers' Web activities—explicit data relationships will need to be established among diverse data collected in Web logs, e-commerce, and legacy operational and financial systems:

- Visitor activity—clicks
- Registered customer profiles
- Customer transactional activity—purchases

The recommendation is that this strategy be designed and put in place concurrent with the first online transaction capability going live, in third quarter of year one of the plan.

Multichannel Business Intelligence

In order to bolster the case for their recommendations, the DA-BI team put together some mockups for some example multichannel BI output. These mockups are shown in Figure 4–6 and Figure 4–7.

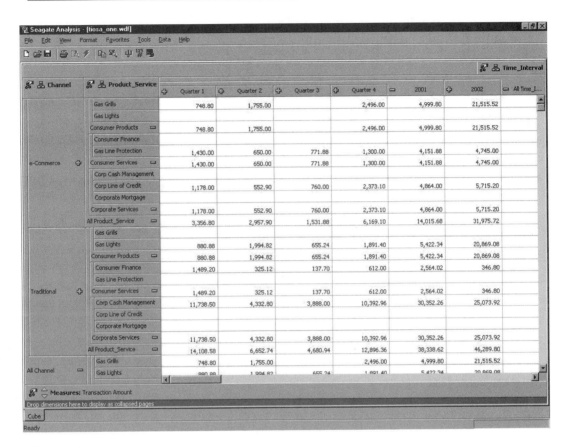

Figure 4–6
A multidimensional business intelligence display. (*Courtesy Crystal Decisions, formerly Seagate Software.*)

When the e-commerce enablement of Tiosa Group nears completion in Year 2 of the plan, data will be available on product sales from all channels, presented in this type of consolidated manner, to provide decision-makers with a broad perspective of the e-commerce initiative in the context of the entire business.

Enterprise-wide Business Intelligence

Tiosa Group executive management has made it clear that by the end of Year 1 of the e-commerce initiative, it will need to provide a report on the status of the initiative to the board and company investors. At that point, management will need to either show that the initiative has been successful in generating

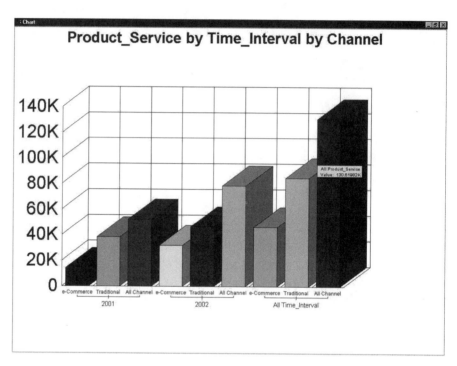

Figure 4–7
A bar chart derived from multidimensional data. (*Courtesy Crystal Decisions, formerly Seagate Software.*)

net revenue or provide a reasonable projection—based on actual trends—about when the effort can be expected to be "out of the red."

Not only will *revenue* figures from sales of the various products and product groups through digital and traditional channels be needed, but *cost* data will need to be allocated as accurately as possible across the products and channels. Cost data will need to be integrated into the sales data, such as presented in the report in Figure 4–6.

The DA-BI team will be developing a recommendation for correlating information from Tiosa's ABC (activity-based costing) system into the scope of data accumulated up to that point across product lines and channels.

Marketwide Business Intelligence

The broadest perspective on Tiosa's business will be made possible by scrutinizing its performance within the context of its overall competitive marketplace. To make this possible, the DA-BI team has also begun researching available and future capabilities for Web scanning, enabling the collection of public data on overall market conditions as well as on competitor financial performance. When this comes to fruition, presentations such as the examples in Figures 4–6 and 4–7 can be enhanced with this external data, giving management a clear and concise picture of the company's performance relative to the competition and to the marketplace in general.

Dan is encouraged when he receives an update on the work of the DA-BI team. If his company has a good idea of where it currently stands in terms of BI capability, and what its future targets are, the path from A to B should be relatively clear. His next questions, of course, will be directed to discovering the plumbing that needs to be in place behind these proposed decision-making tools. This plumbing is what we will cover in the next two chapters.

Chapter 5

KEEPING THE DATA AROUND: REPRESENTATION AND STORAGE

Persistence is the storage of enterprise data in a durable data store, such as a database.
Any serious commerce application requires persistence...
—Ed Roman and Rickard Oberg, The Middleware Company, White Paper

Data storage technologies are the "content engines" throbbing in the basement under the colorful storefronts of the digital economy. Data warehousing solutions have from the outset pushed the envelope on data storage technologies. Whatever the challenge the digital economy may impose on data storage, it's likely that data warehousing has already been there and taken it on. The most critical data storage challenges in the digital economy are those of security, scalability, reliability, and availability. Data warehousing brings to the digital economy especially valuable lessons learned in assuring the scalability and security of large databases.

Large data warehouse environments, spanning multiple value chain links and constituencies of varying technical sophistication typically include robust security capabilities for defining users and user groups, as well as the scope of data access available to their various constituencies. Protection and appropriate utilization of the critical information assets of the digital enterprise require extension of security functionality to very large numbers of constituents outside the enterprise as well.

The increasingly dynamic and vibrant computer-human interactions of the digital economy will demand constant enrichment of basic textual and numeric content. Storage of very large volumes of video, audio, and image data will create significant scalability hurdles. Searching, accessing, and delivering multiple media through digital channels—with predictably rapid response, of course—will challenge the talents and expertise of the most leading-edge and experienced data warehousing professionals. Above and beyond this, automatic scalability will be required of databases powering the digital enterprise, enabling them to absorb unexpected transaction volumes, in spikes and sustained onslaughts, without burps or hiccups.

Data warehousing has historically also faced, and met, challenges in database reliability and availability, but the digital economy has raised the bar to zero tolerance in these areas. If an internal decision-support database is down for the afternoon, business will still go on, but if a database that powers an e-commerce site is down for an hour, business, by definition, does *not* go on. Reliability also dictates predictably brisk response to queries requested by internal and external constituents. In the majority of cases, this necessitates separate but synchronized data stores, each optimized for either input or output. This of course is the familiar data warehousing architecture that pairs operational data store and decision-support database.

Data Representation: Logical Data Storage

A major contribution of data warehousing to information technology has been the advancement of data integration. In order to accomplish this, data warehousing has had to successfully address both the perception of the data requirements of the business ("logical" data models) and how the data is actually stored ("physical" data models), as well as resolve, by hook or by crook, the differences between the two. Without a doubt, all data required by decision-makers should, at the very least, appear to the user as being retrievable from a single location. Indeed, any company whose leaders are unable to locate, in a timely fashion, all the data required for effective decision-making will be at a considerable disadvantage in attempting to prevail in a hypercompetitive, multichannel e-business marketplace.

The explosive growth of e-commerce poses even more new and radical challenges in data representation and storage. Human and software consumers of data, ever more diverse and dispersed, require ever more divergent views of how data "should" appear. Data consumers now expect data to be continuously and immediately available. Demands of ever-proliferating sources of data require new and innovative methods for physically retaining the data. And along with these rapid changes, data modelers, data architects, database administrators, and data administrators continue to do battle to iden-

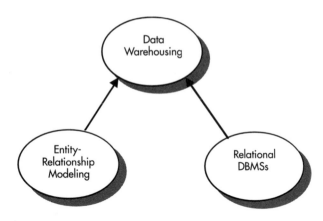

Figure 5–1
Data warehousing benefactors.

tify and eradicate, from the data consumer's perspective, any discrepancies between how the data is stored and in what form it is needed.

The success of data warehousing has been strongly dependent on the rise of relational database management systems (RDBMSs)—Oracle, DB2, SQL Server, Sybase, Informix. These RDBMS products were in turn made possible by the development of the relational model for database systems introduced in 1970 by Edgar F. Codd.

Data warehousing has also been strongly aided and abetted by entity-relationship (E-R) modeling, originated by Peter Chen in 1977. E-R modeling and the relational model strongly complement each other. A data *entity* in E-R terms—that is, something about which the business needs to store data—can very often be directly translated to a table in a relational database. This happy circumstance greatly facilitates the implementation of relational databases from E-R models. The same techniques and technologies have become indispensable enablers for mobilizing data resources within e-commerce applications for both transactional operations and decision support.

Data Models for E-Commerce

Almost without exception, the development and implementation of a dedicated database is a prerequisite for establishment of an e-commerce site. A new dedicated database is sometimes preferable to attaching e-commerce capabilities directly to one or more existing internal databases, for several reasons:

- *Security:* Internal data can remain insulated from potential outside attack.

- *Performance:* External users (customers) have even less a sense of humor about slow response than internal users. A dedicated database minimizes the potential for access contention, and its contents can be "limited" to data relevant to the site.
- *Availability:* Site data is insulated from problems with internal systems.

While much of the content required for this dedicated database must be fed from internal data sources, the database itself needs to be designed to support the site. Most e-commerce sites are based on the implementation of a commercial e-commerce software product, so the physical database schema is constrained to a great extent by the package's out-of-the-box database design. Even in these cases, however, construction of a logical data model is recommended for several reasons:

- To document the data requirements of the e-commerce site, independent of whether or not a given e-commerce package supports these requirements out of the box.
- To document any differences between the out-of-the-box database schema and the data requirements for the site, such as supporting a gap analysis.
- To aid in designing any required extensions to the package database.
- And, perhaps most importantly, to provide a comprehensive, platform-independent view of integration requirements between the site database and the data sources with which it must interact.

Data models for e-commerce sites are similar in many ways to those for data warehouses. Both often span multiple "stovepipe" vertical applications, and both tend to be customer-centric. The diagram in Figure 5–1 is an example high-level (E-R) logical data model representing the data requirements for operating a retail (B2C) Web site. (A brief overview of how to "read" a data model diagram can be found in the appendix.)

Star-Schemas and Entity-Relationship Models

The *star schema*, a pattern for designing and visualizing multidimensional databases, was promoted by Ralph Kimball beginning in 1996. The star schema is now the most widely accepted methodology for designing multidimensional databases.

A star-schema design can be approached as an E-R model with additional

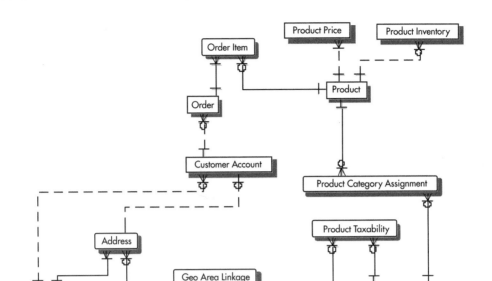

Figure 5-2
A logical data model for a B2C Web site.

constraints. Debate about which model is "better" is counterproductive, confusing to developers and data consumers, and does not help the cause of improved data management.

A star schema design is most appropriate where

1. The scope of decision support is well-defined.
2. The reporting requirements are well understood and stable.
3. A good deal of summary data is required.
4. OLAP tools are the primary means of user access to the data.

An E-R approach or combination approach may be more appropriate if

1. There is a significant requirement for ad hoc (unpredictable) access to the data, and/or
2. The bulk of data is to be accessed at a detailed rather than a summarized level.

Figure 5–3 is an example of a star-schema model derived from the earlier example Web site model. This model would be valuable in analyzing Web site buying activity by timeframe, customer type, and product.

Linking up additional data on marketing promotions results in a hybrid E-R/dimensional model, from which other star-schema patterns could potentially be derived, as illustrated in Figure 5–4.

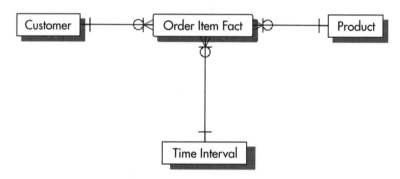

Figure 5–3
An example of a star schema.

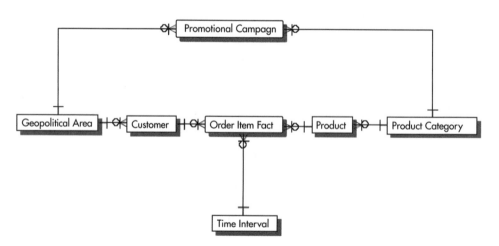

Figure 5–4
A hybrid E-R/dimensional data model.

Structured and Unstructured Data

The increasing proliferation and widespread juxtaposition of data of different types brought on by e-commerce (the Web, specifically) has brought discussions of structured and unstructured data to the forefront. Few IT professionals would disagree that a relational table is an example of "structured" data. Some would propose that a document such as an XML file is an example of "semi-structured" data. Then, is there such a thing as "unstructured" data, and what makes some data less or more structured than other data? This discussion may on first glance appear to be of the angels-dancing-on-pins variety, but clarification of these issues is beginning to be of central importance to effective data management.

"Structured-ness" is a matter of degree—a continuous, relative quality; that is, there is no hard and fast dividing line between structured and unstructured. Structure consists primarily of discretely referable constituent parts. For the sake of argument, the following classes are proposed as being arranged from more to less structured:

- *Regularly recurring data:* relational table rows or sequential-file records.
- *Document-organized data* (may recur but not necessarily *regularly*): marked-up data (XML, HTML), email, word processing.
- Media data: a "bit bucket" with no recurring structure, such as images, audio, and video.

The degree to which data is structured varies inversely with the degree to which loss (see discussion on data compression later in this chapter) can be tolerated.

XML (eXtensible Markup Language) deserves extended discussion here. As a data-representation format, it has been very widely discussed and is beginning to be more widely implemented. XML began as a document format. For the past three decades, the most widespread perception of data organization for business applications has been based on concepts analogous to files and records. However, as it has in many areas, the World Wide Web is bringing about an evolution in these perceptions. On the Web, the document is without doubt the de facto unit of data storage, retrieval, and presentation.

Three characteristics distinguish the concept of a document as a model or pattern for data:

- A document (not surprisingly) is primarily textual, rather than computational, in emphasis.

- A document is generally agreed to be comprised of a hierarchical arrangement of elements. A fundamental distinction between the document model and the relational model is that in documents, elements can be hierarchically "nested," while in the relational model, nesting is specifically prohibited.

- In addition to actual data content, and in contrast to a historically typical database structure, a given document also contains "markup" attributes—tags or labels—describing the intent of each element. In essence, this constitutes "embedded meta-data."

The creation of formal and standard document modeling theory is the focus of much current activity. Work towards a formalized model of the building blocks, manipulation methods, and constraints in the document world began with Standard Generalized Markup Language (SGML). A specialized dialect of SGML, XML has been developed and has assumed a pivotal role in e-business architectures.

Work on theory and standardization of document models is proceeding in a fashion similar to earlier comparable efforts on database models (with the exception of the relational model)—that is, concurrent with product development and practical application. The risks resulting from standards and products evolving in parallel are product incompatibility and instability over time. These risks are even greater in the current environment than in historical precedent, due to the greater number of vendors and products in the marketplace. Efforts of various intent and levels of abstraction are ongoing, primarily of working groups within the World Wide Web Consortium (W3C).

A marked-up file such as an XML file originally was a "document," that is, one (albeit complicated) record per file. With the transformation of markup languages into data representation mechanisms, an XML file is more likely to contain numerous records.

Since a typical XML document is a hierarchical, "denormalized" structure, transforming between XML structures and relational databases has presented a challenge for DBMS vendors. Varied approaches for solving this problem include providing XML-specialized I/O functionality, new data types, and entirely XML-native storage structures.

IBM's XML Extender for DB2 includes XML stored procedures, a document access description (DAD) construct enabling document-to-database mapping, and an XMLVARCHAR column data type for storing entire XML documents in table columns.

Microsoft SQL Server 2000 also includes functions that enable the database as both a producer and consumer of data in XML formats. Transact-SQL keywords are available with SQL Server 2000 to specify the rendering of result sets in XML format. Below is a sample T-SQL statement including an XML extension:

```
SELECT+firstname,+lastname,+homephone,+title+FROM+Employees+FOR+
XML+AUTO
```

The query above may be submitted as part of a URL—in this case the plus signs are required to represent spaces in the URL. "FOR XML" indicates that the result set should be returned in XML format. "AUTO" indicates that the format should specifically be a simple, nested tree structure. Adding the XMLDATA keyword to the end of the statement will cause an XML schema to also be returned for the result document. Extended database capabilities such as this will enable relatively straightforward request initiation and results delivery over the Web.

New XML-specific stored procedures and T-SQL keywords are also provided with SQL Server 2000. The **sp_xml_preparedocument** stored procedure parses an XML document into an intermediate, in-memory tree structure. This intermediate parse tree can then be referenced using the OPENXML keyword, allowing SELECT access to various levels in the in-memory representation of the document, and "normalization" of the data via INSERTs to appropriate database tables.

Vendors of other DBMS products, such as eXcelon from eXcelon Corp. and Tamino from Software AG, have adopted a more direct approach, supporting the storage of XML documents in their native format.

Physical Data Storage

In many cases, the form in which a given set of data is most convenient and intuitive to use is antithetical to the manner most conducive to fast access, secure retention, and flexible growth. The domain of physical data storage is concerned with *performance*.

The physical level of data storage is the level of the data-software interface. Specialized software programs such as file systems and database management systems have been developed and enhanced over several decades, primarily to bridge the gap between the hardware storage level and the logical, data-consumer level.

Physical Management of Data Types

Things were challenging enough for database professionals back in the "good old days"—five years ago, perhaps—when all that could reasonably be required to be stored in a typical business database were text and numbers. Back then, text and numbers were all that were required because text and numbers were all that typically needed to be displayed on a screen. But of course the Web has changed all that. A company putting up a Web site containing nothing but text and numbers is not likely to generate much business there.

Web page visitors have been become accustomed to seeing much more than text and numbers: graphics, such as logos and line drawings; product photographs of varying sizes; even animations, videos, and sound clips. Text-type data, of which the user is not typically aware, but are necessary for dynamically generating Web pages, include page templates such as HTML, ASP (Active Server Pages), Java, and XML. All these forms of content are data of one type or another, and, in addition to the text and numbers content, need to be stored in such a manner that they can be effectively accessed and maintained.

A picture may or may not be worth a thousand words, but it probably takes up at least as much storage space. Another culprit in the voracious consumption of data storage space is email. The growth of email use inside and outside companies in the past decade has been phenomenal. And email is quite valuable as an as-yet-untapped source of business intelligence (BI). It's easy to imagine the wealth of information on day-to-day transaction of business, as well as documentation of decisions and the process leading to decisions, that lies largely dormant in the email system of practically every company. The storage space consumed by emails is a considerable proportion of a company's data resources, growing steadily day by day—and how often is email purged, if ever? Several knowledge-management indexing products (see Chapters 6 and 11) claim to be able to parse, index, and categorize message formats such as Lotus Notes and Microsoft Exchange. But in a larger sense, the technology is the easy part. Will employees—and employees' correspondents—be enthusiastic about offering up their "confidential" email communications on the altar of collective corporate consciousness?

From the perspective of storage space economy, a very interesting ongoing development for "storing" graphics data is Scalable Vector Graphics (SVG). SVG is an XML vocabulary developed specifically to enable description of graphics via plain text. Rather than storing every pixel (picture element), SVG allows the developer to describe how shapes are to be drawn by a browser. The "scalable" part is important since a large version of the same image conceivably consumes no more storage space than a smaller counterpart. It's all a matter of describing how big the graphic needs to be, rather than filling in all those additional pixels. The SVG specification is currently under development by the World Wide Web Consortium.

Storage Techniques for Access

Another important contribution of data warehousing has been increasing the accessibility of data—providing mechanisms to allow users to find the data they need more quickly and easily. New storage types bring new challenges in enabling this type of support regardless of the type of data desired by the user. Much successful effort has gone into providing effective indexing and searching within the context of traditional data types of text and numbers. How can less structured types of data be indexed and searched in a manner quite similar, if not identical to, the search functionality for structured data?

Cataloging

From a purely user perspective, the most important advantage of database systems over file systems is *precision of access*. Databases provide extensive facilities that support finding and returning very precisely specified packages of information, whether large or small.

At the very least, each media-type object needs to have a readable and searchable "catalog entry" stored in a database, including a meaningful name and the physical file name and directory location of the object. A configuration of this type is shown in Figure 5–5.

Figure 5–5
Typical file/catalog physical configuration.

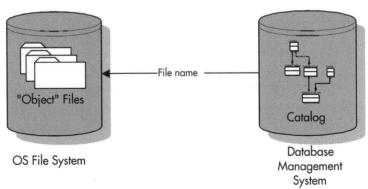

113

Few decision-support functions may yet require access to media data types, but requirements for this are imminent and inevitable. Take these potential query requests for example:

- Which of our Web page click-through banner graphics is leading to the most sales?
- Show me our thumbnail graphic of this SKU (Stock-Keeping Unit, a standardized identifier for a retail product), along with our top five competitors' graphics for the same SKU.
- What are our five top-selling CDs, and allow me to play a clip from the most-requested track from each.
- Which of our products receives the most help-desk calls, and allow me to play back recorded telephone contacts from those calls.

Figure 5–6 is a data model for an application that could provide answers to these types of queries. The Object table contains rows, designating a title and file name and location for each media or text file that is cataloged. The Attribute table contains a row for each characteristic by which any of these files is likely to be searched—for example, publication date, subject, author, keyword, and so on. The Document_Attribute table cross-references Objects to

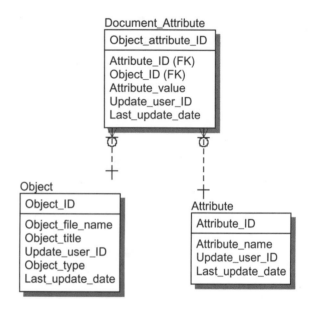

Figure 5–6
Example model for document cataloging.

Attributes, enabling the assignment of an Attribute_value to any given Attribute of an Object (file). For example, the Attribute_name "Author" can relate to an Attribute_value of "Charles Dickens." This provides what essentially constitutes an infinitely expandable card catalog.

The Object_type attribute in the Object table can be referenced to determine what software—viewers, players, editors—is available and appropriate for processing an object of this type.

It is less important how objects are stored (database tables are stored in OS files, after all) than that *entity integrity* is maintained—for example, there should be no header without a corresponding object, and vice versa. Also, this integrity should work for bidirectional access, allowing retrieval of attribute data if the object is found, and, conversely, the object if attribute data has been retrieved.

Text Indexing

As the total amount of document-organized textual data within and across businesses continues to explode, effective techniques for providing fast, efficient, and precise access to textual data—such as email, word-processing documents, HTML and XML files—become increasingly essential.

A prime example of indexing of document-organized data is the architecture used by at least one Web search engine, utilizing agents called "spiders" or "crawlers" to build and maintain what is termed an *inverted index*.

A spider or crawler is a program that methodically "crawls" through the Web (or any other specified collection of documents) and downloads all the documents it finds for parsing. The crawler can crawl through a specified directory, a server—or even through the entire Web, by following all hyperlinks it finds within documents, until it cannot find any more that it has not processed. The documents are then parsed, and an inverted index is built. The index is nothing more than a (potentially very large) table, wherein each row is an entry for a document and each column represents a word. If a value in a given word column for a given document row is "on" (each column needs to be no more than one bit), this indicates that that word is found in that document. The index can be much smaller than the sum of all the documents, since it needs to contain only one bit per distinct word in each document—so searching of such an index can be very quick.

Such an index of course has no awareness of semantics—the meaning, or context, of the words contained—to the annoyance of almost anyone who has performed Web searches. Additional software products are available to support the labor-intensive effort of building contextual and classification schemes, above and beyond the index, to provide additional intelligence to searching capabilities.

Indexing tools that can be applied within the textual data resources of a single company or business unit are available from vendors such as AltaVista and Verity.

Indexing and Searching of Media Files

Indexing and searching of media files is understandably even more challenging than indexing and searching of text files. Even so, some advanced relational database product features enable some of this type of functionality.

The DB2 Image Extender (see "Universal Database," page 118) from IBM includes the Query by Image Content (QBIC) function, enabling search of image libraries by color and layout. Both the DB2 Video Extender from IBM and the Video Foundation DataBlade Module from Informix enable indexing and searching of video by frames and scenes.

Applications of such advanced media functionality within e-business channels are numerous, both at point of customer contact and in after-the-fact analytics. Any time a new content type is introduced within a channel, the opportunity should be taken to implement ongoing assessment of its effectiveness within the selling cycle. The more precise this analysis can be, the better.

Multidimensional Storage: Performance Versus Storage Economy

Multidimensional databases provide for enhanced performance by precalculating and storing some or all required summary data. Doing this work up front eliminates much of the data retrieval and processing required when a query is submitted by a user. The basic structure of a multidimensional database builds on concepts from both relational and entity-relationship theories. Both "facts"—fundamental detailed data—and the dimensions, which categorize and aggregate the fact records, can be perceived as tables. Aggregation tables can be extrapolated and created automatically by the DBMS at the intersections of some or all levels of all dimensions, to store summarized data at these levels.

OLAP-supporting databases can be categorized according to the method with which they address the challenges of storing the considerable volumes of underlying data to be analyzed. These types include MOLAP, ROLAP, and HOLAP.

- *MOLAP, or Multidimensional OLAP*. MOLAP products support the creation and maintenance of specialized (multidimensional) database storage structures that are optimized for fastest performance of OLAP analysis. A prime example of this type of product is Essbase from Hyperion Solutions Corp. MOLAP products require that all data to be analyzed be copied into a separate multidimensional data store. In general, this type of product can deliver the fastest performance.

- *ROLAP, or Relational OLAP*. ROLAP products enable data stored in standard relational databases, such as Oracle, DB2, or Microsoft SQL Server, to be optimized for OLAP analysis. ROLAP products do not require the creation of a separate multidimensional data store. A prime example of this type is the family of business-intelligence products from Microstrategy Inc. To achieve fast performance, a ROLAP product may typically require more maintenance and tuning than a MOLAP product; however, data storage and scalability requirements are not as critical, since relational and OLAP reporting functions can operate over the same data store.

- *HOLAP, or Hybrid OLAP*. HOLAP products allow flexible allocation of data storage between relational and multidimensional structures. For example, fact and dimension tables can be stored in standard relational structures, while calculated aggregated data is stored in optimized multidimensional structures. A prime example of this type of product is Microsoft OLAP Services. (Note: MS OLAP also supports "pure" MOLAP and "pure" ROLAP.) A HOLAP product allows the allocation of data across different storage structures in order to balance data storage and fast response considerations.

Federated Database

I recently acquired my first handheld computing device and have become quite attached to it. The little device contains several "databases": calendar, to-do, contacts, and memos. One of several nifty built-in applications is the search function—it performs as a miniature federated database system. The user can enter search arguments, and the search function returns all occurrences of the arguments—regardless of in which "database" it may find them.

A federated database is a collection of multiple autonomous databases that can be viewed by consumers as a single source of data, through the application of specialized software functions. The concept of federated database developed as an alternative solution for the disparate data problem—a solution that would economize on data storage because it does not require data to be physically copied from one location to another. Whereas the federated database concept allows for update as well as retrieval, a similar concept, the *virtual data warehouse,* is a read-only capability.

This technology has succeeded in breaking out from the research labs into commercially available products. Cerebellum, from Cerebellum Software, Inc., is a federated-database product that supports read/write access to multiple data storage formats. Other currently available federated database technology is embedded in the Cohera E-Catalog System from Cohera Corp. Cohera's underlying federated database technology provides to customers of e-business trading hubs a consolidated, consistent view of product catalogs from multiple suppliers, stored in disparate formats.

Universal Database

The concept of a universal database is in many ways on the opposite end of the spectrum from a federated database. Rather than having specialized software for managing diverse types of data, a universal database is one in which any type of data can be effectively stored, maintained, and accessed. This approach has benefits and drawbacks. The major benefit is the capability of managing, interrelating, and delivering all data assets in a consistent manner without having to traverse hither and yon to assemble everything. The downside, as with all one-size-fits-all types of solutions, is that it is difficult for a single database to provide all specialized functionality truly required for each diverse data type.

Universal database products have been commercially available since the mid-1990s. Several different vendors have tackled the universal database problem, with varying approaches and solutions. An early innovator on the market was the Illustra DMBS, subsequently acquired by Informix. The Informix DataBlades products, originally part of Illustra, provide facilities for storing, managing, and accessing several types of media and text data. In the IBM world, DB2's Universal Database Extenders provide similar facilities.

Data-Hardware Interfaces for E-Commerce

Imagine a multi-petabyte relational decision-support database, one containing hundreds of tables. Some tables may contain hundreds of columns, and perhaps billions of rows. And in this database, every table is structured in third normal form. The database contains no indexes, no prejoined tables, no aggregations; in fact, no thought has ever been given to building and maintaining anything like these.

Sound like a data graveyard? Cabinet upon cabinet of clicking, whirring, RAID-n magnetic disks? Queries grinding to a halt, lights dimming in the data center, server crashing to its knees?

Not exactly. Users of the database expect, and *receive*, sub-second response to *any* query, regardless of the number of joins or aggregations required. And the multiple petabytes of data are stored in a clear crystal about the size of a sugar cube.

Pinch me, it's a dream. Actually, currently and for the near future, this remains a dream—until a revolution in ultra high-tech hardware such as quantum computers and holographic devices becomes commercially viable. In the meantime, storage technologies are moving relatively slowly towards being able to support such a scenario. Advances in capacity and performance of magnetic storage hardware have been made in the past two decades, but it is a little strange to consider that the primary data storage media by far continues to be based on mechanical arms lurching back and forth above spinning, rust-coated disks. And although the capacity of disk drives may have increased by several orders of magnitude during the past decade, the speed at which the data on the drives can be accessed has only increased by just about one order of magnitude.

Storage technologies lag so far behind all other IT components that this interface is the most critical, yet low-priority, bottleneck in IT inventories, and even worse, in the IT marketplace. Performance problems are exacerbated due to increasing volumes of data. Will increasing processor speed and storage capacity ever overtake increase in data volumes? Will primary storage ever become cost-effective enough to enable persistent stores large enough to break the bottleneck? We can write "IBM" in atoms, but still need to be concerned with "seek time."

Predictions have been made that, largely due to e-commerce growth, within the next two to three years companies will be spending more on data storage hardware than on servers. Especially considering steady increases in Internet bandwidth, at some point it may no longer make economic sense for a company to manage all its data storage in house. In many cases, outsourcing to specialized data-storage ASPs (application service providers) known as storage service providers, or SSPs, may be justifiable. In anticipation of this trend, major server and storage hardware vendors have begun to offer more extensive service and support options for scalable storage options.

Storage Availability

In order to provide absolute assurance of continuous data availability, some level of data redundancy is required. Continuous availability requires the elimination of any type of database downtime, either planned or unplanned.

For any set of data that must be continuously available, at least one other "live" copy is required as a backup in the event that the primary data store becomes unavailable for any reason. Such redundancy can be managed at a hardware level or at the DBMS level. Redundancy of course exacerbates the challenge of data volumes.

At the hardware level, RAID (redundant arrays of independent disks) is a widely implemented solution to the data availability problem. Several classifications of RAID, designated as "levels," are available. RAID is implemented at, or very close to, the hardware level; that is, neither the database management system nor application software is at all aware of how the data being created or accessed is actually stored.

The different classifications of RAID (RAID-0, 1, 3, 5, etc.) provide data protection for continuous availability through combinations of functions called striping, mirroring, and parity.

- *Striping:* Subsets of data are "striped," or distributed, across multiple drives. If any one drive fails, the impact of the failure is limited to the data within the "stripe" on that disk.

- *Parity:* Parity bits are encoded data, generated during write operations, that enable the reconstruction of the original data in the event that all or part of the data cannot be accessed due to drive failure. The lost data can be reconstructed on the fly until it can be rewritten to undamaged disks.

- *Mirroring:* Full copies of the data are made on at least two disk drives, and any changes made to the data are made simultaneously to both copies. If one fails, access is automatically shifted to the remaining copy.

An example of a software-managed facility for assuring continuous availability is included with the Oracle DBMS. The Automated Standby feature of Oracle 8*i* allows for maintaining an offline, duplicate copy of an online database in synch with the main database. The standby database is initialized with a "snapshot" of the main database, and kept in synch by periodic application of update log file transactions from the main database. If the main database is ever unavailable for any reason, the DBMS can automatically route all requests to the standby database.

Storage Volumes: Some Perspective

I've found the information in Table 5.1 to be very interesting for establishing a context on where we've come from and where we're going, in terms of volumes of data that needs to be managed in the digital economy.

As the growth of e-business fuels the rapid increase in data volumes within businesses—estimates range from 75% to 150% annually—techniques for effectively managing and economizing on data storage real estate will become increasingly critical.

Data Compression

Data compression is a widely-used solution for managing the amount of resource required to store a given set of data—especially the exploding volumes of media-type data. Many diverse compression techniques are in use; the type of compression technique used depends primarily on the type of data to be compressed. Media data can be compressed using what are termed *lossy* compression techniques. Lossy techniques allow some information to be lost as a result of the compression/decompression cycle. Compression of text and numeric data is accomplished using *lossless* compression techniques. Lossless techniques are necessary for text and numeric data since no information loss can be tolerated in the compression/decompression cycle. (If you compress the table holding my bank account title and balance, I would not want any letters or digits to be compromised!)

Several types of lossy compression techniques for media data have become standardized and very common. These include JPEG, MPEG, and GIF.

- JPEG stands for Joint Photographic Experts Group, the organization that developed the standard. Not surprisingly, JPEG is used to compress photographic image files.
- MPEG stands for Moving Pictures Expert Group—ditto. MPEG includes standards for compressing not only motion pictures, but also audio, such as MPEG-1, a.k.a. MP3.
- GIF stands for Graphics Interchange Format. (Both the term and the acronym are service marks of CompuServe Interactive Services, Inc. a wholly-owned subsidiary of America Online, Inc.)

Two familiar but diverse software products—PKZIP and IBM's DB2 RDBMS—utilize a lossless compression technique known as dictionary-based encoding. In the dictionary-based encoding process, frequently occurring patterns of data, such as spaces, zeroes, or even city names, are replaced in the compressed data set with shorter encoded values. The decoding scheme for each pattern is then stored in a "dictionary," which is dynamically built during compression. During decompression, the dictionary is referenced to reconstruct the original patterns.

Table 5.1 Relative Data Storage Volumes

Unit	Size			Notes
Byte (B)	8 bits (on almost all modern computers)			
Kilobyte (KB)	1,024 bytes	2^{10} bytes		
Megabyte (MB)	1,024 kilobytes	2^{20} bytes	1,048,576 bytes	
Gigabyte (GB)	1,024 megabytes	2^{30} bytes	1,073,741,824 bytes	Disk drives in home PCs are measured in GBs. Single RDBMS tables in tens of GBs are not uncommon.
Terabyte (TB)	1,024 gigabytes	2^{40} bytes	1,099,511,627,776 bytes	Data warehouse are databases in TB size becoming more common.
Petabyte	1,024 terabytes	2^{50} bytes	1,125,899,906,842,624 bytes	2 petabytes is enough to store the contents of all U.S academic libraries.
Exabyte	1,024 petabytes	2^{60} bytes	1,152,921,504,606,846,976 bytes	
Zettabyte	1,024 exabytes	2^{70} bytes	1,180,591,620,717,411,303,424 bytes	
Yottabyte	1,024 zettabytes	2^{80} bytes	1,208,925,819,614,629,174,706,176 bytes	

As an example of input and output operations on compressed data, in DB2's optional data compression capability, data is compressed at the table-space level, and decompression is done a row at a time as rows are accessed.

While compressing of data allows for significant economizing on storage real estate, a potential trade-off is the additional processing overhead imposed by compression on update operations, and of decompression functions upon retrieval. However, the reduction in I/O costs that can occur because rows are smaller and more rows can be accessed with a single read/write operation might actually cause compressed data to be accessed more efficiently than its uncompressed equivalent.

Advanced Storage Hardware

For decades, the majority of business data has been stored on magnetic media. Speedy delivery of data is dependent on retrieval rates, memory capacity, bandwidth, and processor speed. Even with constant and impressive advances in magnetic media technologies, the last three metrics have increased much faster than the rates at which data, once put at rest, can be roused to move to where it's needed.

Two trends in advanced storage hold much promise for helping us out of the data storage quagmire: in-memory databases and holographic storage. While in-memory database solutions are currently available on the market, much work remains to be done in holographic storage before the technologies are commercially viable.

In-Memory Databases

A quantum leap in predictably brisk response to queries against high-volume, read-only data stores may be provided by in-memory databases. As memory prices decline, in-memory databases have become much more feasible. Memory prices have declined to the extent that the cost of memory necessary to completely store a database of significant size is now well within the realm of feasibility. Running on a commercially available 64-bit server, an in-memory database capacity of 64 gigabytes is possible.

A prime example of an in-memory database is TimesTen from TimesTen Performance Software. TimesTen claims significantly faster performance than even conventional RDBMS data cached completely in memory, as a result of its product being exclusively optimized for in-memory storage. TimesTen databases can be accessed via standard SQL, ODBC (Microsoft Open Database Connectivity), and JDBC (Java Database Connectivity).

Holographic Storage

Imagine being able to store 12 gigabytes, or the equivalent of two full-length movies, in the space taken up by a cube of sugar. This is the potential of holographic storage technology.

Holographic storage utilizes the same type of laser-based technology used to create the hologram on your credit card, except that instead of depositing an image on a flat surface, it enables storage of data in multiple layers throughout a three-dimensional storage medium. Benefits of this technology include not only impressive storage capacities, but also blistering retrieval rates and even enhanced data recoverability.

Data stored holographically requires no moving parts; it is read with a laser, similar to other optical technologies such as CDs. And since the multiple pages, stored throughout the depth of the medium, can be read simultaneously by the laser beam, the data in those multiple pages can be read out in parallel, allowing for impressively fast retrieval rates. Retrieval of a one megabit page in one millisecond provides a data rate of one gigabit per second.

In magnetic storage media, any given bit of data is stored at a single unique position on the media. In any holographically-recorded media, any given unit of data is distributed throughout the volume of the medium. (I honestly don't get this part, but I do believe it.) Consequently, if the medium is damaged, the data in the damaged part remains readable from other areas of the medium.

Most of the new techniques being originated within conventional data storage media are for increasing capacity, rather than in improving seek times and data transfer rates. Much innovation in optical storage has taken place in Japan. However, Japan's optical storage industry has so far focused exclusively on multimedia and entertainment applications driven by consumer market, and left the mainstream computing applications to magnetic hard disk drives. Perhaps the significant revenue opportunities presented by practical solutions to the exploding e-business data problem will make the commercial data-storage market more attractive to aggressive research and innovation in alternative media.

The primary challenge facing researchers in holographic data storage is finding material for the storage medium that is economical, erasable, and also stable. In many materials being investigated, the stored data erodes after many readings with a laser beam. Detailed information of research in holographic storage can be found at *www.research.ibm.com/topics/popups/deep/storage/ html/hresearchers.html* and *www.holospace.dwe.co.kr/* (mostly in Korean, unfortunately).

Data Storage for E-Commerce at Tiosa Group

To: larry_pizacca@gasomatic.com
From: dan_roberts@tiosacorp.com
Subject: Next Steps

Larry,

Thanks for taking time to talk last week. I'm very glad you've decided to stay on with our team as director of data architecture management. We can really use someone with your strong database experience in this position. And of course the respect and credibility you bring with you from your tenure as CIO at Gasomatic will help our combined management team gel that much more quickly.

Now, for your first assignment. Please excuse the impersonal communication, but as you know I will be out of town for the next three days, and I wanted to get things in gear right away. With the pressure we're getting from the e-business folks there is no time to spare.

Can you develop 10 to 15 bullet points for a high-level action plan for mobilizing our data resources—according to the architecture framework we agreed on earlier—in support of our e-Business Enablement Plan? Nothing in depth yet, just something we can use to get us pointed in the right direction. An email is fine—please get to me whatever you have by the end of this week.

Looking forward to working together.

Thanks,
Dan

T. Daniel Roberts
Chief Information Officer
dan_roberts@tiosacorp.com
Tiosa Group
One Tiosa Place
Melvinburg, PA 15600

Phone 412-555-1632
Fax 412-555-1800
Mobile 412-555-7026

To: dan_roberts@tiosacorp.com
From: larry_pizacca@gasomatic.com
Subject: Action Plan Bullet Points

Dan—

I appreciate your generous offer and was glad to be able to accept. Your first assignment is sure motivating me to get going and earn my keep at Tiosa Group. And the combined group of folks you gave me in the data architecture management group is already being a terrific help.

This is what I've come up with so far for an action plan for addressing the data resource requirements of our e-business initiative. It's a work in progress, as they say, and I look forward to discussing this with you in detail. Your feedback is appreciated.

Logical Data
• Confirm that all e-business initiatives will have necessary data modeling support.
• Conduct skills assessment of data modeling team, with focus on e-business knowledge and experience.
• Develop recruiting and training plans as required for enhancing e-business awareness of data modelers.

Physical Data
• Conduct e-business readiness assessment of current DBMS assets, including
  • performance
  • scalability
  • continuous availability
  • media data support, e.g., universal database capabilities
    • if and how these DBMS capabilities can interface with specialized "content management" software
    • whether our current DMBS software versions/contracts include these extended capabilities
• Review DBMS vendor contracts, especially those up for renewal.
• Prepare DBMS vendor RFPs as required.

126

Data-Hardware Interface
- Conduct e-business readiness assessment of DBMS server and storage hardware, including
  - redundancy
  - RAID levels
  - automated failover
  - local and remote backups
  - current and future networking options, e.g., NAS, SAN
- Review storage vendor contracts.
  - Consider vendor service options up to and including outsourcing

I realize this is just a start but it can be the basis for ongoing discussions as we develop a more detailed plan. Hope your management offsite is being productive—and you're making progress on eliminating that slice.

Regards,
Larry

Larry Z. Pizacca
Director, Data Architecture Management
larry_pizacca@gasomatic.com
Tiosa Group
Two Tiosa Place
Pittsfield, PA 15999
Phone 312-555-1632
Fax 312-555-1800
Mobile 312-555-7026

Chapter 6

Input—Moving the Data Around

> Data warehousing is a response to the enterprise need to integrate valuable data
> spread across organizations from multiple sources.
> —Press release, September 25, 2000, announcing the merger of the
> Meta Data Coalition into the Object Management Group

E-Commerce Data Integration

In Chapter 2, we introduced the concepts of value chains and channels, as well as discussed the importance to e-commerce of increasing the cohesiveness between value chain links, between channels, and between value chain links and channels. In this chapter, we'll go into more detail on how techniques and technologies for data movement and manipulation—historically associated with data warehousing efforts—can help significantly to increase this cohesiveness.

In addition to value chain and channel integration, data integration has become a key enabler in spanning channels, extending value chain integration outside the walls and firewalls of the enterprise. As e-commerce channels increase the transparency of these fortifications, barriers to the movement of data in and out are relentlessly lowered. As the boundaries of the enterprise

Table 6.1 Data Architectures Compared

Property	Architecture	
	Conventional Data Warehouse	**Integrated Value Chain**
Synchronization Frequency	Periodic (e.g., daily)	Real-time or near real-time
Source/destination model	Many-to-one	Many-to-many
Update mode	Batch	Transactional

become blurred and increasingly permeable, the condition of the data resources inside appear with more clarity and immediacy to customers, partners, and competitors alike. It follows then that the first steps in becoming a digitized enterprise should be taken towards putting these internal resources in order. After the organization's internal situation has been fortified, it can then begin extending its outward reach from a position of strength.

Data warehousing technologies continue to evolve to support the accelerating timeframes inherent in internal and external e-business data integration. Table 6.1 illustrates the similarities and differences associated with this evolution.

Data-Integration Infrastructure

It's not necessarily the intent of this book to provide a comprehensive assessment of middleware or enterprise application integration (EAI). Many good resources are available dealing specifically with these subjects. However, data integration—moving the data around—is the core functionality underlying both middleware/EAI and back-end, input-related data warehousing components. As a result, in attempting to comprehensively address the contribution of data warehousing within an overall e-commerce strategy, it's necessary to describe, to at least some level of detail, several types of technology that span both domains.

Data integration infrastructure is the technical plumbing that's prerequisite to any data-integration effort. The type of technical data integration most applicable in any situation depends on the combination of the available techni-

Table 6.2   Data Synchronization Alternatives

Data Synchronization Timing	Examples	Benefits	Drawbacks
Instantaneous real-time	Database links Transaction monitors	No latency—all data is continuously synchronized.	Tight coupling between source and target. If target is unavailable (off-line, down), processing at source is likely to be affected. Resource-intensive; potential contention for resources
Deferred, near real-time	Message queueing Message brokers	Latency is minimal. Source and target are loosely coupled—if target is down, source is not affected.	Relatively complex and costly infrastructure required.
Scheduled/ triggered update	Extract-transform-load (ETL) products	Source and target are highly independent.	High potential latency. Batched updates cause "spikes" in resource utilization, such as database locking.

cal infrastructure (hardware and software for clients, servers, and networks) and the requirements of the e-business opportunity.

Demands for *timing* of data movement are the business requirements that most directly determine the choices available for data integration infrastructure technologies. Timing requirements span an entire spectrum from instantaneous synchronization through periodic batch updates. Each point in the spectrum has potential benefits and drawbacks, as shown in Table 6.2.

Database Links

Many instances of data movement within e-commerce applications require data to be directly or indirectly copied from one database to another through a connection defined by one or more database management systems

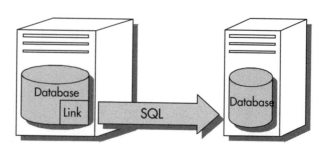

Figure 6-1
A database link.

(DBMSs). Direct database-to-database connectivity allows SQL statements executing on a database server to modify database tables on a different server. Database connectivity should be seriously considered as a technology option in cases where data must be moved in an instantaneous, real-time manner.

Homogeneous database connectivity—where the source and target databases are implemented in the same DBMS—is relatively simple. DBMS vendors, almost without exception, provide facilities within their products for moving data between various installations of their products.

Heterogeneous database connectivity—where data must be moved between databases implemented on different vendors' DBMSs—typically pose more of a challenge, since the idiosyncrasies of two (competing) vendors' connectivity functions must be dealt with and coordinated. Figure 6-1 describes a database link.

Database Replication

All major DBMS products include database replication functions. Replication solutions are especially well-suited for data-integration applications where the source and target data structures are very similar or identical, and are implemented on the same DBMS. Of course these exact conditions are likely to occur less frequently than other scenarios.

Specific database replication functionality is vendor-dependent; however, types of replication such as those offered by Microsoft SQL Server are representative. As you can see, these options run the gamut of the timing spectrum.

- *Transactional Replication:* Any changes made to the source data set are duplicated at the target. The changes could either be made either as they occur or be applied in batches at scheduled intervals. See Figure 6–2.
- *Merge Replication:* Any changes made to either data set are synchro-

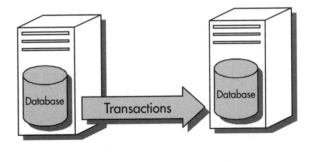

Figure 6-2
Transactional replication.

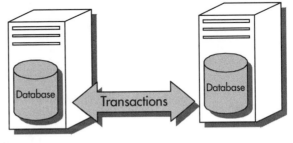

Figure 6-3
Merge replication.

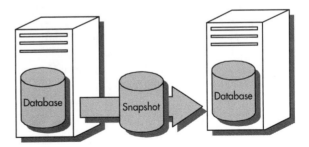

Figure 6-4
Snapshot replication.

nized with the other. Each data set is effectively both source and target. See Figure 6–3.

- *Snapshot Replication:* A copy is made of the source data and applied, in its entirety, to the target. See Figure 6–4.

Transaction Monitors and Application Servers

Transaction monitors exist to manage multiple, concurrent, real-time processes—transactions—including database updates. A transaction is generally agreed to be a process that meets what is called the ACID properties: atomicity, consistency, isolation, and durability. Generally, this means that a transaction—such as data being moved from a source to a target—either completely succeeds or completely fails, and does not affect any other transaction. Transaction monitor products serve to assure that processes under their control meet the ACID properties for transactions. It's critical that in analysis and design, business functions and data are correctly and precisely understood, to enable their transformation into transactions that adequately support business requirements.

In e-commerce multitier architectures, transaction monitors are gradually being merged into a newer class of software products, generally termed *application servers*. This has become a necessity due to the amount of coordination required among the processes taking place at an e-commerce Web site. A glance at Figure 6–13 will serve to confirm this state of affairs.

Message Queues and Brokers

Messaging technologies provide a higher degree of autonomy among the various application components of an e-commerce solution, if required, while also maintaining ACID properties of transactions. Messaging products provide an asynchronous layer of "insulation" between sending and receiving events or applications. For example, in a B2C e-commerce Web site, there may be a requirement for a data update in the source order-processing application to trigger a nearly-instantaneous corresponding update in a target inventory-management application. Yet, we may not want the Web order-processing application to be impacted whatsoever if for any reason the inventory-management application is unavailable.

In a message-queueing scenario, the order-processing application invokes the messaging software and places a message marked for delivery to the inventory-management application on a shared queue, or input/output buffer area. The source application then goes about its business. The target application is configured to read the queue, extract any messages marked for it, and perform the appropriate action in response. If for any reason the target application is delayed in picking up the message, the message will stay in the queue until the target application reads it from the queue. Figure 6–5 shows this at a conceptual level.

Basic data mapping functions come into play in any messaging solution, since source data elements must be mapped first to corresponding elements in the message format; then the message format elements must be mapped to their corresponding elements in the target application (or database).

Message brokers, in addition to the application-independence and message-

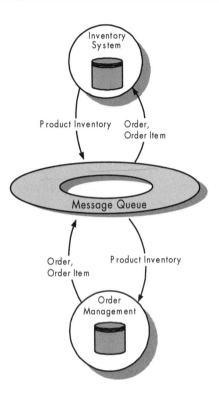

Figure 6-5
Message queueing.

persistence features of message queues, provide additional functions including message routing and enhanced transformation. Routing features permit message types to be preregistered with the broker, along with one or more target applications for the message type. Source applications send messages to the broker, which, acting as a central message clearinghouse, routes messages to their appropriate multiple target applications or databases. A message broker solution is conceptually presented in Figure 6-6.

In addition to basic data mapping facilities, message broker products typically also provide support for data transformations, such as data type conversions and value translations, which may be necessary to change the data, as it is moved, into formats compatible with the target applications or databases. In order to accomplish this, message brokers may have extensive meta-data-management facilities, supporting the definition, design, and storage of multiple data structures, as well as mapping and transformation specifications, in a centralized meta-data database.

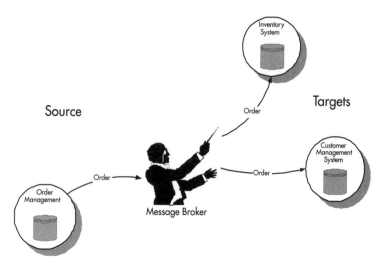

Source

Targets

Figure 6-6
A message broker.

Enterprise Application Integration: All Together Now

While there are many flavors of enterprise application integration, or EAI, the common goal of solutions of this type is the application of technology to achieve enterprise-wide integration of both data and process. The overlap between EAI and data warehousing is of course in the data-related integration components. In an EAI solution, these components are arguably the most critical, since some level of data integration is a precondition to any significant process integration.

The components of a complete EAI solution can be looked at as layers, as in Figure 6–7.

The top two layers of EAI enable a company to connect and integrate processes. At a technical level, this is accomplished primarily through interprocess messaging, and at the business level, through workflow definition—describing and implementing what business processes trigger other business processes under what conditions.

The underlying two data layers include, at the lowest level, the various types of data integration infrastructure technologies discussed earlier, and directly above this, support for data integration at a business level, implemented through data modeling, meta-data, and data transformations.

Workflow—*Business Process* Integration
Processing Middleware—*Technical Process* Integration
Data Modeling, Metadata and Data Transformation—*Business Data* Integration
Data Integration Infrastructure—*Technical Data* Integration

Figure 6-7
EAI layers.

XML, XML, and More XML

> Many companies report a strong interest in XML. XML, however,
> is so flexible that this is similar to expressing a strong interest
> in ASCII characters.
>
> —Microsoft BizTalk Framework Overview

If one were to summarize the convergence of e-commerce and data ware-housing in three letters, those letters would be XML. There is little doubt re-maining that XML—eXtensible Markup Language—will be a fundamental building block of e-commerce, but how does it relate to data warehousing? What should data warehousing practitioners have to do with XML? As much as they should, since XML is bringing about radical changes in techniques pre-viously closely held within the domain of data warehousing specialists: meta-data management and data transformation.

At a fundamental level, XML is a method for *formatting and moving data*—and, some may contend, also for storing data. And since data ware-housing is also fundamentally about *formatting and moving data*, the parallels are evident.

What's XML Good For?

The primary value of XML is in moving data around. That is, its greatest value will be in exchanging data—to some extent among applications within enter-prises, but primarily in exchanging data between enterprises. It is a catalyst for convergence; XML is a prime example of the *network effect:* the more partic-ipants in the network, the higher its value becomes. The more businesses that adopt XML, the more valuable it becomes, and the more businesses will adopt XML, and so forth.

XML, in being accepted by a critical mass of e-commerce participants and industries as a technological enabler, has as a result begun to act as an organizational motivator. This motivation is indeed picking up steam. The primary evidence for this momentum is the increased activity surrounding industry-specific vocabularies implemented in XML Schemas.

XML Documents, Syntax, and Semantics

Beginning in mid-1999, much hype was generated indicating that XML, due to its ability to combine data and meta-data in the same document, would remove once and for all the barriers to enterprises sharing not only data but also the meaning of that data. Supposedly, all business organizations "speaking" XML would be able to understand what the data means and easily match and correlate it with similar data from other providers. Rather like the intent of the international language Esperanto *(www.esperanto.org)*, the goal of which was to remove all barriers to the understanding of spoken and written languages by providing a worldwide second language.

The meta-data associated with XML documents is in the form of labels, or *tags,* which enclose each data value (see Example 6–1). This labeling, while certainly a big step toward conveying meaning, by no means insures communication of *complete* and *unambiguous* meaning. For example, take a verbal, decidedly low-tech interchange in a restaurant regarding coffee: "May I have a cup of coffee, please." To me, the label coffee is unambiguous; it always means "regular, and black." But that's just me—it's a "local variable." A waitress, working in the precise vocabulary of the food-service professional, has no way of receiving specific-enough meaning without eliciting the details "behind" the label: "Regular or decaf; cream or sugar?" The label "coffee" is insufficient to allow the sharing of complete and accurate meaning.

What does this have to do with XML? Well, if the meaning (i.e., meta-data) included in an XML document is only in the form of labels, in order to be globally shared, these labels must be (1) very specific, and (2) comprehended the same way by all parties, to avoid misunderstandings. (Practitioners of corporate law make a good living by arbitrating the consequences of corporate misunderstandings!) This is why the development of "vocabularies," or "grammars," is absolutely essential to the successful and widespread adoption of XML. So, we can see that the technology and the syntax are the easy parts and that, once again raising its ugly head, is the hard part—those pesky ol' semantics. The bad news is that we will see a proliferation of vocabularies; the good news is that there is a standard tool—XSL transformations (more on this a little later) with which vocabularies can be translated.

Example 6–1 Example of an XML Purchase Order Document

```
<?xml version="1.0"?>
        <purchaseOrder orderDate="1999-10-20">
          <shipTo country="US">
            <name>Jane Jones</name>
            <street>123 Mill Street</street>
            <city>Mill Mountain</city>
            <state>CA</state>
            <zip>90952</zip>
          </shipTo>
          <billTo country="US">
            <name>Robert Smith</name>
            <street>8 Pine Avenue</street>
            <city>Big City</city>
            <state>PA</state>
            <zip>95819</zip>
          </billTo>
          <comment>Help, my toilet is overflowing!</comment>
          <items>
            <item partNum="872-AA">
              <productName>Toilet</productName>
              <quantity>1</quantity>
              <price>148.95</price>
              <comment>Confirm this is electric</comment>
            </item>
            <item partNum="926-AA">
              <productName>Baby Monitor</productName>
              <quantity>1</quantity>
              <price>39.98</price>
              <shipDate>1999-05-21</shipDate>
            </item>
          </items>
        </purchaseOrder>
```

Describing XML Documents: DTDs, Schemas, and Schema Registries

XML-formatted data is often characterized as self-describing. A stand-alone XML document does indeed contain descriptive content—tags—but that's about the extent of its self-contained descriptive facilities. For XML-formatted data to be effectively shared between applications and enterprises, it is important to consider the facilities available for describing and validating XML document types: document type definitions (DTDs), XML schemas, and schema registries.

A document type is analogous to a record layout or a relational table definition; it describes the content and structure of a specific valid data format, such as an invoice record or purchase order record. Many standards for and around XML are in a state of development by the W3C and others, and the standards for describing document types are no exception. Until mid-year 2000, the most widely accepted standard for describing XML layouts were DTDs, but beginning with the W3C publications on XML schemas at that time, schemas have begun to overtake DTDs as the preferred XML document description vocabulary. Although DTDs and schemas serve essentially the same purpose, schemas have several advantages, including additional descriptive power, primarily in their support for a wide range of data types. XML schemas are also XML documents themselves, and as such can be managed by the same software tools as any other XML documents. See Example 6–2.

Schemas (and DTDs) are where the "real" XML meta-data resides. In addition to the element tag names also found in the instance (data file) XML data itself, schemas include extensive additional specifications for elements: data types, allowable values, occurrence constraints (how many times the element can occur), and edit patterns.

XML schemas are vitally important in defining the rules of engagement for e-business data exchange. This importance is evident in the establishment of schema repositories such as those found at *www.oasis.org* and *www.biztalk.org*, where numerous XML schemas are posted for the prospective adoption and use by e-business partners. If two or more trading partners are able to

Example 6–2 Part of the Schema for the Purchase Order Example

```
<xsd:element name="purchaseOrder" type="PurchaseOrderType"/>

    <xsd:element name="comment" type="xsd:string"/>

    <xsd:complexType name="PurchaseOrderType">
    <xsd:element name="shipTo" type="Address"/>
    <xsd:element name="billTo" type="Address"/>
    <xsd:element ref="comment" minOccurs="0"/>
    <xsd:element name="items" type="Items"/>
    <xsd:attribute name="orderDate" type="xsd:date"/>
    </xsd:complexType>
```

share a common schema—layouts—for exchanging business transactions, data interchange is greatly simplified.

It is more likely that trading partners, rather than settling on an identical shared schema, will use layouts that are similar but not identical. This is likely to become the most common scenario, and will require the application of XML data transformations. In the next section, we'll consider the importance of XML schemas in e-business data transformations.

Transforming Data

In order to complete the data-integration picture, additional facilities are required above and beyond the prerequisite data-integration infrastructure.

Data transformation technologies predate the origination of the term *data warehousing* itself. Transforming data among different but related forms has, from the outset, been one of the core components within the data warehousing domain. As the digital economy expands and continues to generate data in ever more forms and formats, data transformation will continue to increase in importance; at the same time, the advent of XML raises new challenges for traditional thinking about data transformation. In fact, the emergence of B2B exchanges may go so far as to elevate data transformation to a directly revenue-generating service.

The acronym ETL (extract-transform-load) lumps together a pretty broad set of functions, the end result of which is the periodic synchronization of one data set (the target, or destination, data set) with one or more others (the source data set). Each of the constituent functions is in turn comprised of several other functions.

Extraction

If the term extraction sounds like going to the dentist, many times it is like pulling teeth. Extraction is the ETL step in which the data-integration infrastructure is most important—it's the only part of the process that actually comes in contact with the data source. Conventional data warehousing has almost always relied on a data-integration infrastructure so basic that we did not even cover it in the earlier section: batch file transfer, such as FTP (File Transfer Protocol). Use of this infrastructure actually requires a two-step process: (1) create an *extract file*—a complete or partial subset of the data source, and (2) transmit the extract file, over local-area-network, wide-area network, or even the Internet, to the data-warehouse server platform. Once the source data, usually in something resembling its original form, is colocated with the target data, the extraction process is complete.

Push or Pull?

The extraction scenario described previously is what could be termed a *pull* scenario. The data is periodically pulled (somewhat like a tooth, during that dentist visit) from the data source, largely unbeknownst to, and with little or no participation by, the data source. This is in stark contrast to the e-commerce data-integration scenarios described earlier, where the data source was an active participant in the data-integration process.

When the extraction process is initiated at the data source, we have what can be termed a *push* scenario; the data is pushed from the source to the target. (The concept of "push extraction" may cause some cognitive dissonance, so let's not go there.) Since the data source is much more aware of the real stuff going on, and knows when it happens, the push scenario can achieve a much higher degree of synchronization between source and target, with much less elapsed time, or latency, between the event and its propagation.

One method by which such a push scenario can be implemented is by using a database trigger. A database trigger is a program, related to one specific table and stored in the database, that executes automatically when that table is updated. In the Web site example discussed earlier, a trigger could be created on the Order table in the order-processing application, which, when an update to the table occurred, would "push" an update of the inventory level of the item ordered through a database link, to the Item Inventory table in the inventory management application.

The push idea is the basis of both the Active Warehouse concept marketed by NCR Teradata, and the idea of the Operational Data Store, popularized by Bill Inmon. As e-business continues to affect the inexorable acceleration in the rate of change (velocity) in almost all markets, managers of decision-support data sources such as data warehouses must continually strive, with techniques such as this, to decrease the latency of the data provided to decision-makers.

Transformation: Gentlemen and Ladies, Start Your Coding

Development of a data transformation process begins with source-to-target data element mapping. In order to do this, the data element content in both the source and target data structures must be accessible. This is one instance where availability of meta-data is absolute mandatory. Mapping columns to columns in relational database tables is relatively painless, since all table layouts are by definition stored in the database catalog.

Mapping of sequential files as sources or targets requires access to record layouts from programs or application documentation. Mapping of XML files is made easier by the existence of embedded tags. Many automated ETL tools are able to directly import layouts from database catalogs, programs, and more recently, XML schemas or DTDs. Most automated ETL tools—and more and more XML tools—allow import of source and target layout meta-data to support mapping. Any formats for which mapping is not supported must be entered manually.

After the mapping is done, the real work begins. ETL tools typically allow specification of pseudocode or SQL statements to allow manipulation of values between input of the source and output to the target. Common data warehousing transformations include decoding of coded values, resolution of multiple coding or identification schemes from sources into a single target scheme, and aggregating detailed values into summarized tables. Often, when more complicated transformations are required, ETL tools allow exits to code script to accomplish the transformation.

As e-commerce-related data-transformation tools and technologies mature, more types of data sources, targets, and transformations are being supported and implemented. As previously mentioned, message brokers and EAI tools also support development and execution of data transformations. Transformations of data among various e-commerce data interchange formats such as XML and EDI formats—including ANSI X.12, EDIFACT, SWIFT, and others—and between e-commerce formats and relational databases, are becoming increasingly common, and software tool vendors are rushing to support this growing market.

One of the most important developments in data transformation for e-commerce is XSLT.

eXtensible Stylesheet Language Transformations (XSLT)

Many of us may remember the universal translator of *Star Trek* fame—a tiny handheld device that could translate any alien tongue into any other language. XSLT (eXtensible Stylesheet Language Transformations) may become the universal translator of e-commerce. XSLT offers a standard, declarative, and largely self-documenting format for specifying transformations of XML (and potentially many other types) of data formats. XSLT may indeed become the universal format for describing data transformations.

From a data warehousing perspective, XSLT may be the most significant aspect of the XML phenomenon. According to the W3C, XSLT is an XML vocabulary that is a means by which one XML document can be transformed into another XML document. In reality, XSLT can be used to transform just about any data format into any other; for example, one of the most common uses of XSLT is to transform XML data into HTML for display in a Web browser.

Example 6–3 is an XSLT file that transforms the previous purchase order XML document into an HTML document for browser display, selecting out for display only the name of the ship-to party (the value of the <name> element within the <shipTo> element).

Example 6–3 XSLT File Transformation of XML Purchase Order Document

```
<xsl:stylesheet xmlns:xsl="http://www.w3.org/TR/WD-xsl">

    <xsl:template match="/">
     <HTML>
      <BODY>
       <TABLE WIDTH="100%" CELLPADDING="5">
        <xsl:apply-templates select="//shipTo" />
       </TABLE>
       </BODY>
      </HTML>
     </xsl:template>

    <xsl:template match="//shipTo">
     <TR>
      <xsl:apply-templates select="name" />
      </TR>
     <TR><TD COLSPAN="3"><HR /></TD></TR>
     </xsl:template>

    <xsl:template match="name">
     <TD ROWSPAN="2">
      <xsl:value-of />
      </TD>
     </xsl:template>

</xsl:stylesheet>
```

Due to the combination of the following factors, it's quite likely that XSLT applications will rapidly proliferate in the coming decade:

- E-commerce is causing data-exchange channels and transactions to proliferate.
- XML is becoming the data-formatting technique of choice for such data exchanges.
- The diversity of data formats among trading partners will inevitably require data transformation.

Rather than being a transformation procedure or program, an XSLT document is a listing of declarative "rules," or instructions, specifying how an input file format, or potentially multiple input file formats, are to be transformed into an output format.

The content of an XSL style sheet (which is also an XML document) may not yet be intuitively understandable by a data warehousing analyst accustomed to working with venerable ETL tools such as Informatica or SQL Server Data Transformation Services. But just as XML is taking its place among the languages of electronic commerce, so too will XSLT assume a pivotal role in translating among the various dialects in which electronic business events are articulated and stored. Database professionals should become familiar with XSLT. More reference materials are becoming available every month.

An example of how XSLT transformations could work in the context of a B2B exchange, for example, is as follows. Say a company wishes to subscribe to a B2B exchange as a purchaser. One of the services the exchange may offer to its subscribers is transformation of transaction data to and from the formats used by other subscribers. It may even maintain a library of widely used XML schemas for common transaction types.

At subscription time, the newly subscribing company specifies to the exchange the transaction types and formats it will be sending to, and receiving from, the exchange. These types and formats could include, for example, purchase orders and Requests For Quotes (RFQs) in the format of a (more or less) industry-standard XML schema. If these transaction types and formats are currently supported by the exchange, charges for data transformations into and out of these formats may be free or inexpensive; if the transaction formats are new to the exchange, there may be a charge for setting up the necessary transformations.

After subscription setup is complete, the company begins sending and receiving transactions, in their specified formats, through the exchange. The company does not need to know or care about the formats to and from which

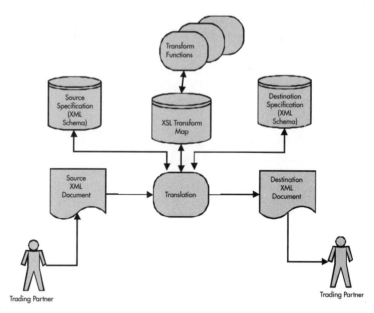

Figure 6–8
B2B transformations.

their transactions may have been transformed in order to complete the transactions with other members of the exchange.

A pictorial representation of such an interaction and transformation is shown in Figure 6–8.

XSLT Constraints

Most commercial XSLT processors are currently constrained to manipulating data solely in main memory. They must load an entire source file into main memory in order to transform it into an output file. This constraint of course potentially seriously limits the size of the files that can be processed using XSLT. XSLT in its current form is likely to be much more effective for single-transaction applications, rather than for processing files that include large batches of transactions. However, considering the combination of the momentum gathering around XSLT as the de facto transformation language of e-commerce, coupled with the relatively immature market of current XSLT processors, it would be truly surprising if these products did not soon begin to find ways around current source-file size limitations.

Loading

The term *loading* is an oversimplification, implying a process in which an empty database is filled up periodically. This in reality is one technique, but a quick-and-dirty, blunt-force method. This type of bulk loading can either replace or append to data already in the database, but precludes the update of existing data. It is rarely applicable in today's fast-paced business world.

Data warehousing technologies are continuing to mature and evolve, continuing to keep in step with the accelerating pace of e-commerce data integration requirements. In the e-business world, instantaneous or near-instantaneous synchronization of autonomous data stores—in contrast to just loading—is the order of the day. Data warehousing has been compelled to evolve from its original, stand-alone weekly or monthly snapshot-and-load configuration to include any and all e-commerce data movement, resolution, and synchronization needs.

Meta-data and Data Transformation

Meta-data—specifically, data structure layouts and data element documentation—are essential prerequisites for data movement. When data is moved, it is actually copied from a source data structure to a target data structure (no brain surgery here). The source and target formats are sometimes nearly identical, but in the vast majority of situations, they range from similar to quite dissimilar.

Meta-data is initially necessary in the mapping process to accurately determine which source and target data elements are close enough in intent to be reasonably mapped. After mapping is completed, the remaining source-target differences must be resolved by data transformations. An example screen from Microsoft's BizTalk Mapper is shown in Figure 6–9. BizTalk Mapper supports the mapping and transformation of e-business data, primarily emphasizing the transformation of XML files through the generation of extended XSLT scripts.

This function reveals the essential nature of meta-data in the mapping and transformation process. In the top half of the screen, the source specification meta-data—an XML schema—appears in the left window. The destination specification, in this case also an XML schema, appears in the right window. The workspace between shows mappings between fields in the source and destination, as well as transformations—"functoids" in Microsoft's parlance—which take place between source and destination. The lower section of the screen shows the XSL stylesheet code generated by the mappings and trans-

147

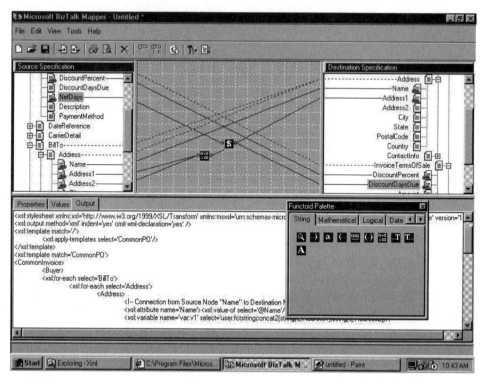

Figure 6-9
BizTalk Mapper.

formations, as well as the Functoid Palette from which various transformation templates—string, math, logical, date, custom VB script, and so on—can be chosen.

Extraction, Transformation, and Analysis of Web Interactions

One of the most common requirements for ETL processing in e-commerce is to support the analysis of user interactions with Web sites—clickstreams. Even the most basic Web server includes the capability to create and retain detailed records of all interactions with browser sessions from which it receives requests and provides responses. These interaction records are stored in Web server log files—sequential, fixed-format text files. The basic log file format—common log file (CLF) format—is specified by the World

148

Wide Web Consortium and is implemented in most Web server software products. Data fields included in the CLF format specification include

- IP address or Internet domain name of the client
- First line of the client request (e.g., a text string including a Web page URL requested by the client)
- Status code of the interaction
- Number of bytes returned to the client
- URL of the referring page

The detail in a Web server log file is definitely much deeper than wide—that is, contains many more records than fields. While because of this depth the Web server log is a potentially rich source of data for analysis of site-visitor interactions, several major hurdles exist when attempting to apply this data for analysis.

- The data is in a sequential file format not able to be directly queried joined to other data sources. This can of course be overcome by loading the data into a data source that can be queried, such as a relational database table.
- In the log file, records of multiple concurrent user interactions are appended to the file in chronological sequence; therefore, the records representing the interactions of any single session are not contiguous. Not only this, but absolutely precise "sessionization"—that is, determining the boundaries, or the first and last request or response of a given user session—is difficult, if not impossible.
- Log file data is difficult to directly correlate with data from other sources, specifically business transaction data such as purchases.

Precise identification of sessions and users for retrospective (or real-time) analysis requires implementation of more extensive capabilities than those provided by the basic Web log. These capabilities include cookies and explicit user registration.

- *Cookies:* A cookie is a small file transmitted by the Web server to the browser client and stored on the client workstation. A cookie file can retain required data not available in a basic log file, such as a session identifier, which can be created and accessed by the e-commerce application. When retrieved during visitor interactions, such a session identifier can then, for example, be stored in an extension to the basic log file records for each session. Retrospective extract processes can then use the session identifier to group and "sessionize" all log file records for a given session.

* *Explicit User Registration:* Any true e-commerce site requiring exchange of payment is likely to require users—customers, at this point—to explicitly identify themselves via a registration process. The registration process can create a customer identifier that can then be stored in the user's cookie file and from there be populated into each log file record for that user. The customer identifier can also then be saved with order transaction records that (it is hoped) result from the user's interactions with the site. The log file session records for the user can then be correlated (joined) for meaningful retrospective analysis activities.

Several advanced e-commerce server software products provide functionality, such as that just described, enabling analysis of Web interactions. This analysis, often designated *Web analytics,* is provided either through components bundled with the server software or through an interface with specialized third-party analytical software. Examples of different configurations include Blue Martini e-commerce server software, which includes data warehousing and Web analytics modules, and Broadvision, through interfaces with Broadbase analytical software.

Successively Broader Scopes of Data Integration

The scope of data integration in which an enterprise may be engaged can be approached in a manner similar to that discussed in Chapter 4 with regard to analytic data. It may be advantageous for a business to get its own internal house in order with an enterprise scope of data integration—integrating its internal value chain—before exposing this data to customers, suppliers, and partners. However, given the intense time-to-market pressures and "land-grab" nature bearing on e-business initiatives, both internal and external data-integration scopes must often be addressed concurrently.

Enterprise Data Integration

The increased criticality of enterprise data integration brought about by the expansion of e-commerce coincides with a widespread trend away from custom-built business applications toward package application implementation. In cases of custom-built applications, there may have been opportunity for building in cross-application integration. But when multiple vendor-built products enter the scene, this opportunity, while not completely disappearing, becomes dependent on

- Industry technical standards to which the various vendors may adhere.
- The "openness" of the product—that is, the facilities provided by the vendor with which data and functions within a packaged application may be accessed.

Under this type of common scenario, data-integration infrastructure technologies become increasingly important for establishing a foundation upon which internal data integration can proceed.

Extra-Enterprise B2B Data Integration

As e-commerce data exchange continues to expand, several alternative configurations are becoming available to support interchange of data among buyers and sellers. Two major configurations of extra-enterprise B2B data integration can be characterized as point-to-point and hub-and-spoke.

Point-to-Point

A point-to-point configuration exists when two trading partners exchange data directly, without a middleman such as a B2B exchange. In this case, the two companies must work out together the formats and conventions for exchanging data through e-commerce channels. If the two companies maintain different formats for their common transactions, they must determine and implement the necessary mappings and transformations between the dissimilar transaction layouts. The configuration resulting from such an approach may not be highly reusable in situations where the company on either end of the data exchange—buyer or seller—may wish to connect to additional alternative partners for a given transaction type. A unique translation may be necessary for each additional partner; this configuration provides limited scalability. In the example in Figure 6–10, the buyer must maintain a unique mapping/transformation for each seller with whom he or she wishes to deal.

An alternative is a hub-and-spoke configuration provided by B2B exchanges.

151

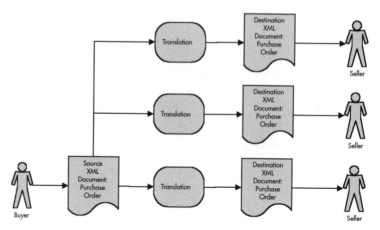

Figure 6-10

A point-to-point configuration for e-commerce data exchange.

Hub-and-Spoke

The prime example of a hub-and-spoke configuration (See Figure 6–11) is a B2B exchange. In cases when buyer and seller companies participating in a B2B exchange will use dissimilar formats for the same transaction type, each participant needs to map and translate to only one "common" format (such as an XML schema). This allows an unlimited number of partners to participate, with only one mapping/transformation required for each. The exchange provides tools and services to participants that facilitate mapping to its common formats.

When a trading partner sends a transaction through the exchange to a designated receiver partner, the sender can reference an information-exchange agreement previously defined and maintained at the exchange. The transformation map indicated in the agreement is then applied; the map uses the source and destination specifications and the appropriate functions to translate the source document into the target document. The target document is then forwarded to the receiver.

Such a hub-and-spoke configuration, offered by a middleman such as a B2B exchange, adds value by increasing the reusability and scalability of participants' mapping and transformation specifications.

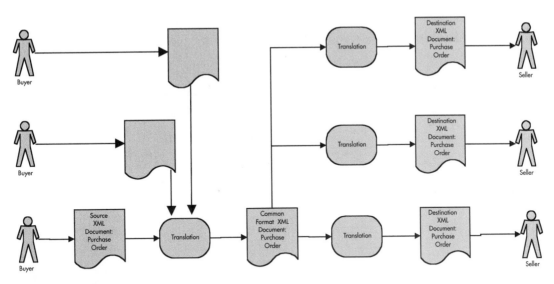

Figure 6–11
A hub-and-spoke configuration for e-commerce data exchange.

UDDI

A relatively new initiative with a potentially significant impact on extra-enterprise integration is Universal Description, Discovery, and Integration (UDDI). UDDI is a joint effort of a number of vendors, including Ariba, Microsoft, and IBM. It is a set of specifications, the goal of which is to allow companies doing e-commerce to create, in a public registry, XML-format entries that describe their business and the Web-based services they offer. Among other benefits, this registry would likely provide a means for companies to describe the formats and procedures they offer for exchange of e-business data. As in the case of the more specialized schema registries, the success of this initiative is dependent on the network effect: The more companies that actively participate, the more likely additional companies will be to sign up.

Data Integration for a B2C E-Commerce Web Site

For a true B2C e-commerce Web site—one capable of accepting orders for products in return for payment—the data integration challenges are not at all trivial. Implementation of package software solutions for one or more components definitely eases the development burden and accelerates time-to-market; however, even this scenario requires a significant amount of down-and-dirty data mapping, trigger event and transformation coding, middleware configuration, and in some cases even data modeling and database design.

A B2C Web site has many characteristics in common with a data warehouse—it requires integration of data from many source systems and presentation of this data to the user as a coherent whole. It follows, then, that a reasonably meticulous design methodology for such a site resembles in many ways a data warehouse design methodology, and can be adapted from such in a relatively straightforward manner. Figure 6–12 outlines the general flow of such a methodology.

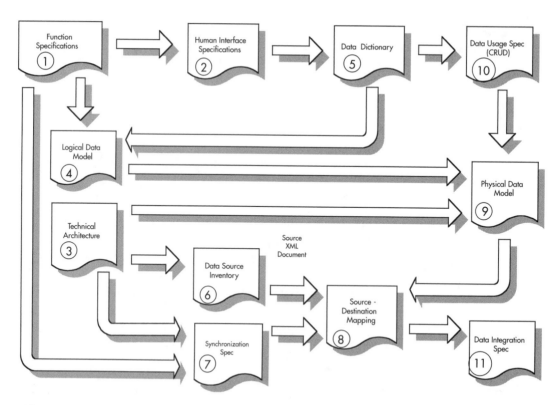

Figure 6–12
B2C Web site data deliverables.

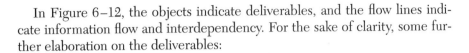

In Figure 6–12, the objects indicate deliverables, and the flow lines indicate information flow and interdependency. For the sake of clarity, some further elaboration on the deliverables:

1. *Function Specifications:* Description of the scope, content, and navigation of the site from a business perspective.

2. *Human Interface Specifications:* Description of the scope, content, and navigation of the site's pages.

3. *Technical Architecture:* Current and proposed hardware and software inventory and assumptions.

4. *Logical Data Model:* Comprehensive data model, down to the key and attribute level, of all the data required for the site—spanning all commercial and/or custom application components.

5. *Data Dictionary:* All data elements required for all pages included within the site.

6. *Data Source Inventory:* All data stores (files, database tables, content directories, external providers, etc.) from which data is to be obtained (or to which it is to be sent).

7. *Synchronization Specification:* Requirements for timing of data movement—what events trigger other events, acceptable lag times between initiation and movement (for example, synchronous, near real-time, or intervallic).

8. *Source-Destination Mapping:* Specification of which source data structures (fields, message parameters, table columns, Web page elements, etc.) are to be moved to which destination data structures.

9. *Physical Data Model:* Derived from completed logical data model, with any required adjustments made for performance, scalability, availability, and application partitioning.

10. *Data Usage Specification:* What operations (Create, Retrieve, Update, Delete) are applied to what data structures within the context of users' interactions with the site.

11. *Data Integration Specification:* Final compilation of data sources, targets, events, timings, mappings, and any and all data transformations that may be required.

The resulting overall design of such a Web site might look somewhat like Figure 6–13.

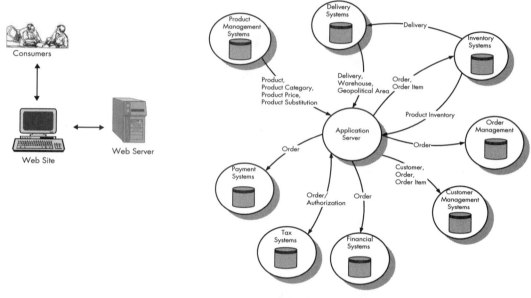

Figure 6-13
B2C Web site overall design.

Enhancing the Data: Customer Matching and Householding

Some of the most important and advanced applications of data transformation are what are known as customer matching and householding. These applications have been around for decades, but the concurrent growth of e-business and customer-centricity has combined to thrust them together into center stage.

The high-level steps in the customer-matching and householding processes are as follows:

1. Available attribute values for multiple customer "versions"—such as names, addresses, and Social Security numbers—are compared, according to flexible matching rules determined by the business. Versions may have been accumulated as a result of multiple interactions with a single customer.

2. Data from these multiple versions are merged, again according to flex-

ible business-defined rules, to yield a designated "single version of the truth" customer record.

3. Once the "true" customers are identified, these can be grouped, according to business-defined matching rules, into likely households.

The data model diagram in Figure 6–14 includes the input to the matching and householding processes.

Customer Version. In many companies, over time there may have been multiple interactions with the same customer in which data about that customer was captured in digital format. If at these times no attempt was made to look up prior records on the customer, yet another record of that customer probably came into being. This is a common occurrence in diversified companies—notoriously, financial institutions—and in the case of mergers and acquisitions when the merged companies' customer constituencies overlap. The result is multiple "versions" of the same customer—multiple snapshots at different points in time, probably associated with different transactions and/or products.

In order for the company to form a single, complete, and consistent image of its customers, such versions must be merged into a single instance of the customer.

Customer. A single version of a customer of the company. How does the company arrive at this single version? It depends on the

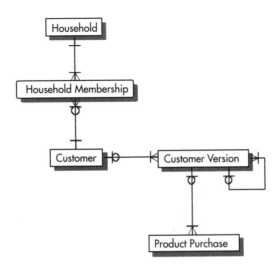

Figure 6–14
Customer householding and versioning
data model.

matching criteria applied to the various versions. The most common matching criteria include name (first, last, middle, nicknames), address, and if available, Social Security number. Matching character strings such as names and addresses requires dictionary/thesaurus facilities; customer-matching software products typically include an extensive starter set and allow for customization by the company based on the company's customer base.

Household. The existence of a household is in most cases derived from the clustering of the individual customer records remaining after true customers are consolidated from a number of customer versions.

A traditional household is sometimes defined as a set of individuals with the same last name, living at the same address. Of course, many exceptions can be found to this definition—so various types of households can be defined, such as "contemporary"(same address, perhaps different last names), and "extended" (maybe not even the same address—this is a bit difficult to fully automate).

Household Membership. Household membership represents the inclusion of an individual customer in a household. Membership is determined at the same time as the household, since in most cases households are actually created by grouping their individual members.

Product Purchase. These are sales transactions with which associated (often redundant) customer information is captured.

Equivalents to households and customer versions are also common in the B2B world. A corporate organizational structure, including subsidiaries, divisions, and so on, is analogous to the household. Versions of corporate names commonly exist as well—for example, IBM, International Business Machines, and IBM Corp. are versions of the same corporate entity name.

Assimilating External Data

The growth of e-commerce has greatly expanded the market for commercial providers of various types of data. The largest areas for vendor-provided data include marketing, credit, product, and taxes. While in the past data warehousing focused primarily, if not exclusively, on internal enterprise data, e-commerce will inevitably expand the scope of data warehousing applications to include the absorption of these and other types of data into the organization's value chain.

Marketing and Demographics. Vendors of marketing and demographics data probably have the longest track record of commercial data providers. E-commerce and the related increased focus on customer awareness have combined to expand the market for this prosperous group of companies, as well as to increase their numbers with new entrants.

Product Data. A large market has developed around providing product data, both character-based and graphical, to e-commerce sites. Retail Web sites are likely to maintain proprietary internal data on their product catalogs, as well as obtain additional data from one or more external providers. Purchased external data must be matched—on SKU, or Stock Keeping Unit, for example—and merged with the in-house data to provide a complete product profile for their online customers.

Another type of product-data consolidation scenario found in both B2B and B2C markets is that of the catalog content aggregator. Aggregators may provide an online "hub" though which several vendors' product catalog data can be browsed. In many of these cases, the combined velocity of changes across all catalogs makes physical replication of all vendor participants' data at the aggregator's site prohibitively problematic, making a federated database approach (as discussed in Chapter 5) an attractive alternative.

Taxes. Tax calculations, if applicable, for online purchases on B2C Web sites need to take place instantaneously. For these tax calculations, the data that needs to move between e-commerce and tax applications includes item type (often identified by SKU), purchase amount, and identification of the applicable state and municipal taxation authorities. Similar to product data, changes to this type of data happen infrequently, and sites will most likely choose to host the required data onsite and refresh on a periodic basis through downloads available from the vendor of the software.

Credit Card Data. Financial consideration for e-commerce transactions is definitely not exchanged by cash or check. And unless and until experimental alternative payment mechanisms break through, credit cards have a lock on e-business transactions. It's obvious that movement of data between e-commerce merchant sites and credit card service providers needs to be immediate. When a customer enters credit card data at a Web site, the data needs to be verified real-time, and an authorization sent back in time to avoid, at all costs, trying the patience of the customer. Even though per-transaction fees are quite small, the enormous and ever-increasing volume of e-commerce transactions and the resulting upside potential has mobilized and energized the large existing credit card infrastructure to strongly support e-business. Many alternative software products, services, and combinations are available to merchants. The single common denominator is data, and moving the data around. When it comes to data formats, the service providers hold the cards; they determine the data formats and required values, and the merchants have little room for negotiation. In fact, the more data-compliant the merchant is able to be, the more kindly the services will look upon reducing his per-transaction fee.

Knowledge Management: The Input is the Issue

Data is the raw material that allows humans to be informed—for *inform*ation to take place. E-commerce continues to fuel escalating volumes of stored and transient digitized data. Institutionalized knowledge results when information is accumulated, assimilated, and interconnected by organizations—groups of humans—over time. As individuals continue to become ever more career-mobile, the links between employees and employers as a result become more and more short-lived. To leverage as much as possible their investment in their employees, organizations more than ever require effective methods for capturing knowledge—both that gained by informed associates and that publicly available. Methods are also required for digitizing that information back into data and for disseminating the data back out to those associates with a need to be informed.

Knowledge management (KM) will continue to be increasingly important for organizations to remain competitive in e-commerce. Two of the most challenging areas in the management of this knowledge cycle are taxonomy building and knowledge capture.

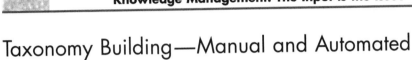

Taxonomy Building—Manual and Automated

Indexes of words, such as those created by basic Web search facilities, provide a fundamental starting point for supporting users' needs to be informed. But more advanced capabilities are available for organizing and managing the growing mass of electronic information confronted by business users. Effective methods for collecting, classifying, and managing meaningful groups of data are becoming increasingly essential.

In Chapter 4 we touched briefly on the value of classification hierarchies—taxonomies—in accessing and making sense of proliferating masses of data. Since creating these taxonomies is likely to take place on the back end, or input side, of the data-management equation, we'll go into some of these techniques and technologies in more detail here.

A taxonomy is a hierarchical classification of concepts. The taxonomy probably most familiar in e-commerce is found at Yahoo!. Yahoo retains an army of analysts to create and maintain classifications—groupings—of subjects contained in Web sites. When a site submits its content to Yahoo!, the analysts consider the submission and reach a decision on the category into which the site best fits. Needless to say, this is a relatively labor-intensive—and expensive—method for creating and maintaining a knowledge taxonomy; however, Yahoo! has obviously been very successful in applying this method.

Maintaining such a staff of analysts, however lean and mean, may not be such an obvious choice for a more traditional business organization—one whose core competency and value proposition may not necessarily be knowledge classification. However, realizing the potential for increased information throughput to be gained from knowledge classification, some companies are indeed pursuing this route. The impact of a relatively small KM staff can also be significantly increased by the application of commercially-available automated taxonomy-building tools.

The first step in an automated taxonomy process is quite similar to that of Web index-building engines: accessing and parsing—picking apart—a set of data sources to which it is directed. Whereas in the case of Web crawlers this set is usually quite large—the entire World Wide Web—for a business application, this set of data typically begins with the data for a subset of the organization, such as a department or division. The set of data sources can include databases as well as text files from email, word processing, hypertext, or collaboration systems.

As the taxonomy builder works its way through the data sources, it applies linguistic rules for determining, for example, relevant terms, groups of terms that form phrases, and terms and phrases that are interrelated, either as synonyms or conceptually. Some taxonomy builders employ statistical clustering techniques, such as those used in data mining, to automatically determine groupings of terms that are significant.

The results of this analysis can then be used to create one or more new classification hierarchies, or they can be connected to one or more predefined classification schemes. These taxonomies can then be made available to business users through a browsing tool such as an information portal or business information directory discussed in Chapter 4. Users can then browse through a catalog or table of contents of the information assets that have been categorized, and, if configured correctly and with sufficient authorization, can click through, or hyperlink, to the data source within the classification.

Knowledge IS Power, After All

Within the realm of KM, capturing, managing, and disseminating database, desktop, and email data is just the tip of the iceberg. Knowledge that can impart or deny competitive advantage to a business remains, in large part, closely retained within employees' wetware.

Who owns the knowledge you've gained on the job—you or your company? One of the most challenging issues in KM is incentive for input. Say I am a knowledge worker whose status in my job—and probably my level of compensation—are predicated in large part on what I know. What motivation do I have to unload what I know into some medium, such as a knowledge repository of some sort—the use of which is outside of my control? If I do share my knowledge with current and future coworkers, by essentially cloning these parts of my work persona, does this not dilute the value of my knowledge?

If business organizations are to survive the accelerating rates of turnover endemic in a full-employment e-commerce marketplace, procedures must be in place through which the capture of employees' knowledge is an integral, nonintrusive, and even compensated part of doing their job. There's no doubt that companies that are able to effectively solve these challenges will become and remain more competitive.

E-Commerce Data Movement at Tiosa Group

Tiosa has decided to investigate the feasibility of developing an elongated, integrated value chain, by addressing intra- and extra-enterprise data integration

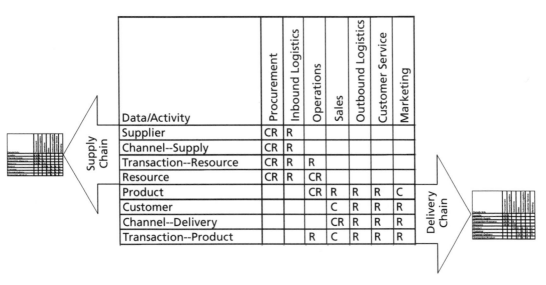

Data/Activity	Procurement	Inbound Logistics	Operations	Sales	Outbound Logistics	Customer Service	Marketing
Supplier	CR	R					
Channel--Supply	CR	R					
Transaction--Resource	CR	R	R				
Resource	CR	R	CR				
Product			CR	R	R	R	C
Customer				C	R	R	R
Channel--Delivery				CR	R	R	R
Transaction--Product			R	C	R	R	R

Figure 6–15
Dan's chart: Linkages between internal and external value chains.

concurrently, within a limited vertical scope. CIO Dan has extracted and transformed the CRUD matrix in Figure 6–15 based on the enterprise-wide matrix discussed earlier. He's presented it to the e-commerce task force as a means of focusing their efforts toward mobilizing technology—specifically data-movement and data-integration technology—to gain the most momentum and leverage for the e-commerce initiative.

Dan and Larry worked closely in developing this proposal. Here's a transcript from Dan's presentation on "Extending Our Value Chain Through Data Integration."

> On the left of the chart you can clearly see the supply chain, and on the right, the delivery chain. The data for supply-chain integration flows not only farther into our organization, but also outward to the left, into the delivery chains of our suppliers. The data for delivery-chain integration flows back into the organization, as well as forward into the supply chains of our customers.
>
> What it comes down to is providing those value chain activities that *create* the data with the capability to make that data available to the other downstream activities that need the data. Not only that, if the upstream process creating the data is outside our own firewall—within a supplier's or exchange's value chain, for example—we need access to that data too, if at all possible. And we also need to be suppliers of data to our client's value chains downstream from us.

Dan went on to emphasize that, on the one hand, Tiosa' requirements are rigorous due to its need to establish a presence in both B2B and B2C e-commerce markets. Mitigating this, however, due to the nature of its products and services, Tiosa's data movement-immediacy requirements are not as rigorous—yet—as many others in B2B or B2C.

"We need to take a hard look at each of these linkages and determine the data-immediacy requirements, now and in the future, as our first step toward deciding what type of data-movement infrastructure to establish. The infrastructure needs to be flexible in accommodating as many different scenarios as possible for getting the right data, at the right time, to the people we work with inside and outside our organization."

Dan's presentation was enthusiastically received. Afterward, the CEO confided that he thinks he finally "gets it" when it comes to Dan's budget request for data-movement infrastructure hardware and software. "Let's talk about it again in more detail as soon as you have some recommendations based on those immediacy requirements. Good job, Dan."

Chapter 7

DATA AS A PRODUCT

Get your facts first, then you can distort them as much as you please.

— Mark Twain

Data continues to be the most stable, slowly evolving resource component of an IT architecture. It is also unique to each business enterprise—a significant source of its competitive differentiation—and as such an invaluable resource. Data is accumulating at an accelerating rate, faster than software and hardware technology can address it; hence bottlenecks arise. Not only is a history of facts being accumulated with the passage of time, but more and more "counterfeit" copies of facts are being created as a result of hardware-data bottlenecks. These copies require software to create and interpret, causing the need for more software and interfaces with that software.

Much time, effort, and expense are expended in carefully managing more perceptible corporate assets such as personnel, capital, and physical plants. As is the case with these assets, prudent business practice dictates that costs associated with the data resource be minimized as much as possible and that the value of the data resource be maximized as well. As the spread of e-commerce causes more and more data to be produced and consumed, it makes sense to take a look at some of the methods, historic and current, with which the costs and value associated with the production and consumption of data can be managed.

E-Commerce and the Data Value Chain

What does it mean to consider data as a product? A product is something that is created by assembling raw materials into finished goods, which are then provided to consumers. Good product management strives to make the most cost-effective use of the raw materials in the *production* process, as well as to provide high value to consumers of the finished goods.

Up to this point, we have intentionally assumed a "data warehousing-centric" point of view on managing data resources—focusing on the three aspects of input, storage, and output. But to truly do justice to the importance of data in e-commerce, we need to take one more step back. And for total, front-to-back coverage of data as a product, there is perhaps no better tool than the value chain introduced earlier. It should be enlightening to walk through the value chain, one last time—this time in the role of an enterprise whose sole product is our data. See Figure 7–1.

From the perspective of the core activities in a data-product value chain as a whole, the input-storage-output, data warehousing viewpoint we have assumed so far concentrates almost exclusively on operations and its links to value activities on either side. Due to the considerable impact of e-commerce on the data product, we will now present some important additional operational considerations—specifically dealing with the quality of the data product and who is accountable for its quality and use. To complete the picture, we will briefly address the other value activities in the data-product value chain as well.

- *Marketing, Sales, Customer Service, and Support*
  In some industries, most notably in marketing and finance, data has been a revenue-generating product for a long time. E-commerce has greatly increased the market for these more traditional data providers. And now, because of the ubiquitous fluidity of e-commerce data delivery mechanisms, data is evolving into a product in many places where previously it has been only a byproduct. This fledgling product must be packaged, marketed, sold, and supported.

  Traditional data products that have established new, high-volume channels to retail e-commerce businesses include online Web-based credit card and sales tax data. Storage service providers (SSPs) are beginning to provide one-stop shopping for outsourced data storage infrastructures. B2B exchanges provide transaction and business-intelligence data to their participants. Basically, the future is bounded only by the imagination of the risk-takers investing in data consolidation and dissemination infrastructures—as

Figure 7-1
Generic value chain.

well as the limits of ethics and self- and government regulation, which are
daily being put to the test.

- *Outbound Logistics*
  E-commerce enables and requires that data products be output to more and
  more diverse human and computer consumers. The logistical implications
  of disseminating, presenting, and safeguarding data that traverses multiple
  firewalls is just beginning to become evident.

- *Operations*
  We've covered data operations—getting data into and out of inventory in
  the most effective manner—extensively up to this point. (Hint: This is what
  data warehousing is all about.) The majority of this chapter covers additional topics within the scope of this value chain activity to help complete
  the data operations picture.

- *Inbound Logistics*
  The flip side of the logistical coin: Just as the complexities of outbound data
  logistics relentlessly increase, so too do the logistics of data acquisition from
  an increasingly voluminous and diverse data supply chain. And, more applicable than ever, is the legendary IT concept of garbage-in, garbage-out,
  or GIGO. Will this increasing diversity serve to diminish the quality of the
  raw material, by pushing the procurement ever closer to the source (e.g.,
  customer data entry), or will quality increase as info-mediaries disappear?

Ah, things used to be much simpler.

A History of Data as a Product

In 4Q2000, the last remaining manufacturer of large IBM-compatible computers announced its intention to exit that marketplace. The mainframe market is no longer large enough to support more than one vendor of this type of
commercial computer hardware. The UNIX and Intel hardware platforms,

which were termed *alternative* platforms in some shops not too long ago, are now ubiquitous. Just about every company has numerous UNIX and Intel computers—even those companies continuing to run one or more mainframes. To get some perspective of the impact of this platform evolution on data management, please accompany me on a brief stroll down the hallowed halls of historical commercial computing.

The Data Processing Era

Through the late 1980s, the IBM MVS mainframe continued its domination of information technology—or *data processing*, as it was, ironically, then known. Regardless of the benefits and drawbacks of the mainframe as a computing platform, one fact is nearly indisputable: A centralized, monolithic, and homogeneous computing platform strongly tended to limit the challenges faced in attempting to undertake a disciplined approach to the management of data as a product. In fact, the early heyday of data administration, coincident with the apex of the mainframe's dominance, almost succeeded in getting its hands around what, even then, was a pretty hairy problem: precisely defining and quantifying the enterprise data resource in order to truly manage data as a product.

But then of course the Intel platform ingratiated itself into the corporate world, and suddenly there were two or more miniature data centers springing up on every floor of corporate headquarters, with attendant staff, budget, consultants, standalone applications, and data—an autonomous computing Nirvana for each department. Centralized data management staff wrung their hands, shook their heads, and watched as the corporate data resources—that they may have just about gotten a handle on—morphed, replicated, and proliferated.

Okay, so back to the drawing board. We no longer just had direct-access data formats such as IAM, VSAM, IMS, as well as sequential tape file layouts to try to catalog, cross-reference, and standardize; we had data in various proprietary, b-tree, X-base, and other mysterious, even less-well-documented new data formats to learn and try to make some sense of. Commercial business software packages, part and parcel with their own often labyrinthine and sparsely-documented data layouts, became much more available, affordable, and easy for the semitechnical to install and maintain. And last but not least, making friends with all the new, department-level mini-CIOs brought a new dimension of people-skills development opportunities to the erstwhile glass-housed data management staff.

Up through the late 1990s, the concurrent rise of three trends served to mitigate this potentially chaotic state of affairs:

- The proliferation of relational DBMSs.
- The expansion and relative overall success of data warehousing efforts.
- Vendor database middleware initiatives, beginning with Microsoft's ODBC (Open Database Connectivity) and IBM's DRDA (Distributed Relational Database Architecture).

These interconnecting trends began to allow some order to be made from this client-server (there, I said it) near-chaos. Some light began to appear at the end of the data-management tunnel.

Relational Databases and the Data Product

These three characteristics of the relational database model have provided the greatest value to the management of the data product:

1. Support for storing data as normalized relations.
2. Inclusion of a database catalog for storing descriptive specifications of the stored data.
3. Proliferation of a widely accepted, relatively easy-to-use language for data access and data definition. (In practice, this happens to be Structured Query Language—SQL—but in theory, other, perhaps better, languages are made possible by the relational model.)

Widespread application of relational databases has encouraged a disciplined approach to database design, specifically resulting in more normalized (in the genuine meaning of the word) data resources. Normalization is a widely abused and misused term.

I'll spare you a walkthrough of the normalization process (sighs of relief). Simply put, normalization is a (nearly) scientific technique for increasing the likelihood that data that *belongs* together *stays* together, and is inventoried in a straightforward, simple manner, as well.

Elemental, or *atomic*, data packages—*relations*—developed according to this standard approach tend to be more understandable and to also allow flexible reconfiguration into multiple combinations. Consequently, relations—implemented as database tables, for example—are likely to be highly reusable by data consumers.

Inclusion of a catalog as a part of all relational database systems assures that specifications of all data stored in the system are inventoried in the database

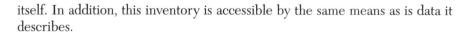

itself. In addition, this inventory is accessible by the same means as is data it describes.

Data Warehousing and the Data Product

Data warehousing has been the first large-scale packaging of data as a distinct product in and of itself. The impact of data warehousing on data product management has been somewhat of a mixed blessing—in some ways a setback, in others a vital benefactor.

The primary benefits to data product management resulting from data warehousing have been

1. The promotion of disciplined creation and distribution of—and ongoing conformance to—data specifications documentation (i.e., meta-data).
2. An increased awareness of data quality issues.
3. The potential for increase in data inventory turnover—its primary goal.

Construction of a data warehousing solution in any sort of disciplined fashion requires development of quality data specifications—including data models, entity and attribute definitions, domain definitions, and business rules. Several important benefits to the organization result from disciplined development and maintenance of these specifications: better understanding by data consumers (more *informing* happens), which in turn leads to increased reuse; and increased data quality, due to conformance of the data product to the specifications.

The existence of quality data specifications results in an increased awareness of data quality issues. Data specifications become benchmarks against which the actual data values can be measured. Data warehousing efforts invariably expose data values that deviate from the specifications—defects. A short-term resolution is to alert data warehouse consumers to the existence of specific potential defects. In an ideal situation, the flawed processes causing the defects can be corrected at the source.

It's indisputable that data warehousing has "unlocked" a great deal of previously inaccessible or nearly inaccessible data resources and put them to much wider use than ever before. The most significant challenge, albeit a justifiable one, posed to data product management by data warehousing has been the rampant proliferation of data redundancy. In an ideal technological world—with nearly infinite computing and bandwidth capacity—it would not be necessary to make copies of data as a means of increasing its accessibility. Until that day arrives, of course, "managed redundancy" will be the means justified by the ends of making data highly available.

Data inventory turnover is a prospective metric for quantifying data reuse—by comparing a given amount of data with the frequency of its use (access) over a specified time period.

$$Data\ Inventory\ Turnover = \frac{Usage\ /\ Amount}{Time}$$

A prime example of effectively managing to this metric is making a shared data source available to a greater number of users over time. The same amount of data, say 1 megabyte, could, for example, be accessed perhaps 40 times per day, as compared to 20 times per day previously. The data inventory turnover ratio has therefore increased by 100%:

Previous: 20 accesses / 1 MB / 1 day = Data Inventory Turnover Ratio of **20**

Current: 40 accesses / 1 MB / 1 day = Data Inventory Turnover Ratio of **40**

This metric is analogous to return on investment (ROI), but specifically for an organization's data resources. As a business organization strives to manage its ROI, it should strive to increase its overall data inventory turnover.

Establishment of a successful data warehouse will significantly increase the frequency of reuse of the data it contains. In a data warehousing solution, however, the potential data inventory turnover improvement resulting from increased reuse is offset significantly due to increased data redundancy.

E-Commerce Impact on Data Resources

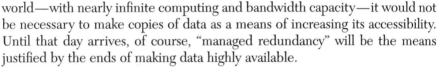

In addition to the central focus on the data resource itself, all interfaces to other IT architecture components need to be considered within each perspective and transformation.

Much of the impact of e-commerce on corporate data resources has resulted from its transformation of the interfaces of data components (see Figure 7–2) with other architectural components. The interfaces that have under-

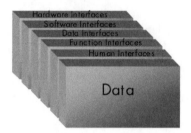

Figure 7-2
The data resource and its interfaces.

gone the greatest changes are the human-data interface and the function-data interface.

Imagine: *customers* entering massive volumes of data—about themselves and their purchases—directly into a company's computer systems. Up through the mid-1990s, such a suggestion would have been received with a high degree of skepticism. But this type of data entry is the basis of what has become today's business-to-consumer e-commerce marketplace. Data entry functions that were previously performed by internal customer support or order-entry units are now distributed outside the company into the homes of consumers.

From the standpoint of data quality, this evolution of interfaces is not at all necessarily a bad thing. Whereas internal staff may have multiple, potentially conflicting priorities regarding data acquisition and capture, it is usually clearly in the best self-interest of an external constituent—B2C customer or B2B partner—to do a quality job of data entry. Data-entry software for internal functions, including embedded validation logic, has been evolving for up to two decades or more. The newly distributed external data entry interface points, both human and machine, are having to quickly catch up to this point. The stakes are high: Suboptimal data quality translates directly to lost revenue and increased costs, and the closer to the source that problems can be identified, the less costly they are to resolve.

Data Ownership

The goal of data ownership is the assignment of authority and accountability for the state of corporate data assets. Ownership of data within companies has always been controversial, due to organizational dynamics (read *politics*) combined with the less-than-tangible nature of the data resource. The impact of

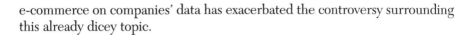

e-commerce on companies' data has exacerbated the controversy surrounding this already dicey topic.

Corporate Internal Data Ownership

Not too long ago, just about any candidate for ownership of any company data resource was likely to be an employee holding a responsible position within the company. The head of the finance department owned the chart of accounts; the human resources director owned the payroll files; the VP of customer service owned the customer accounts file. Within this context, important considerations for designating ownership of data resources internal to an organization would be

- The designee should have the organizational authority to control the content of data resources in question.
- Increasing the quality of the data resource should be within the best professional interest of the designee. Best case would be that the quality of the data resource is actually among the performance evaluation criteria of the designee.

Data Ownership in the New Economy

As if these types of considerations were not challenging enough, now e-business has once again shuffled the deck and extended the data-ownership discussion outside the ramparts of the business organization. Some of the most controversial questions arising in B2C e-commerce relate to whether the company's *customers* retain ownership of data *about* them, and if so, under what circumstances, and to what extent? This type of challenge will most certainly extend into the B2B world. In the "virtual corporation" of the near future, made possible by business models such as B2B exchanges and collaborative commerce, who will own *which* data about *what*—transactions, products, partners, prices, volumes? And at what points in extended transaction cycles will constituents assume, or relinquish, ownership?

Who *owns* the data? Which parties have what responsibility, accountability, privileges? Buying and selling of data has become a hugely controversial issue in the digital economy. Does data that has been collected by a business organization perhaps form part of its intellectual capital? Let's take a closer look at one way these issues can be addressed.

173

A Model for Data Ownership and Custodianship

While e-commerce may appear to have changed the circumstances surrounding ownership of data, parties and relationships exist that continue to endure at a fundamental level. These constant notions are

- Data as a representation of something of value in the "real world."
- The existence of two parties: the owner and the custodian.
- An agreement—implicit or explicit—between the owner and custodian, in which the owner confers rights and responsibilities to the custodian relative to the data.

In such an agreement, responsibilities conferred to the custodian typically include

- Assuring accessibility to the data by the owner, on demand.
- Assuring the accuracy of the data relative to the thing of value that the data represents.
- Assuring the protection of the data from deliberate or accidental interference with, or disclosure to, any third party.

The expansion of e-commerce has, unfortunately, precipitated the exploitation by the business community of the generally implicit nature of these agreements. These developments have, fortunately, led in turn to a more positive trend, the appearance of explicit agreements—data privacy policies—on B2C Web sites. These developments are a clear indication that the data a customer enters at a Web site are representations of "real world things of value" to which he doggedly retains property rights. These things of value include, first and foremost, his identity and his actions. They include, as well, the merchandise and financial consideration associated with the transaction between the customer and the party to which he assigns the role of data custodian.

Another sticky issue relates to rules for how a data privacy policy can be changed. Can the organization simply change the policy, post it to its Web site, and have it become effective without first informing their customers? If so, can it be retroactive? If it can't be retroactive, how can separate policies be enforced on separate sets of the same data, acquired under different privacy policies? These issues fall within the domain of business rules (discussed in the next section and also in Chapter 10). Business rules can be defined as time-specific, that is, with effective dates and expiration dates. But before busi-

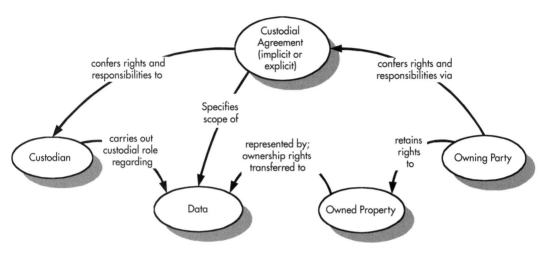

Figure 7-3
Data ownership entities and relationships.

ness rules can be implemented, they must be identified and unambiguously defined.

Figure 7–3 is a pictorial representation of these entities and relationships (warning: includes entities and relationships, but not intended strictly as an entity-relationship diagram! Professional driver...closed course.).

Examples of this model in action in various scenarios include

- Company and shareholders: A custodial role for the data describing the financial assets of the corporation is conferred by the shareholders of a public company through the board of directors and the company leadership to the management of the finance department.

- Company and customers: In a B2C e-commerce scenario, I as an online customer may choose to bestow a custodial responsibility to the company for data that represents myself, my financial condition, my buying habits, and the goods for which I have traded with the company. Buyer beware—this custodial agreement is more often implicit than not.

- Company and a B2B exchange: The data representing the exchange of goods between a company and its suppliers is highly confidential. A digital exchange acts as an intermediary, expediting the transmission of this data. In doing so, it is granted custodial responsibility for the data by its participants—including responsibility for its accessibility, accuracy, and protection.

Data Specifications and Quality Data

In Chapter 3, we discussed various *perspectives* that are part of an IT architecture, and more specifically, a data architecture. Among other benefits, the concept of perspectives is helpful in understanding and managing data quality. Within a data-architectural context, quality of the data product is important at all perspective levels and is highly dependent on *the correlation among the perspectives for any given scope of data.* As you may recall, the perspectives were defined as

- *Conceptualization:* A description of the problem. Having a clear understanding of a challenge or opportunity greatly increases the likelihood of successfully conceiving effective potential means (solutions) for addressing the challenge or opportunity.

- *Specification:* A description of a solution. Having a clear and precise understanding of one or more solutions greatly increases the likelihood of successfully implementing an effective solution.

- *Realization:* An implementation of a solution. This may sound like the end of the story; however, as anyone who has implemented a system understands, the implementation of a solution, if at all successful, leads to additional challenges and opportunities to be addressed, which leads us to the conceptualization perspective once again.

Product quality has been defined as conformance to specification. Conversely, a product defect has been defined as a *variance* from specifications. So—quality is relative. This makes sense—any measurement is done relative to some benchmark—for example, a ruler (at one time a surrogate for the king's, i.e., ruler's, foot), lines on a barometer, and so on.

If we apply this relative comparison within the data architecture domain, it follows then that the quality of data within any perspective can only be measured relative to the corresponding data within the *other* perspectives.

To bring this down to specifics, the quality of the data within the realization perspective—the "real" data values in files and databases—can really only be measured relative to the meta (literally "higher") data in the specification perspective. What, no meta-data? Then, with nothing to measure it against, realization-perspective data quality is darn difficult to quantify. Furthermore, even if quality meta-data does exist in the specification perspective, if it does not closely correlate to a quality problem description at the conceptualization level—for example, if it addresses the *wrong* problem—data quality at both "lower" levels is jeopardized.

Let's briefly discuss what constitutes quality data descriptions at the "meta" levels—the specification and conceptualization perspectives. If your interest is piqued, detailed accounts of these concepts by Larry English, Ron Ross, and Barbara von Halle are highly recommended.

There are three data specification types, often overlooked, that are fundamental to producing quality meta-data. This holds true for data in any configuration—commercial software, data warehouse, custom back-office applications, and, of course, e-business applications.

1. Precise lexical definitions of data entities and attributes

2. Business rules

3. Domains

An *entity* is a type of thing about which the business needs to record data—customer, for example. An *attribute* is a property of an entity—such as customer first name. Entities usually are "realized" (implemented) as tables or files; attributes as columns or fields. Not surprisingly, if an entity is precisely defined, its set of attributes usually winds up "naturally" being a normalized relation.

The importance of naming of data resources—entities, attributes, files, tables, columns, XML tags, databases, and so on, is often emphasized as good meta-data-management practice. This is true to a great extent, but an inherent constraint of names is that they are necessarily brief. A text definition, on the other hand, can be of indefinite length. In fact, the best practice is to develop a precise text definition for a data entity or attribute even before it is named.

To be most useful as a benchmark against which actual data may be compared, a good text definition of an entity or attribute should be complete, clear, and lexical—actually emulating an entry in a dictionary entry. Definitions should include both an "intentional" section, which states a set of criteria that a member of the entity or attribute type must exhibit, plus an "extensional" section, listing examples of members of the type. A typical example:

> Customer: a person or organization that has purchased products or services from the company. Examples include retail-store shoppers and those who place orders on our Web site.

Business rules expand on entity definitions by describing the valid "behavior" of business data entities. Business rules include descriptions of the restrictions on, and dependencies among, entities and attributes. They include instructions about events that may or must happen as a cause or effect of other events. Business rules can be enforced by program code, or in many cases, in the database itself by means of stored procedures and triggers.

One of the most common and basic examples of a business rule is the text description of a relationship in an entity-relationship (ER) model. For example: *A customer may place one or many orders.*

A more complete, restrictive, and therefore more valuable set of business rules in this instance would include, for example,

- A customer may place one or many orders.
- An order is placed by only one customer.
- A customer may place an order through either the retail store channel or the e-commerce channel.
- If a customer places an order through the e-commerce channel, and the order is his or her first order, he or she must provide a valid credit card type, credit card number, and credit card expiration date.
- After the customer's initial order, subsequent orders placed by the customer do not require resubmission of credit card data by the customer.
- A customer may cancel an order until any item in the order is shipped.
- If an order is cancelled, the count of each order item is added back to the item inventory.

Business rules can take many forms:

- Preconditions: prior events
- Postconditions: subsequent events
- Optional or mandatory conditions
- Prescriptive (should or must happen) or proscriptive (must *not* happen) constraints

Definitions and business rules provide a clear benchmark specification for data development or acquisition. Benchmarks also provide a clear target against which production data can be assessed.

The final ingredients of a quality data specification are domains. A domain is simply a set of values. Each data element has a domain from which it can take its values; if any element takes a value outside its domain, a defect results. Typical examples include the 50 values of U.S. state codes, the set of valid zip codes, or status codes for a bank account—open, closed, suspended, and so on.

Profiling of Production Data Resources

Profiling is to data as testing is to software. Data profiling measures the extent to which data conforms to the types of specifications outlined in the previous section. Best-practice data warehousing efforts include some form of data profiling to discover the true state of the data prior to beginning its consolidation into a data warehouse. Profiling of input data early in the development lifecycle can greatly decrease the risk of uncovering unexpected surprises buried in the source data when it is too late to avoid a negative impact on project implementation.

Sample profiling can also be undertaken to determine the quality of production data resources of an entire business, for a subset of the organization, or for a particular project such as migration of an application. A certain amount of profiling can be done on production data even with a limited amount of meta-data specifications against which it can be compared. If at least basic layouts, such as COBOL records or relational database catalogs, are available, the production data can be broken up—parsed—into its constituent data elements and analyzed manually, by automated tools, or both.

Manual profiling tools include SQL queries for relational database data and basic file-editing tools such as File-Aid in the IBM mainframe environment, or grep in the UNIX environment. Several commercial products are available for more sophisticated profiling using statistical and pattern-matching techniques. Regardless of the approach taken, the most important considerations are the availability of format layouts and a disciplined plan for scrutinizing the selected data characteristics.

The initial steps in data profiling are acquiring production sample data sources and matching these to their format meta-data. In complex cases such as multiple record formats within single files, extraction, normalization, and creation of separate files may also be necessary. This setup enables independent data attributes to be observed and assessed both separately and in combination.

The most important factors that can be assessed in data profiling are domains of attributes, dependencies between data elements, and redundancy.

Data element domains should be inspected to assure that

- There are no occurrences of values outside the specified domain of the element.

179

- The frequency of occurrence of values follows the expected distribution.
- There are no occurrences with missing values (unless this is valid).

Tools ranging from SQL queries to statistical software such as SAS and specialized data-audit products can be used for this type of analysis.

Identification of data element dependencies requires a somewhat more sophisticated type of analysis, such as pattern-matching techniques. Dependencies exist when data elements are related; that is, the values of one data element vary directly with the values of another. An example of this might be job grade and salary. In almost all cases these should rise or fall together; any exceptions that are identified could be candidates for further validation.

Data redundancy occurs when the same data is recorded in multiple places, with no process in place to correlate the multiple occurrences. A perennial example of this is multiple customer files—different copies for different sales channels, geographic locations, business units or customer types. In cases such as this, data on the same customer may actually occur redundantly in multiple places. Comprehensive data profiling can identify situations such as this, and a matching and reconcilement process can be put in place to synchronize the data resources going forward.

Last, but certainly not least, production data resources should of course be audited against whatever source documents are available, including application forms, data entry forms, and contracts. A company's auditing department is a valuable resource, and will be quite interested in being involved with this type of activity. Auditing and IT should therefore be engaged early on in a partnership, rather than in an adversarial affiliation.

Refinement of Production Data Resources

Figure 7–4 describes a data-quality enhancement effort in the form of a data architecture cycle. Step 1 of the cycle begins with the current production data resource, and subsequent steps proceed sequentially from there. Larry P. English describes such data-quality assessment and enhancement processes in detail in his book *Improving Data Warehouse and Business Information Quality*.

An example of data profiling and refinement common to just about any business is address validation. The first step in this process typically includes both domain and dependency profiling.

Valid address and zip code listings are available from many sources (some of which are listed in Chapter 11). The domain of zip codes is finite, and de-

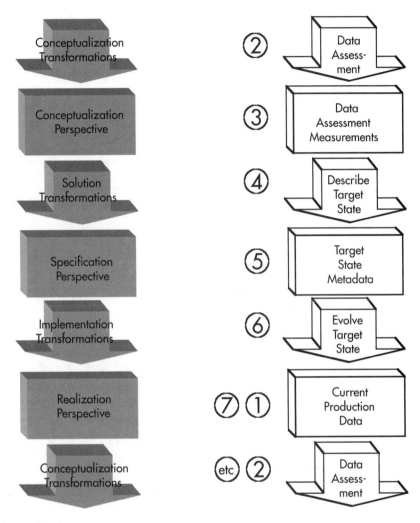

Figure 7-4
Data refinement transformations.

pendencies exist—although not completely strict, of course—between zip codes and street addresses. (For example, there either is a Michigan Ave. in the 15232 zip code, or there is not. If a customer address contains a zip code of 15232 and a street address of Michigan Ave., perhaps there is an opportunity for some data-defect elimination.) Profiling a company's production data against the specifications expressed in a vendor's address-validation files can uncover many instances of potential defects in address data.

An overview of this type of data refinement process is presented in Fig-

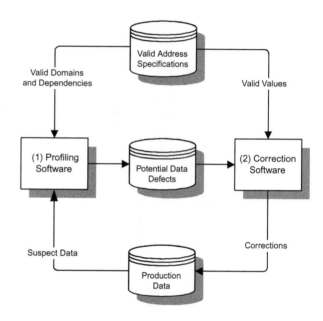

Figure 7–5
Data refinement technology.

ure 7–5. Using specialized data profiling software (1), production data is compared to a vendor's file of standardized, up-to-date geopolitical data. A file of suspected defects is produced. After the suspects are analyzed and confirmed, correction software (2) uses the standardized data to correct the defects in the production data.

At the end of this process, the production data has been "cleansed." To prevent the introduction of more defects and to maintain the quality of the production data over time, the process is repeated for newly added data either on a scheduled basis or triggered as the data is added to production.

The Data Product at Tiosa Group

A company in "acquisition mode," as is Tiosa Group, often finds itself with an embarrassment of riches in its potential for product-izing its burgeoning data resources. To see what this means at Tiosa Group, let's map out some very high-level current and hypothetical e-commerce data flows in Figure 7–6.

As the diagram shows, the Gasomatic subsidiary sells directly to consumers as well as to distributors of natural gas-related parts and appliances, such as hardware stores and retail appliance stores (1). The Tiosa Financial subsidiary sells its corporate financing products to gas and electric utility companies such

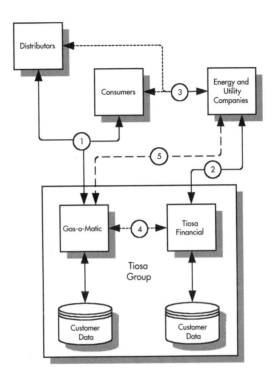

Figure 7-6
Customers and customer data at Tiosa Group.

as local distributions companies, transmission companies, and exploration and production (E&P) companies (2). Sales of energy-related products and services taking place between utility/energy companies, consumers, and distributors (3) are not currently visible to Tiosa Group. Both Tiosa Corp. and Gasomatic retain a significant amount of data on their current customers and on the transactions and lending agreements made with those customers. Currently, there has been no requirement to share this type of data between the two subsidiaries in any way (4).

Before the merger of the two businesses, the customer base (and customer data) of each was essentially dissimilar and not overlapping. But since the merger and the initiation of the e-business enablement strategy, Tiosa Group management is beginning to assess its future combined customer base, and how to best manage and leverage the potential interrelationships among their constituent markets and channels.

You may remember from Chapter 4 this overview (Table 7.1) of the implementation plan for Tiosa Group e-commerce enablement.

We can imagine a group of Tiosa Group's upper management gathered in a conference room, gazing at a chart somewhat like this. We can also imagine

Table 7.1 Tiosa Group's E-Business Implementation Plan

Phase	E-Commerce Capability	Former Company	Target Date
1	Online Catalog—Consumer Products and Services	Gasomatic	Current (Year0)
2	Online Catalog—Corporate Services	Tiosa Financial	Y1Q1
3	Online Transactions—Consumer Products	Gasomatic	Y1Q3
4	Online Transactions—Consumer Services	Gasomatic	Y2Q1
5	Online Transactions—Corporate Services	Tiosa Financial	Y2Q3

our CIO Dan—who, with his staff, is responsible for developing the diagram —is part of the group in the conference room.

Not too many years ago, the likelihood would have been very small that a session such as this would have taken place within such an organization. But these days, this is not at all unusual—such is the impact of e-commerce on the corporate data products.

Discussion points on the agenda for this session include

1. How can we most effectively manage the evolution of our combined data resource going forward, given the merger and the e-commerce enablement strategy?

2. What current and future opportunities may be available to leverage the data available at any given point in time to generate additional revenue for the company? If such revenue-generating opportunities will be available, what are the associated risks and rewards?

3. Gasomatic will begin to offer financing in conjunction with its product sales, both in stores and on its Web site, in Y2Q1. Tiosa Financial will provide servicing and support for these loans (4). At this point—when these customers become customers of both Gasomatic and Tiosa Financial—where should data on these customers be kept, and which organization will be responsible for this data?

4. Tiosa Group management is considering the feasibility of offering to private-label its product sales and services to its corporate energy and utility customers. This would allow these companies to sell, under their own brand names (5), Gasomatic-supplied products and Tiosa financial services to their customers. At this point, these companies' *customers* will become indirect customers of Gasomatic.

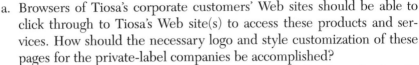

a. Browsers of Tiosa's corporate customers' Web sites should be able to click through to Tiosa's Web site(s) to access these products and services. How should the necessary logo and style customization of these pages for the private-label companies be accomplished?

b. Scalability, capacity, and throughput must be carefully planned to handle the increased data volume and network traffic resulting from these services.

c. Can Tiosa Group leverage the resulting cross-company consumer and sales data in its custody to provide value-added services, such as data mining, customer profiling, and e-marketing campaign management, to its corporate customers?

5. What potential antitrust, regulatory, data privacy, data quality liability, and other legal implications might need to be considered in conjunction with these strategies?

All items are presented and, given the limited time available for the session, briefly discussed by the participants. Three action items result from the session:

1. Comprehensively working out these and other related opportunities and issues will require an extended period of discussion. Agreement is reached that a 1- to 2-day offsite meeting will be scheduled to do this within the next two months, and Dan is asked to coordinate this conference.

2. The advisability of retaining outside consulting assistance will be discussed at the offsite.

3. Tiosa Group's legal department needs to be represented at the offsite to address legal and regulatory issues.

Chapter 8

MANAGING THE DATA SIDE OF E-COMMERCE PROJECTS

Man is still the most extraordinary computer of all.
— President John F. Kennedy

When establishing or maintaining a presence in the e-commerce marketplace, a company can achieve time-to market expediencies by using commercial, off-the-shelf (COTS) software and hardware. A limited amount of commodity data, such as demographics, taxes, and creditworthiness, may also be part of a solution. But in contrast to these types of commodities, an enterprise can achieve significant differentiating benefit by leveraging its unique data product as the central component in any e-business initiative.

Within an e-commerce initiative, a great deal of concentrated effort is typically expended on a specific subset of IT architecture components and interfaces—most notably, the human-software interface, as well as Web and application server software and hardware. Focus on textual and graphical content is also justifiably found. In many cases, structured data is pretty much regarded as a necessary evil or an afterthought.

Data integration is the fundamental differentiator, and data is a fundamental integrating component in an e-commerce effort. Effective, dedicated management of the scoping, analysis, design, and deployment of e-business data resources is essential to assure this differentiation is attained.

Project Management, in General—And Briefly

Project management is not just about managing projects; it's about predicting the future and minimizing risk. The risk of course is that the future may differ from the prediction—the future may turn out to be more expensive, farther away, or may appear significantly different from the prediction.

Project risks are minimized through minimizing the number and range of project variables. Scope management and standard, proven-repeatable project plan tasks, deliverables, roles, and skills tend to reduce the number and range of variables, and thus reduce risk. In this chapter, we'll cover these project components specifically within the scope of the data side of e-commerce projects.

In the project-management equation, if the input variables of tasks, deliverables, roles, and skills are "solved"—by assigning standard values—the output-dependent variables of time, effort, and cost can be better predicted.

Project management is concerned with planning for—and following through on—*what* gets done, *who* does it, and *when* it gets done. Effective management of the data side of an e-commerce project ensures the establishment and delivery of appropriate data resources and interfaces—contributing to the decreased risk and enhanced success of the entire effort.

Tasks and Deliverables in an E-Commerce Project

Figure 8–1 maps the data architecture perspectives and transformations onto an IT project phase structure.

The lifecycle of an e-commerce project is, after all, much like that of any other technology deployment. In a scoping and analysis phase, the realization perspective (the current or as-is state) is assessed and cataloged. In the conceptualization transformation, the *concept* of a future (to-be) state is defined and superimposed on the realization perspective. The results of the transformation are cataloged as requirements, creating the conceptualization perspective.

A design phase begins with the conceptualization perspective; designers then superimpose one or more solution sets onto it. The results of this transformation are cataloged as the specification perspective.

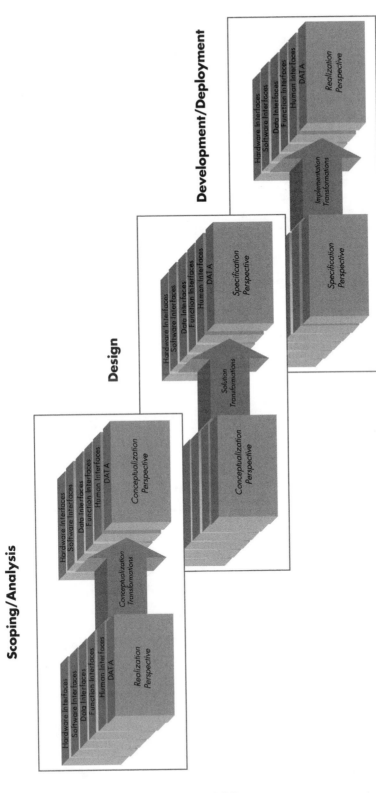

Figure 8-1
Project phases and data architecture.

189

In a development phase, the specifications are transformed by developers into a new realization perspective; the solution is implemented.

This progression is of course applicable across all components of the IT architecture; but we will be concentrating on the data component and its interfaces. When should data specialists be involved? From the beginning to the end of the project. At minimum, a data architect should be involved in e-commerce projects, full-time, from the very beginning of scoping and analysis. The data architect and his or her team can compile, design, and administer the data inventory and its interfaces, as well as position it as the common denominator for integrating the other components.

Data Resource Tasks and Deliverables

The trajectory of the data resource through the e-commerce project can be tracked by the progression of the following deliverables: data inventory, logical data model, physical data model, and implemented data storage.

The company can make use of the data resources they have only if they know

1. That the resources exist.
2. What those resources are.
3. Where the resources are located.

The data analyst assembles the current data inventory, concurrent with the development of the logical data model by the data modeler. The logical data model represents the sum total of data requirements for the effort, regardless of their format or location.

Together, the data analyst and the data modeler perform a gap analysis to determine the difference between the data inventory and the logical data model. The result comprises the new and enhanced data required for the effort.

If off-the-shelf e-commerce server software packages are under evaluation, the data analyst and data modeler, in partnership with the business function analysis team, determine and document the gaps between overall data requirements and the databases that underlie the e-commerce server products.

The data modeler and database architect work together to transform the logical data model into one or more physical data models, as appropriate. The data administrator has acquired data-usage patterns and performance requirements from the business function analysts, and provides this input to the database architect for consideration in the design for physical data storage. If one or more physical database structures are acquired as part of off-the-shelf e-commerce software, these same team members determine and design the necessary extensions to the database layout of the base product.

As deployment nears, plans and procedures are developed for data acquisition, conversion, loading, and testing. After these steps are completed, the implemented and/or enhanced database(s) are put into production.

Data-Human Interface Tasks and Deliverables

The data-human interface is critically important in e-commerce applications. In hypercompetitive digital markets, the loyalty of a company's constituencies is tenuous. In many cases, if they cannot convert displayed data into information quickly, customers, partners, and even employees will click over to a competitor's site and try again there.

Should the data be presented in a chart, a graph, or both? If a chart, should it be scrollable, hyperlinked to underlying details, both, or neither? Assuring that an interactive (directed at humans) e-commerce site allows the maximum amount of information to take place requires skills and experience in organizing data for presentation and interaction. The role filled by the data team member with these skills is often designated as information architect.

The information architect begins with current data presentation norms and standards, and designs new and enhanced data presentations that are required. These data-presentation specifications are integrated into the overall style guide. The information architect then works with the software developers to assure that the presentation objects—HTML, Java, and/or ASP (Active Server Pages) screens—are developed consistently with the specifications.

Data-Function Interface Tasks and Deliverables

The high-level functionality of an e-commerce channel often includes the following:

- Storefront: product presentation
- Catalog and content management
- Sales transaction lifecycle management
- Interfaces to back-office functions such as procurement and fulfillment
- Contact center: customer assistance, typically through multiple channels

All of these functions, of course, consume and create data. During the scoping and analysis phase, the data administrator will be joined at the hip with the functional analysts to assure that all data requirements, by function, are identified, documented, and communicated to all other members of the data team.

The data administrator evaluates current data usage by function and determines data usage requirements for the new and enhanced functions as they are identified. As design of the new functions progress, the data administrator develops and maintains a comprehensive, high-level data-function usage matrix, sometimes referred to as a CRUD (Create, Retrieve, Update, Delete) matrix.

As the structure of the application's human interaction takes shape in the design phase, the data administrator and data access designer develop the data/page cross-reference dictionary. This deliverable is expanded into data access pseudocode for each page, from which the data access developer creates executable data access scripts in embedded SQL or stored procedures. In conjunction with the data conversion/quality specialist, the data access developer tests the completed scripts for accuracy and performance, first as individual units, then within the context of the entire e-commerce application. Any required tuning adjustments are made, and the data accesses are implemented as part of the overall deployment.

Data-Data Interface Tasks and Deliverables

E-commerce is commerce, of course, and commerce is transactions; so everything in an e-commerce database relates directly or indirectly to transactions. But in almost all cases the e-commerce functions interface with multiple other functions. In other words, much of the data used in an e-commerce site comes from, or goes to, somewhere else.

The person filling the role of data transformation specialist identifies and works closely with technical and business staff knowledgeable in the applications and data—often legacy applications and data—with which the e-commerce functions must interface. She or he should be the e-commerce team member most familiar with data outside the scope of the e-commerce application proper.

The transformation specialist identifies and assesses current data interfaces, triggers, and transformations to identify opportunities to reuse existing mappings and transformations. In conjunction with the software design team, she or he identifies requirements for new and enhanced interfaces, triggers, transformations, and data replication, and captures these in a high-level interface model.

During the design phase, the transformation specialist creates layouts, or schemas, for messages—data in motion—between the e-commerce application and other applications, both internal to the organization, and external, to partner organizations. The design specifications developed by the data interface specialist also include

- Data mappings, describing which data source elements correspond to which target elements.
- Procedures and rules for *how* data is to be changed from source to target.
- Triggers specifying when, and under what conditions, data is to be sent from source to target.

Executables are created from detailed specifications for mappings, transformations, and triggers during the development phase, using software frameworks and tools selected as part of establishing the data-software interface. These tools and frameworks can include extract-transform-load (ETL) tools, enterprise application integration (EAI) and middleware products, messaging software, and/or custom-developed components.

Data-Software Interface Tasks and Deliverables

The data-software interface encompasses the software tools and frameworks supporting the data resource in both development and operational environments. Early in project inception, the current data-management software support—including current database management systems and data access middleware—is inventoried and assessed. A gap analysis is performed to determine what new and enhanced data management software may be required.

If additional capabilities are identified as being required, based on the gap analysis, a list is developed of requirements for data management software. Vendor RFPs may be extracted from this list and forwarded to candidate product vendors. The appropriate data-management software products are selected, installed, configured, and tested.

The data-software interface tasks and deliverables are primarily the responsibility of the database architect and the data middleware specialist.

Data-Hardware Interface Tasks and Deliverables

The data-hardware interface includes the storage, cache, and connection hardware supporting the data resource in both development and operational environments. Because they both deal with more or less commodity, off-the-shelf components, the tasks and deliverables associated with this interface resemble, at a high level, those for the data-software interface.

Early in project inception, the organization's current data hardware capacity, throughput, and growth rates are inventoried and assessed. A gap analysis is performed to determine whatever new and enhanced data-specific hardware may be required.

If additional capabilities are identified as being required, based on the gap analysis, a list is developed of requirements for data storage, cache, and connection hardware. Vendor RFPs may be extracted from this list and forwarded to candidate product vendors. The appropriate data-specific hardware products are selected, installed, configured, and tested.

The data-hardware interface tasks and deliverables are the responsibility of a team consisting of the database architect, the data middleware specialist, and the data storage specialist.

Table 8.1 describes the data-related deliverables across all phases of an e-commerce initiative.

Skills and Staffing: The E-Commerce Data Dream Team

The establishment and delivery of appropriate data resources and interfaces can best be accomplished with a sub-team of skilled and experienced data specialists who form an integral part of the overall project team. The cumulative skill sets of this team clearly overlaps with that of a data warehousing team: data modeling, database administration, data transformation, middleware, and data presentation skills and experience are essential for both types of projects.

The allocation of skilled individuals to roles is, as always, dependent on the size of the project effort and the available staffing budget. On a large project, one or more individuals may be designated for each role. On a smaller project, single individuals may perform multiple roles. The important point is that these or similar roles are clearly defined, the listed deliverables are clearly assigned to the roles, and individuals are clearly slotted to fill the roles.

Data skills and aptitudes are somewhat tangential to those required for function analysis or software development. Data skills and software skills are conflicting yet complimentary. Data specialists tend to consider process as something that happens to data; function analysts and software developers

Table 8.1 Data-Related Deliverables Throughout Project Phases

	Scoping/Analysis		Design			Development/Deployment	
	Realization Perspective "As-is" Deliverables	Conceptualization Transformation Tasks	Conceptualization Perspective Deliverables	Solution Transformation Tasks	Specification Perspective Deliverables	Implementation Transformation Tasks	Realization Perspective "To-be" Deliverables
Data	Current data inventory.	Perform gap analysis and determine new and enhanced data required.	Complete scope of required data: logical data model.	Determine gaps between data requirements and package database(s). Transform into appropriate physical data model(s).	New and/or enhanced physical data model(s).	Develop and execute data acquisition, conversion, population, and testing plans and procedures.	Implemented and populated new and/or enhanced database(s).
Data-Human	Current data presentation norms and standards.	Determine required new/enhanced data presentations.	Consolidated current/required data presentations.	Design appropriate data-presentation formats.	Data-presentation format specifications integrated with style guide.	Generate presentation objects—HTML pages, screens, etc.	Implemented presentation objects.
Data-Function	Current data usage by function.	Data usage by new/enhanced functions.	Comprehensive, high-level CRUD matrix.	Design data-function usage.	Data/page cross-reference dictionary, data access pseudocode.	Develop executable data access scripts, e.g. SQL, integrated with functionality.	Implemented data accesses

(continued)

Table 8.1 Data-Related Deliverables Throughout Project Phases   (continued)

	Scoping/Analysis		Design			Development/Deployment	
	Realization Perspective "As-is" Deliverables	Conceptualization Transformation Tasks	Conceptualization Perspective Deliverables	Solution Transformation Tasks	Specification Perspective Deliverables	Implementation Transformation Tasks	Realization Perspective "To-be" Deliverables
Data-Data	Current data interfaces, triggers, and transformations.	Determine new and enhanced interfaces, triggers, transformations, and replications required.	High-level model of data source-target mappings and triggers.	Create detailed design for data interfaces, triggers, transformations, transaction, and messages schemas.	Detailed design for data interfaces, triggers, transformations, transactions and messages schemas.	Create executable data interfaces, triggers, transformations, transactions, and messages schemas.	Implemented data interfaces, triggers, transformations, transactions, and messages.
Data-Software	Current DBMS, data access, and application software inventory within scope.	Perform gap analysis and determine new and enhanced data management software required.	High-level model of data-management software requirements.	Select appropriate data-management software products integrated with application software.	Selected/confirmed data-management software products, data usage by application software.	Install and configure data-management software.	Operational new and/or enhanced data-management software.
Data-Hardware	Current data hardware capacity, throughput, growth rates.	Perform gap analysis and determine new and enhanced data-specific hardware required.	High-level data storage and connectivity hardware model.	Determine and select data storage, cache, and connection hardware.	Detailed order listing of data storage, cache and connection hardware.	Install and configure data storage, cache, and connection hardware.	Installed and configured data storage and connection hardware.

tend to look at data as a byproduct of processes or programs. If both "camps" are strongly represented on an e-commerce project, the resulting deployment is likely to be well-balanced and robust in construction.

As is the case with staffing for specialized skills and peaks in development effort, contracted staff, ranging from minimal staff supplementation to all or nearly all of an entire team, should be considered as an option. Because of the similarity of much of the data-related work on e-commerce projects to that of data warehousing, many of the necessary skills required can be found in staff with data warehousing experience.

A graphical depiction of this staff and their relationships is shown in Figure 8-2.

Figure 8-2
The "big" e-commerce data team and communication interface.

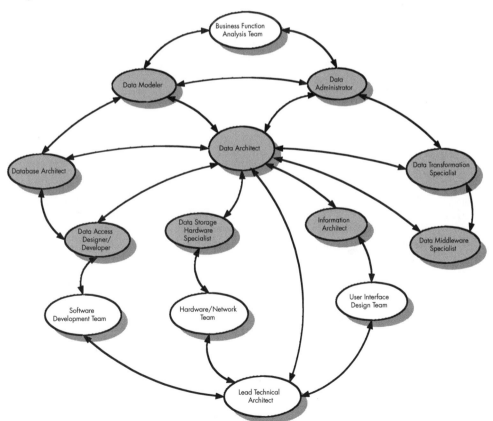

Data Architect

The most visible generalist role throughout all phases of an e-commerce project is that of lead technical architect. Not to be overly stereotypical, but . . . technical architects (designers) are, by and large, more skilled, experienced and acclimated to working in detail with software and hardware—rather than with data in and of itself. For e-commerce projects, establishment of a complementary role of data architect is strongly advisable

- because of the importance of the data components and interfaces throughout the project lifecycle, and
- as a means to assure that the ubiquitous and proprietary nature of the organization's data assets are leveraged as the fundamental integrating component of the effort and the result.

Most of the staff of an e-commerce project will, of necessity, be specialists in either a business area or a technical area. In contrast, one of the major requirements of the data architect is the ability to span both domains. Like the lead technical architect, the lead data architect is staffed full-time on the project throughout the lifecycle, from initiation through implementation—and beyond. Doing so provides critical continuity across the phases.

Data Modeler

The framework for the entire data team (and, dare we say, for the entire project) is developed and maintained by the data modeler. New technologies, languages, architectures, development techniques, and business channels have not eliminated the need for fundamentally sound database design practice.

Data modeling tasks include the analysis and design of extensions to e-commerce package database designs.

Data Administrator

While the data modeler provides the framework for the data team, the data administrator fills in all the details. The data administrator should have a background in meta-data repository or data dictionary development and administration, as well as data usage and lineage identification and tracking.

The data administrator oversees all data components within the project, as well as all interrelationships among data components and between data and

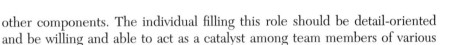
other components. The individual filling this role should be detail-oriented and be willing and able to act as a catalyst among team members of various roles.

Information Architect

The information architect functions as a link between the creative-and-cognitive front-end designers and the data team. She or he must understand the full set of data available and required for the site, and how to best present this data in a manner integrated well into the overall interactive design. An ideal candidate for this role would combine a graphics background with experience in the design of decision-support output, such as report screens and multidimensional displays.

The information architect has primary responsibility for the presentation of content to the consumer, including conventional data (text and numbers) as well as media-type data. A person filling this role designs information classification schemes—taxonomies—with the goal of presenting them as information directories or navigation paths. Information architects attempt to anticipate the labels, groupings and routes that are likely to be most intuitive to the greatest number of information consumers.

The folks who design and maintain the Yahoo! Classifications discussed earlier can definitely be, well, classified, as information architects.

Database Architect

The role of database architect is likely to be filled by a seasoned DBA (database administrator)—a practitioner who knows one or more database management system products inside and out. This individual has been through all the hard knocks of installing, configuring, performance tuning, and debugging high-volume, high-performance, and high-availability databases.

If a decision has been reached that the deployment will utilize a packaged e-commerce application product, it will also be beneficial if the database architect has experience in the pros and cons and idiosyncrasies of deploying this specific solution.

The first assignment of the database architect, in the design phase, is to work closely with the data modeler and data administrator to transform the data requirements of the project—captured in the logical data model—into a physical data model. The physical data model will in turn be used to create or enhance the production database or databases for the e-commerce site.

During the development phase, the database architect supports the software development team by creating and maintaining one or more test versions of the physical database. The database architect also works closely with the data conversion specialist and the data access developer to assure that the test database is populated with data necessary for executing test cases for

- data integrity
- processing accuracy
- "stress testing" for peak concurrent accesses
- satisfactory response to accesses

The database architect is indispensable in the early deployment period. Regardless of the detail and extent of testing scenarios developed and executed before going live, and the robustness of automated database error-handling and failover mechanisms, in early production there will be stress and exception situations encountered that are impossible to foresee. The database architect will need to be on call to monitor, respond to, and correct these types of situations as they arise.

Data Access Designer/Developer

This team member is a software development specialist—a programmer— who knows all the ins and outs of data access development; and in today's technical environment, this undoubtedly means SQL and all of its acronymic flavors, including:

- ODBC (Open Database Connectivity)
- OLE DB (Object Linking and Embedding Database)
- JDBC (Java DataBase Connectivity)
- SQLJ (SQL for Java)

There may be several different ways of accomplishing any given database access requirement. In order to choose the most appropriate alternative, the data access designer/developer needs to be intimately familiar with

- The physical data model for the project.
- The performance requirements of the application.
- The characteristics and configuration of the connectivity technologies with which the data access requests and responses will be communicated between the application and the DBMS.

- The DBMS in which the data will be stored—especially how the DBMS internally interprets and executes data access requests.

Data Transformation Specialist

Because an e-commerce application is typically assembled from multiple large component parts, the role of the data transformation specialist is critically important. The person filling this role requires experience both with commercial ETL tools and in designing and developing custom software to provide these capabilities. The data transformation specialist works closely with the data conversion/quality specialist to take advantage of opportunities to codevelop and reuse similar capabilities for data conversion and transformation. The skill sets for these roles are similar, so in many cases they may be combined in a single person.

The team is likely to look to the data transformation specialist for skills and experience in messaging-type data formats and standards, most universal of which are likely to include XML and related technologies, such as

- XML meta-data formats: XML schemas and DTDs
- XSLT—eXtensible Stylesheet Language Transformations
- SOAP—Simple Object Access Protocol
- SAX—Simplified API for XML
- DOM—Document Object Model

Data Middleware Specialist

Just as the database architect is the more technical alter ego to the data modeler, the data middleware specialist is the technical counterpart to the data transformation specialist. This role specializes in designing and implementing high-performance physical transport systems that put data in motion between software and data storage components of the e-commerce application. The individual in this role is experienced in the connectivity options of several database management systems and middleware solutions, such as EAI frameworks and message brokers.

Data Storage Hardware Specialist

This role is the hardware expert on the data team. The person filling this role has knowledge and experience in high-performance, high-volume data storage

Table 8.2 The Data Team Throughout Project Phases

Category	Scoping/Analysis	Design	Development/Deployment
Data	Data Modeler		
Data-Function	Data Administrator	Data Access Designer/Developer	
Data-Human		Information Architect	
Data-Data		Data Transformation-Mapping Specialist	Data Conversion/Quality Specialist
Data-Software		Database Architect / Database Middleware Specialist	
Data-Hardware		Data Storage Specialist	
Leadership/Communication/Coordination	Lead Data Architect		

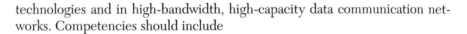
technologies and in high-bandwidth, high-capacity data communication networks. Competencies should include

- SANs (Storage Area Networks)
- RAID (Redundant Arrays of Independent Disks)
- "Hot-swappable" storage devices and arrays
- Offline and "near-line" storage
- Backup media

Data Conversion/Quality Specialist

An e-commerce application is never deployed with an empty database. The initial data needs to come from somewhere, and the starting places are existing databases and files, both internal and external. It's absolutely essential that the site starts with a quality set of data. The data conversion/quality specialist brings skills and experience in developing quality-measurement metrics, data profiling (such as described in Chapter 7), testing plans, and initial load/unload/reload procedures.

In summary, Table 8.2 illustrates the roles within the data team, and when they are typically required across the various phases of an e-commerce effort.

Figure 8–2 describes these roles as they relate to each other within a framework of communication and accountability. All relationship lines indicate necessary flows of communication. Personnel who fill (shaded) data team roles are, in addition, directly accountable to the data architect. The data architect reciprocates by assuming responsibility for the appropriate and effective correlation of tasks and deliverables with skilled resources—with the end goal of career-enhancing success for all involved.

Planning and Scheduling

If there is one common denominator across all e-commerce projects, it is that their schedules are driven by *time-to-market*. In many ways, there is indeed less time to "do it right" than there is to do it over after it's done the first time. Quality is likely to be sacrificed for the sake of time-to-market. Under the "land-grab" circumstances of today's e-business, it is futile to condemn these conditions.

On the other hand, it is reasonable to utilize the best methods available to combine speed and quality—to have it both ways. The keys to this are specialization, coordination, cooperation, and communication. A relatively large team, such as that described here, can allow for intense concurrent effort, culminating in shorter delivery times . . . but only if

- roles
- responsibilities
- tasks
- deliverables
- lines of communication

are very specifically and clearly planned for and defined up front, *and* all team members clearly comprehend and concur on the roles they will fill.

The "Next" Project: E-Business Intelligence

E-business intelligence (e-BI) functions—such as Web log analysis, warehousing of e-commerce transactions, and integration of these with other transactional activity—are typically left for subsequent follow-on projects after the initial e-commerce functionality is up and running for a significant period of time. While this does make sense from an implementation-phasing standpoint (one cannot analyze data that one has not accumulated, after all), planning for the analysis of e-commerce activity should begin at the same time data requirements analysis begins. If this is done, the subsequent implementation of business intelligence functionality is much more likely to proceed in a smooth and expedient manner.

What also may make sense is to transition available members of the e-commerce data team into subsequent e-BI efforts. Having been through the initial implementation, these folks have built up a significant store of knowledge of the data and interfaces within the scope of the completed e-commerce project (although the majority of this knowledge should have been captured in deliverables created along the way!).

Representative BI-related functions that should definitely be considered for follow-up projects after an initial e-commerce effort might include the following. Those functions that require a significant volume of data as input will need to be postponed until this data has been accumulated. Examples of relatively early possible functionality include

- Ad hoc query and reporting
- Product profitability
- Customer profitability
- Channel profitability

  Later possibilities, requiring a larger volume of data, may include

- Customer profiling
- Customer lifetime value (LTV)
- Customer segmentation
- Campaign effectiveness
- Cross-sell and up-sell opportunities
- Next likely purchase
- Ad hoc data mining

Tiosa and the E-Commerce Data Dream Team

"You're kidding! *Ten people* just for the *data* side of the project?" CIO Dan was incredulous.

"Not ten people, Dan, ten *roles*," explained Larry, the director of data architecture. "We might need ten *people*—one per role—if we were to do everything at one time. But remember, our plan is to achieve full e-commerce enablement through a series of steps over the next several years.

"I've been giving this some serious thought and have some recommendations for the e-commerce data team I'm proposing. What we should do in the first phase is utilize both our in-house staff—ah, we may need a couple new hires down the road, I'll get to that—and some outside, experienced consulting talent.

"For the initial phase, we should retain a consultant full time as the lead data architect, and additional consultants, part-time, in the areas we're light on right now. The rest of the data team should come from our own staff. We have some good people who have accumulated a lot of data-integration skills and experience working on the data warehousing projects that are beginning to wind down somewhat.

"The internal people will get hands-on experience during the earlier phases, and as they accumulate and broaden their skills, we can move then

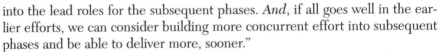

into the lead roles for the subsequent phases. *And*, if all goes well in the earlier efforts, we can consider building more concurrent effort into subsequent phases and be able to deliver more, sooner."

Dan raised his eyebrows. "Okay, you're beginning to almost make sense. But humor me . . . for the initial phase, *how many* people map to *how many* roles?"

"Well, let's see. There's the full-time consultant data architect, of course. We can slot two full-time in-house folks from data warehousing. One can perform both data modeler and data administrator roles, and the other can cover the interfaces and middleware. That's three full time.

"The rest of the staff can probably come and go part-time on the project, both outside help and inside staff. One of the DBAs—who probably won't mind learning what's going on with JDBC—and storage/network guys can work this into their multi-project loads. And we'd better get some outside help on data presentation—that can be part-time too. How's that sound: three full-time, three half-time—four and a half FTEs. Better?"

"Okay, now you're talking. Now get out of my office and find one of those experienced e-commerce data architects. And by the way, find out how much somebody like that is going to cost us."

Chapter 9

CASE STUDIES: E-BUSINESS DATA MANAGEMENT AND DATA WAREHOUSING

> Reality leaves a lot to the imagination.
>
> — John Lennon

The concepts of data warehousing in the world of e-commerce presented up to this point are not just concepts—they are being successfully put to use on a daily basis to accelerate the establishment and operation of the e-commerce presence of myriad companies worldwide.

This chapter presents several real examples of companies in a range of industries—financial, retail, manufacturing, and services—that have applied data warehousing techniques and technologies in support of their unique e-commerce business models.

The examples include

- A bank subsidiary that uses "traditional" data warehousing to provide consolidated, comparative reporting data to its customers across multiple delivery channels.

- An online retailer using data-integration technologies to join together a number of diverse functional components into a comprehensive solution for business-to-consumer e-commerce.

- A consumer financial institution whose data warehouse has evolved into an integral data source for its Web presence.

- A large corporate bank utilizing a transaction database hub to consolidate and distribute data electronically among thousands of customers and partners.

- A manufacturing company optimizing the effectiveness of its sales force with data-replication and information-distribution technologies.
- A Web site outsourcer whose business intelligence service forms a cornerstone of its value to clients.

These are actual companies; the solutions at this writing are at various stages from detailed design through operational stability. Their names (as the reader might guess) have been changed, along with other details at various points, in order to protect sensitive, proprietary, and competitive information.

Electronic Banking: EbizPioneer

Amidst the current Sturm und Drang surrounding the World Wide Web and the Internet, historical perspective on e-business can often be overlooked. Electronic commerce existed for many years prior to the explosion of the Web. The prime example of pre-Web e-commerce is of course electronic data interchange (EDI), which has been a ubiquitous electronic business channel between larger enterprises for many years.

In addition to business-to-business channels such as EDI, throughout the 1980s and 1990s financial institutions such as banks were also pioneers in electronic business-to-consumer channels, most notably through telephone banking and automated teller machines (ATMs). In what was a foreshadowing of more ubiquitous B2C e-commerce, Intuit's Quicken enabled online access to consumers' bank accounts, well in advance of the advent of the Web. And, as its technologies and practices matured in the early to mid-1990s, data warehousing contributed significantly to the marshalling of transaction activity derived from these earlier e-commerce initiatives into valuable decision-making information.

A large, diversified banking institution, EbizPioneer by the late 1990s had established an impressive presence in many market areas of North America. Part of its success had been a result of its Electronic Bank, into which it had consolidated its ATM, bank-by-phone, and call center businesses. The management of the Electronic Bank was interested in monitoring the effectiveness, and eventually the profitability, of the three consumer channels within its business.

To assist with this effort, Electronic Bank management established a partnership with a software vendor that not only specialized in financial services, but offered an off-the-shelf data warehouse product for banks as well. This vendor had not yet extended its data warehousing product into the e-business realm, but was keenly interested in doing so. The opportunity for a successful partnership was realized through the extension of the product to support the three electronic channels of EbizPioneer.

The first area to be addressed was telephone banking. The bank's telephone customers transacted their business with the bank through specialized computer-telephony integration (CTI) hardware and software. As a customer progressed through a "session," checking balances, paying bills, or transferring funds between accounts, for example, the CTI software logged each and every key stroke the customer entered on his telephone. (The similarities between this scenario and customer Web site sessions—and log files—should be apparent.)

Management needed to know how effectively the bank-by-phone channel was serving their customers. Self-service channels such as ATMs and telephone banking are much cheaper to offer than face-to-face, bricks-and-mortar interactions, and of course when costs drop, profits rise. The Electronic Bank at EbizPioneer was anxious to retain those customers who chose to interact through bank-by-phone, and they knew that enhancing a customer's experience would increase the likelihood of his or her picking up the phone again. Management felt that if they gained an understanding of customer keystroke patterns leading up to both successful and unsuccessful interactions, they could perhaps change menus, menu choices, and navigation paths to increase the intuitiveness of the human interface. To be avoided as much as possible was the customer's being led to "zero out" to a call center representative. When this happened, the cost of the interaction to the bank would spike significantly.

The software vendor's staff began by analyzing the data stored in the CTI logs. The available data on customer keystrokes within sessions was reverse-engineered into a logical model that was then used to extend the standard data warehouse database design. Processes were designed and developed to extract the log data, transform it into a normalized format, and load it into the enhanced data warehouse. Queries and reports were then developed to provide detailed and summary analysis of the customer session data to guide informed decision-making by the management of the Electronic Bank.

At this point, EbizPioneer's data warehouse also provided more than just an analyzable source for telephone-banking customer-behavior data. It also made available a comprehensive picture of the customer's entire relationship with the bank—demographics as well as accounts and transaction history. Not only could the bank now understand the usage patterns of the telephone bank by customers, but it could also begin to develop profiles of the banking relationships of typical telephone banking customers. This would help target future marketing campaigns to similar customers who were likely to expand the customer base of the Electronic Bank.

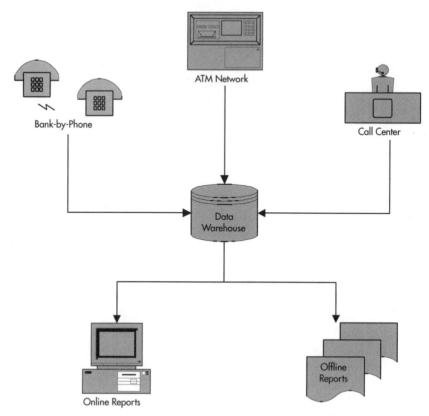

Figure 9–1
EbizPioneer Electronic Bank's data warehouse.

The next channel to be addressed by the Electronic Bank was its ATM network. An initiative was begun to better understand activity volumes and patterns at ATMs in various types of geographic locales, as well as in diverse venues such as bank offices, free-standing kiosks, and various types of retail outlets. Management wished to better understand and compare the cost and revenue trends at ATMs in location and venue types. With such information, informed decisions could be made, such as phasing out low-profitability ATMs and providing additional machines in high-traffic venues.

Different operating costs, such as rental space, machine repairs, and maintenance staff driving distances, were associated with each different machine location type. These costs were collected and captured in a custom-developed ATM maintenance-tracking application. On the revenue side, the location, time, duration, and activity types within all transactions taking place at every ATM were recorded in the central ATM transaction-processing system.

In a follow-on project to the telephone-banking data warehousing project, the data warehouse model was enhanced to include data on ATMs, including their locations and maintenance costs of various types, as well as ATM transactions. Extract-transform-load (ETL) processes were developed and implemented to consolidate the cost and customer transaction data into the data warehouse. Analytical reports and graphs of various types were developed to allow comparison and summarization of cost and activity data across the ATM network.

Future plans include integrating data from both EbizPioneer's activity-based costing (ABC) and call center systems into the data warehouse. The ABC system allows the fine-grained assignment of costs to activities such as those performed by customer service representatives (CSRs) on the call center staff. Consolidated analysis reports of such data from the data warehouse allows call center management to better monitor and optimize call center operations. This should in turn lead to both better customer service and lower cost to the bank.

Figure 9–1 gives an overview of the EbizPioneer Electronic Bank data warehouse.

Retail B2C: EbizDelivery

EbizDelivery is a new, Web-based subsidiary of a retail business with an established bricks-and-mortar presence in a three-state area of the U.S. Many of the products offered by EbizDelivery are perishable, which imposes strict storage and timeliness requirements for delivery of the products to customers. As a result of these requirements, EbizDelivery management decided to develop and maintain completely in-house capabilities for warehousing and delivery of its products.

Being a new subsidiary, EbizDelivery has also taken the opportunity to establish its own dedicated IT architecture. In order to enter the market quickly, it has chosen to construct the majority of this architecture from commercial software. This strategy inarguably offers a significant time-to-market advantage; however, there is no way to avoid the painstaking task of integrating data among these multiple, disparate packages.

The large functional units of the solution include

- *Order management:* allowing for customers to originate orders for product items, and keeping track of the orders throughout their lifecycle.

- *Product management:* keeping track of the "catalog" of products to be offered online; includes dimensions, colors, packaging alternatives, pricing, and images, among other data; a complete catalog requires both internal and external data on many products.

- *Credit card approval and payment:* validating customer credit cards and clearing payments through card providers and banks.

- *Tax calculations:* determining the potentially multiple taxing authorities—state, county, and municipal—having jurisdiction over the items in an order; determining the taxable or exempt status for any ordered items; if taxable, determining what rate to apply, and applying the rate.

- *Inventory management:* checking current and projected inventory levels for an item at the time an order is placed for the item; decreasing the amount of the item on hand by the amount ordered; triggering purchase orders to suppliers when inventory dips below a preset level

- *Delivery management:* allowing customers to select "delivery windows" (date/time slots during which their order will be delivered; scheduling delivery vehicles, drivers, and optimized routes; generating "pick lists" for items to be included in a delivery; determining "cartonization," that is, how many of which items should go into which type of "tote" or delivery bin, and how many bins would go into the delivery.

- *Customer support:* providing both Web- and telephone-based assistance to customers with questions or complaints; tracking the lifecycle of customer "cases" from origination through resolution; adding customer FAQs and suggestions to content of the Web site.

Each large functional unit both *required* data from one or more other units and *provided* data to one or more others, as well. A few synchronous, real-time interfaces were required, notably those triggered during customer interactions. However, most called for near real-time integration; data-sharing was required on a timely basis—usually within 30 minutes to 1 hour—but not instantaneously. This allowable latency in turn permitted a level of isolation, or "loose coupling," between interfacing functional units, so that the unavailability of one would not necessarily jeopardize the performance of another.

Figure 9–2 outlines of the major functional units and their interfaces.

As the diagram shows, the data for the combined solution was highly disparate and distributed, being the sum total of the data in several different packaged products. Designing and managing the data moving between the various parts was an obviously nontrivial set of tasks.

The data-related tasks emphasized during solution transformation, among others (see Table 8.1 in Chapter 8) included

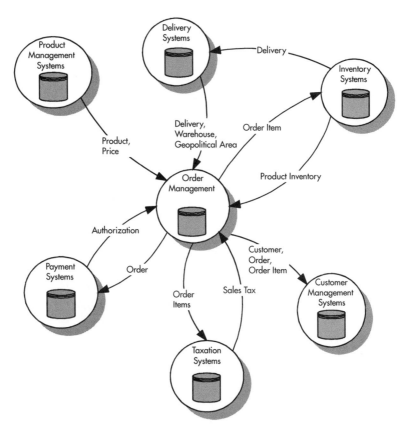

Figure 9–2
EbizDelivery functions and interfaces.

- Determining the events which would trigger the movement of data.
- Cataloging all available data structures and elements.
- Mapping source and target data elements and specifying any required transformations.
- Determining and designing the underlying physical data-movement infrastructure.

As design began, responsibilities for these were allocated as follows. Trigger-event determination was assigned to the team of specialists for each functional unit. Development of an overall logical data model—to which disparate data structures would be mapped—was the responsibility of the data team. Cataloging of data structures and design of mappings and transformations was a

213

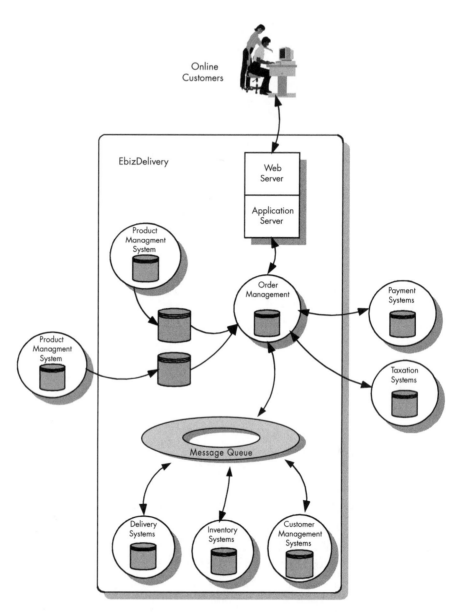

Figure 9–3
EbizDelivery data-movement infrastructure.

joint effort, coordinated by the data team working with the teams for the functional units. Design of the data-movement infrastructure was a joint effort of the data team and the hardware team. The interface infrastructure was comprised of the following three facilities, based on the rates of data interchange required:

- *Offline/batch interfaces.* The rate of change for product catalog data was relatively low, so an offline, periodic, file-transfer interface would be established. An extract process would write from the data source to an intermediate file format, which would then be read by a separate process to update the target.

- *Online/real-time interfaces.* Tax calculations and credit verification required prompt data exchange during an online customer session. Direct APIs (application program interfaces) would be used in these cases. Use of an API required that the data source communicate directly with the target, in the format specified by the target.

- *Near real-time/message-based interfaces.* A message-based infrastructure was specified for exchanges of inventory and delivery data that required inter-day currency and loose coupling, but could also tolerate some degree of latency. In these cases, a message broker could carry out any required data format mappings and transformations.

A specification database was developed and used to keep track of data structures, trigger events, and data mappings. The database, for which the data team maintained administrative responsibility, was a coordination tool used by both the data team and the business function analysis and development teams.

Figure 9–3 shows the resulting overall data-movement infrastructure. EbizDelivery's initial online effort is proceeding on schedule.

Financial B2C: EbizMoney

EbizMoney is a mid-sized regional financial services organization. Most of this company's competitors have offered their customers the ability to log in and check their account balances and transactional activity on their Web sites for some time. A relatively conservative organization, EbizMoney has until recently postponed expanding its Web presence to offer these capabilities.

The "application stovepipe" phenomenon has presented a perennial challenge to full-service financial institutions, more than businesses in practically any other industry. This means that, like most of its competitors, EbizMoney has purchased or built a specialized application to support each of the individual financial products or product families offered. These include checking, savings, loan products of various types, and investments. Each of these applications keeps track of its own accounts, transactions, and customers separate and apart from all the others.

EbizMoney has successfully dealt with this challenge through the combination of customer-matching/householding software (see Chapter 6) and a data warehouse. Each weekend, an offline process reads all new customer records within each of the independent application systems, and either matches these with existing customer and household records or creates new customer and household records for those for which it does not find a match. The consolidated customer records and household records are stored in the data warehouse, along with records for most of the accounts held by each of the customers. Figure 9–4 presents an overview of this process.

The data warehouse has become an important reporting and decision-making tool internal to the company.

These facts have come to light during analysis of the current realization perspective at EbizMoney. It appears that the current data warehouse processing accomplishes much (but not all) of the work necessary to provide a consolidated view of a customer's entire relationship with EbizMoney. As a re-

Figure 9–4
EbizMoney data warehouse update process.

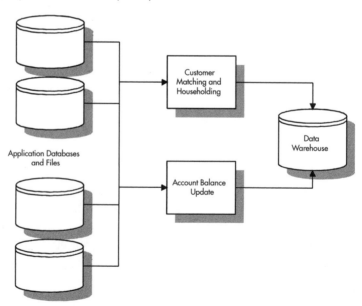

sult, the data warehouse was strongly considered as a potentially integral part of the conceptualization perspective for the company's e-business strategy.

Not surprisingly, however, elevating the data warehouse from internal to external use raised several issues. Among these were a number of constraints on the data warehouse identified during realization perspective analysis:

- The data warehouse was currently updated only on a weekly basis. Web customers would expect to see their balances and activity current at least as of the prior night's posting. Could this time lag be addressed directly in the data warehouse? If not, should the data warehouse be circumvented entirely due to this and other constraints?
- Investment accounts and holdings were not currently represented in the data warehouse. These were critical components of customers' comprehensive view of their relationship with EbizMoney.
- The data warehouse included only account balance information. Transactions, such as checking or savings deposits and withdrawals, investment purchases, and sales, for example, were not included in the data warehouse.

Other significant concerns surrounding data warehouse reuse included data custody and access contention issues. Perhaps the data warehouse itself should remain physically isolated internally, to assure that any potentially proprietary, sensitive corporate data contents could never be compromised. Also, the superimposition of small, but potentially numerous, concurrent external queries upon large, infrequent internal queries could cause contention on the database that would be problematic to optimize for.

As these aspects of solution transformation progressed, the decision was reached that the framework for the human interface and functionality for the company's e-commerce site would be provided by a leading B2C e-commerce server product. This product, as is typical of commercial software, included a predefined database design to support its out-of-the-box functionality, along with capabilities for

- extending the product's database design by adding columns to existing tables and/or adding new tables, and
- adding real-time links to databases outside the product's database.

The decision to use this commercial product obviously had implications not only on the functional side but also on the data side. The product was designed to support "generic" e-commerce functionality—primarily the selling of products and taking of orders. As a result, any data and function necessary to present detailed financial account balance, holdings, and transaction information needed to be developed as extensions to the basic functionality of the product.

At this point in the solution transformation, a major decision regarding Web-enabling the data warehouse was required. Considering the current constraints on the data warehouse and the "extend or link" capabilities of the e-commerce application software, one of the following solution options needed to be chosen:

1. Link the Web site directly to the data warehouse tables.
2. Duplicate some or all of the data warehouse tables in the e-commerce application database and refresh these from the warehouse on a periodic basis.

Given the limitations in scope of the data warehouse data, and concerns for data custody and access contention, the decision was reached that the data warehouse would best fit into the overall solution as one of several data sources for the e-commerce application database. Figure 9–5 describes this design.

Conceptualization perspective requirements directed that Web customers should be able to view all their account balances as of the prior night's posting. Since this data could lag by up to a week in the current data warehouse, solution transformations therefore resulted in specifications enabling the data warehouse to be updated on a nightly basis.

Requirements dictated that customers should also be provided with online access to all their accounts' transaction history, as well as investment accounts and holdings, as of the prior night's posting. Since the current data warehouse did not include this data, solution alternatives included

1. populating the data warehouse with this new data on a nightly basis, then propagating from there to the Web database, or
2. bypassing the data warehouse entirely and directly populating this data into the Web database on a nightly basis.

Time-to-market requirements resulted in the choice of the second alternative solution—bypassing the data warehouse.

The result of these solution transformations was a specification providing for a database of all accounts and transactions for all customers, current as of the prior night's posting.

An additional mandatory requirement was for 24/7 (24 hours a day, 7 days a week) availability of the site to customers. This eliminated any possibility of taking the Web database offline during the nightly update process to avoid contention between the update process and customer inquiries.

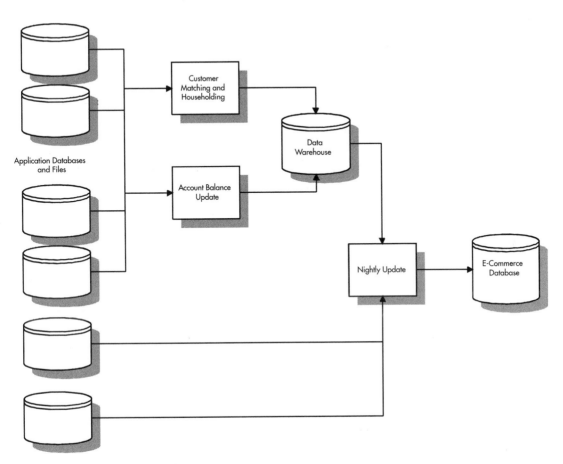

Figure 9–5
EbizMoney's data warehouse in e-commerce context.

The solution to this challenge was to take advantage of the prudent practice of maintaining an offline copy of the main database to assure continuous availability. The design specifications directed that the nightly update be done first to the offline database B. Then, upon successful completion of the offline update, the online processes were to be dynamically redirected from the currently online database A to the newly online database B. This redirection would take only as long as it would take to update a single row in a "switching" table. After this point, database A was offline, and the nightly update could then be applied to this database.

EbizMoney's retail banking Web site is up and running, 24/7. The data warehouse has provided a crucial link in providing important information to its customers in a timely, reliable manner.

Financial B2B: EbizGlobal

EbizGlobal is a financial services organization that provides outsourced money management functions for many companies, both large and small. Many of EbizGlobal's larger corporate customers are diversified organizations with subsidiaries across the U.S. and the world. Such customers may hold corporate deposit and loan accounts at dozens of banks and other financial institutions worldwide.

Accumulating a timely and accurate picture of the funds position and activity across all these accounts, and presenting this to corporate financial decision-makers, is a daunting task—and one at which EbizGlobal takes pride in excelling. One of the ways this company provides value for its customers is with its Transaction Hub service.

Beginning early each business day, EbizGlobal receives data transmissions from the many financial institutions with which their customers hold deposit accounts. The earliest files contain transaction records for the deposit and withdrawal activity in customers' accounts from the prior business day. Transmissions containing the current day's activity continue to be received as the day progresses. All these transactions are appended to a sizeable database containing several months' rolling history.

Concurrent with this input-side activity, many output processes are also initiated on both a scheduled and ad hoc basis. Corporate customers are able to specify the desired timing and content of transmissions of the transaction records for which they have been designated the recipients. The timing and content specifications for these transmissions can be set up proactively as needed. The transaction content of an input or output transmission can be in one of a number of financial industry-standard formats. Additional formats, including XML, are planned for future releases.

In addition to requesting file transmissions of their consolidated transaction activity, corporate customers also have access to an online Web-based reporting facility, which directly accesses the consolidated transaction database. Customers can submit requests for reports qualified by date, date range, account range, and transaction type.

The consolidated transaction database—including several months of transaction history—is a sizeable relational database, and not surprisingly is the core of the system. Due to its multiple diverse and concurrent access requirements, the design and optimization of this database was a challenging task. Large volumes of transactions must be quickly inserted into the database throughout the day, concurrent with both batch transmission extracts and online report requests. With a winning combination of sound logical design, generous application of RDBMS physical design techniques, including table partitioning and multiple indexes, the database is able to perform impressively in support of these processes.

Figure 9–6 presents an overview of EbizGlobal's Transaction Hub facility.

Figure 9–6

EbizGlobal Transaction Hub.

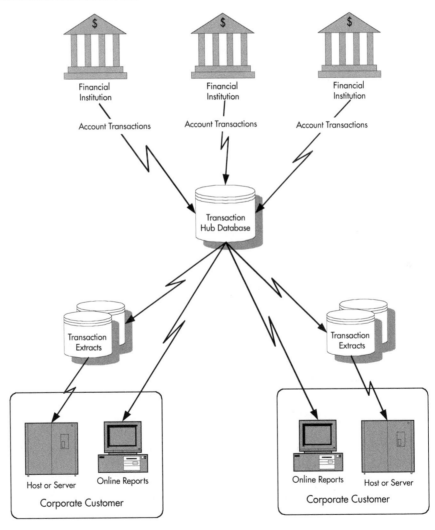

Manufacturing B2B: EbizToolz

EbizToolz is a manufacturer of specialty hardware items for the construction industry. Its product catalog contains several hundred items, some of which are also manufactured by other competing companies, but many of which are proprietary to EbizToolz.

EbizToolz's sales channels are relatively complex, which is common among manufacturing enterprises. EbizToolz retains a permanent staff of sales personnel, many of whom operate from remote offices, including offices in their home. The company also sells through manufacturer's representatives, who are not employees but operate on a commission basis, and can also sell products of other manufacturers. EbizToolz also sells directly to end customers, who include hardware stores, builders' supply outlets, and construction firms.

The expansion of e-commerce channels has, in many such cases, compressed such multilayered sales channels by giving end users increased direct access to product manufacturers. Many companies have taken control of such "disintermediation" of middle layers, such as sales staff and representatives, to the extent even of "re-intermediating" the sales channel—redefining, optimizing, and in some cases increasing its value-added device.

EbizToolz recognized that, due to the specialized and technical nature of its product set, the skills and expertise of its combined internal and external sales organization in the technical specifications, application, installation, and configuration of its products constituted a significant competitive advantage. So, rather than allowing the sales force to be disintermediated by shifting its emphasis to direct sales, EbizToolz initiated a strategy to assure a continuing balance between its direct (Web-based) and indirect sales channels by optimizing its sales force to the greatest extent possible.

One of the first initiatives in its sales-force optimization strategy was to increase the scope, quality, and integration of the information EbizToolz tracked on customers and prospects. The distributed and diverse sales force created significant challenges for managing this type of information. Data warehousing techniques of data replication and information dissemination were applied to help address these challenges.

A commercial ERP (enterprise resource planning) software had been successfully utilized by EbizToolz for several years, but had a number of restrictions when it came to supporting the distributed sales force. The system had been quite effective in tracking and managing orders for the company's products. However, it was accessible only from workstations at the corporate office. In addition, it was able to store only limited, static information on current customers (parties who had actually placed orders) and could not

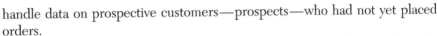

handle data on prospective customers—prospects—who had not yet placed orders.

As a result, data on customers and prospects was captured not only in the ERP system, but also in a number of disparate, redundant, and widely dispersed data stores—spreadsheets, Microsoft Access databases, cell phones, Act! databases, and Palm Pilots—managed by staff in both marketing and sales. This situation made implementation of any cohesive customer acquisition or retention strategy practically impossible to consider.

In conjunction with a partner consulting firm, EbizToolz was able to design and implement a consolidation and dissemination architecture for its customer data. The architecture

- brought the data under control, eliminating redundancy, variation in quality, and disparity in content and format, and
- enabled widespread access to the same enhanced-quality data, across not only the corporate-office organizations, but also the remote, mobile sales force—either connected or "untethered."

This architecture was enabled through data storage, input, and output technologies. A central customer database was maintained at the corporate office and synchronized with the ERP system on a nightly basis. Mobile sales representatives were equipped with a subset "data mart" of the customer database, limited to the customers in their sales territory, stored and maintained on their laptop computer. Subset data marts were also deployed to several independent (non-employee) sales representatives on a selective basis.

Sales personnel captured data on leads, prospects, and customer contacts in their personal data mart via a small data-entry application on their laptop computer. They were also able to connect, over the Internet, to the central customer database at will. While connected, a synchronization process could be initiated with the click of an icon, and updates since the last synchronization would be "shared" between the central and remote databases. This enabled sales personnel to get a current picture of their customers' orders and their status, and at the same time, consolidated new customer and prospect data from the field into the central database. Then, on a nightly basis, "canned" reports were generated from the consolidated data in the corporate office and distributed locally and remotely via email attachment.

Figure 9–7 presents an overview of the customer data consolidation and distribution architecture.

The timely, comprehensive, and high-quality data provided by this architecture helps EbizToolz to effectively leverage its distributed sales channels and compete effectively in its complex, multichannel business environment.

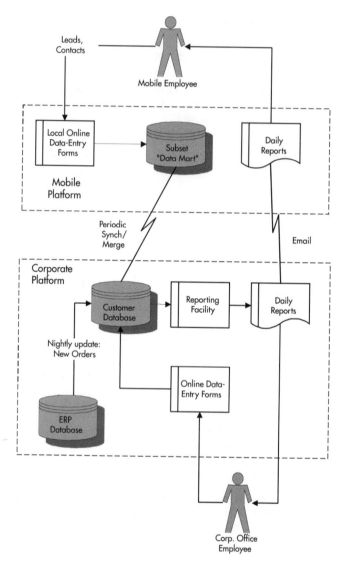

Figure 9–7
EbizToolz customer information architecture.

Outsourced E-Business Intelligence: EbizBI

EbizBI provides outsourced Web site services, offering an alternative for companies who wish to establish a Web e-business presence, but choose not to develop, staff, and maintain their own hardware and software. EbizBI's customer list includes both Web-based "pure-plays" and established bricks-and-mortar enterprises that may have decided to streamline their business processes in order to focus more closely on their core competencies.

Among Web outsourcers, a significant competitive differentiator for EbizBI is the depth and breadth of the business intelligence (BI) services it is able to offer its clients. These services, either in production or planned, include many of the e-BI capabilities presented in Chapter 8.

- *Campaign effectiveness:* assessing click-throughs on banner ads placed on other sites for example; also assessing responses to special offers advertised directly on their clients' sites.
- *Product and channel profitability:* integrating product cost data from clients' internal systems with sales data gathered from product orders placed on their hosted Web site, and in some cases other channels.
- *Customer profitability and lifetime value:* identifying and tracking return customers who tend to purchase high-margin products.
- *Customer segmentation, cross-sell and up-sell opportunities, and next likely purchase:* determined based on past history of customers with similar profiles.
- *Customer matching and householding:* by consolidating data on Web site customers with clients' internal customer data from other channels.
- *Ad hoc query, reporting, and data mining:* providing clients direct access to data on their Web site activity and providing facilities to extract this data and combine it with the client's internal data.

These capabilities are made possible by two types of assets leveraged by EbizBI:

1. A large amount of collected data, providing statistically significant samplings for just about any type of predictive algorithm.
2. A number of specialized software products—both stand-alone "offline" products and real-time products, as well as features embedded in Web application server software underlying EbizBI's sites.

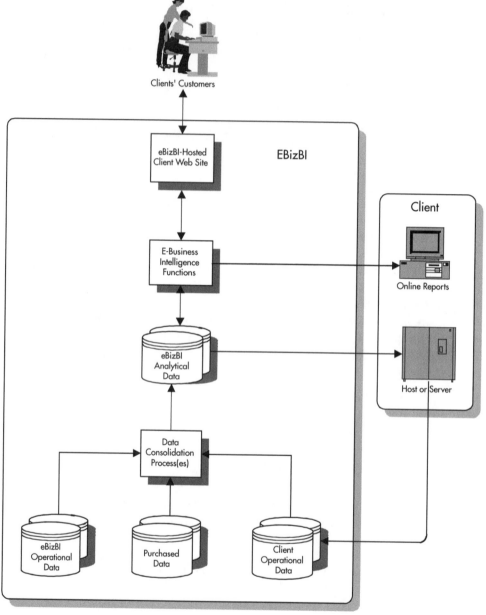

Figure 9–8
EbizBl data flows.

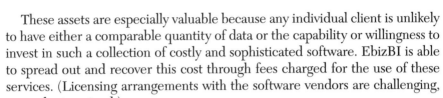
These assets are especially valuable because any individual client is unlikely to have either a comparable quantity of data or the capability or willingness to invest in such a collection of costly and sophisticated software. EbizBI is able to spread out and recover this cost through fees charged for the use of these services. (Licensing arrangements with the software vendors are challenging, as can be imagined.)

Another value-added capability provided by EbizBI is its subscription to outside sources for marketing and demographics data—this service is also resold to its clients. Outside data is consolidated with clients' proprietary data to enrich and enhance its value for marketing and predictive activities.

Figure 9–8 outlines the overall data flow for EbizBI.

As these examples show, numerous enterprises have discovered that experience gained and resources accrued as a result of data warehousing-related data-management efforts continue to pay off—by significantly advancing and expediting their e-business efforts.

Chapter 10

DATA WAREHOUSING *VERSUS* E-COMMERCE?

We must beware of needless innovations, especially when guided by logic.
— Winston Churchill

Up to this point in this book, we've examined many aspects of business and technology where e-commerce applications and data warehousing converge. These common aspects are significant enough, after all, that a book could be written about them. In this chapter, though, we'll lift up a few rocks and see what's underneath: areas of contradiction and controversy where, rather than converging, the paths of e-commerce and data warehousing apparently diverge.

The most significant area of controversy and divergence has been labeled "the object-data divide." This apparent schism results from the contrast between two sets of standard practices:

- *Object-oriented* (OO) standards that are being established for the analysis, development and deployment of e-commerce software.
- Established standards—grounded largely on the *relational database model* and its relatives and derivatives—for the analysis, development and deployment of databases.

The nature of the issue can also be summed up in questions.

- What is the appropriate role of the data resource relative to e-commerce functions and software? Is data a resource in its own right, or is it simply a byproduct, a result of functions and software?

- What are truly the "best" practices for capturing requirements for data and its interfaces with functions and software, and implementing these requirements?

In this chapter, we'll first present an overview of the current practice of e-commerce software development and deployment. With this as a background, we'll then examine the nature of the object-data divergence, its effects on e-commerce application development in theory and practice, and some potential steps that can be taken toward convergence of best practices.

E-Commerce Software Standards

To a great extent, standards for e-commerce software development have been driven by the *distributed computing* requirements of e-commerce applications on the World Wide Web.

The Java language is uniquely suited for distributed applications because of its cross-platform capabilities. Widespread adoption of *OO software development* practices has resulted in turn from the widespread adoption of the Java language. Distributed computing is also driving a resurgence in the adoption of CORBA (Common Object Request Broker Architecture) standards for distributed object computing—the most significant instance of which is seen in the Java 2 Enterprise Edition, or J2EE.

The growth of OO software development has also influenced standards for analysis and design techniques, evidenced in the creation and growing adoption of the Unified Modeling Language, or UML.

Figure 10–1 summarizes these interrelated trends and influences in e-commerce software standards.

The Realization Perspective: Distributed Computing

From the late 1980s through the 1990s, hardware and software architectures have evolved from monolithic—all processes and data on one computer, to *n-tier*—including two or more specialized, interacting computers.

The great majority of e-commerce solutions—and Web-based solutions, by definition—are distributed computing systems, making use of multiple layers of hardware and software. Many challenges must be successfully addressed

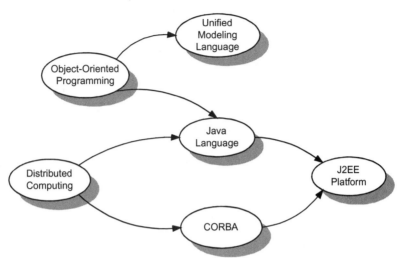

Figure 10–1
Representative trends and influences in e-commerce software development.

and solved to provide distributed computing systems that perform in a consistent, reliable manner, including

- Transaction management
- Session management
- Interprocess communication
- Security
- Directory and naming services

Distributed computing environments require a reliable, integrated and complete set of these infrastructure services, implemented in a manner that is independent of hardware and operating-system software.

CORBA is a widely accepted group of such infrastructure standards, developed specifically to support distributed OO computing. Its standards are centered on an Object Request Broker (ORB), an OO type of message broker. The CORBA standards are administered by the Object Management Group (OMG). As we shall see, the combination of CORBA infrastructure services with a cross-platform language results in a powerful environment for the development and deployment of e-commerce software applications.

The Solution Perspective: Java and the Java Platform

Distributed computing environments, in addition to their complexities of realization, also impose significant challenges on the development and deployment of software solutions. Software developers should ideally be able to focus on providing solutions for the business problems and opportunities within any development effort, and be isolated as much as possible from the hardware and software-service intricacies attendant to a multitiered execution platform. Providing this isolation is one of the primary goals of e-commerce, or *enterprise*, software platform standards—primarily J2EE and DCOM.

The Sun Microsystems J2EE and Microsoft DCOM (Distributed Component Object Model) standards are both firmly grounded in OO programming techniques. And since J2EE is quite representative of current e-commerce software development as a whole, and J2EE and DCOM are very similar at a high level, the remainder of this overview focuses on J2EE and the Java language.

Java technology has been developed with the goals of scalability, reliability, and platform independence for the realization environment. Java technology also provides software developers with a level of isolation from hardware and operating system platforms.

Java was developed to conform to the widely accepted characteristics of an OO language. In general, an OO language is one that supports encapsulation, polymorphism, inheritance, and instantiation. (Explanations of these concepts can be found in most introductory materials on OO software development.) A fundamental goal of languages and development environments that implement these concepts is to facilitate the expedient development and deployment of *reusable software modules*.

The concept of a class is fundamental to OO software development—classes are the elemental units of code that exhibit inheritance, encapsulation, and polymorphism. The Java platform utilizes and extends the class concept in a number of ways, several of which are specifically in support of distributed computing. Table 10.1 summarizes and relates several of these extended concepts. These terms are important in understanding some of the issues arising when attempting to deal with objects and data in combination.

These are the important concepts underlying today's emerging e-commerce software architecture standards. So, you may ask, where is the data?

Table 10.1 A Quick and Dirty Java Glossary

Term	Definition	Context
Class	A module of OO code containing both variables (data) and methods (functions). Theoretically corresponds to a class of objects in the real world.	Object-Oriented Programming
Object	An instance of a class, i.e., a module currently in memory. Theoretically corresponds to a single member of class of objects in the real world.	Object-Oriented Programming
Component	Within an OO context, a component is specifically a group of (one or more) classes that conforms to a standard (e.g., Java) interface definition, one of the primary goals of which is software reusability. Components range in scope from GUI buttons to complex business application functions.	Object-Oriented Development Standards
JavaBean	A Java component with standard interfaces that enable it to operate within a container environment.	Java
Enterprise JavaBean	A server-side Java component with standard interfaces that enable it to operate within a container/server environment. Also known as an EJB.	Java 2 Enterprise Edition
Container	An environment that provides an operating system process or thread for executing components and provides interfaces to server-level services, including transaction management, session management, connectivity, and security.	JavaBeans
Entity Bean	A specialized EJB that is an object representation of persistent data, i.e., stored data such as that in a database.	Java 2 Enterprise Edition

The Software-Data Interface: Entity Beans and Stored Procedures

An *Enterprise Java Bean*, or EJB, is a server-side, distributable, transactional software component conforming to a specified interface format and set of functions. An *Entity Bean* is a specialized type of EJB that, within the Java world, generally correlates to a relational DBMS *table* and its access functions. Entity-bean EJBs are the standard Java representation for the software-data interface.

The code of an entity bean can contain both variables that correspond to the columns of a relational DBMS table and functions (methods) that implement the various types of read and write accesses required for the table. These functions can utilize Java Database Connectivity (JDBC) calls, SQL for Java (SQLJ) calls, or both.

JDBC is a Java derivation of the earlier Microsoft ODBC specification, and specializes in supporting DBMS-independent, dynamic (e.g., ad hoc) data access.

SQLJ is a relatively newer proposed standard, syntactically much closer to conventional SQL, and specialized for static data access, where the access request can be compiled and stored in the database, enabling potentially faster performance.

The more awareness the DBMS has of any database access code—ideally before execution time—through compilation and optimization processes, the more effectively it can choose its internal access paths. A database stored procedure is a program which, being stored and managed by the database software itself, can be compiled and optimized for efficient data access.

Other significant benefits of using stored procedures for database access are enhanced security and data integrity. Implementing integrity rules, such as those discussed in Chapter 7, within stored procedures, and allowing access to database tables only through these stored procedures, prevents integrity and authorization checking from being circumvented by any but the most devious efforts.

Stored procedure capabilities of earlier DBMS versions required that they be coded in proprietary and/or platform-dependent languages. DBMS vendors recognized Java as a means to provide additional platform independence for their customers. Vendors have begun embedding a Java Virtual Machine (JVM) with new releases of their products, enabling Java modules to be developed and executed under control of the database. This in turn enables the development of Java stored procedures, compiled and optimized prior to runtime, that can significantly enhance data access performance and also are portable across the various tiers of a distributed e-commerce application.

A potential SQL-only alternative to Java stored procedures is offered by a standard SQL procedure language now defined within the ANSI SQL standard. Stored procedures utilizing this language would operate within the features, benefits, and drawbacks of SQL as a general-purpose processing language.

The Conceptualization Perspective: The UML

Now that we've looked at some important current developments in e-commerce software standards, let's take an "architectural" step back into project scoping and analysis—and the conceptualization perspective. Why retreat through the software lifecycle, from the solution perspective to the conceptualization perspective? Because this direction follows that of current OO standards development activity.

The predominant current standards for the solution and realization perspectives of e-commerce solutions are direct descendants of OO concepts and languages. Given this progression of events, it's not surprising that OO concepts have been extrapolated backward in the software lifecycle into the conceptualization perspective. The currently predominant OO method for conceptualizing and documenting software requirements is the UML.

Modeling languages are standardized formats for documenting and working within the conceptualization and specification perspectives of IT efforts. They are, effectively, specifications for specifications. The most notable early modeling language used extensively in IT was part of the Information Engineering Methodology originated and promulgated by Clive Finklestein and James Martin.

(In Chapter 8, Table 8.1, *models* are the contents of the cells in the "deliverables" columns. *Methodologies* are standardized processes for the transformations between perspectives—the contents of the "tasks" columns.)

The UML is the result of the merger, or "unification," of OO methodology work done primarily by three OO "gurus"—Grady Booch, James Rumbaugh, and Ivor Jacobsen—under the auspices of the Rational Software Corporation. The results of this work are now owned and administered by The Object Management Group (OMG).

According to the OMG, the UML is "a language for specifying, constructing, visualizing, and documenting the artifacts of a software-intensive system." The emphasis on the software and function components of IT architecture is evident when scrutinizing the form and content of the UML.

As a result of their lineage in OO software development, modeling constructs within the original UML specification tend to emphasize the specification of *behavior* (i.e., function). The focus is on software, function, and their interfaces. The class diagram is the artifact in the original UML specification that most closely resembles a data model. *Persistent attributes* are addressed as a byproduct of the behavior of a given class.

The OMG UML specification document, Version 1.3, states that "data-flow and other diagram types that were not included in the UML do not fit as cleanly into a consistent OO paradigm." As a consequence of this type of decision, the options available within the UML for clearly and specifically describing data-function interfaces have initially been limited.

This situation is changing, and this change is inevitable. OO specialists, faced with the need to clearly specify data resources, the spectrum of possible interactions among data, and the possible interactions of data with functions,

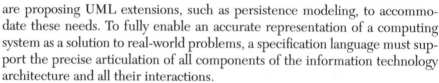

are proposing UML extensions, such as persistence modeling, to accommodate these needs. To fully enable an accurate representation of a computing system as a solution to real-world problems, a specification language must support the precise articulation of all components of the information technology architecture and all their interactions.

While the UML may not yet be comprehensive in its coverage of the data resource, one quality it certainly does have in abundance is widespread acceptance and momentum. Communication and accommodation between data specialists and the promoters of such a phenomenon will without doubt result in significant benefits for both the participants in its development and the users of the end product.

Data *Versus* Objects?

In the presentation of IT architecture in this book, software and data resources have been consistently and deliberately segregated. You may have noticed, during the prior discussion on OO concepts, that this segregation is antithetical to object orientation.

From an OO viewpoint, there is no concept of data existence, independent of function, within any IT architectural perspective from conceptualization through realization. On the contrary, the existence of data (variables) is dependent on the functions (methods) that operate on that data, and are grouped together with it within one or more classes. The notion of a class is the fundamental building block of object orientation. Data is a persistent class.

Does data about something in the "real world" exist independently from its behavior? You may recall this thought problem presented in Chapter 1:

A business has a choice of one and only one of the following disaster plans.

1. In the event of a disaster, all hardware devices and software programs in the company's IT inventory—but no data—are instantly duplicated at an alternate site, or

2. In the event of a disaster, all of the company's data only is instantly copied to an alternate site.

Which is the most prudent choice? Which will enable the business to continue functioning at all? Does it then follow that it makes sense to focus our priorities on the data resources of the business?

Another way of approaching the problem is from the view that a company's competitors could probably acquire the equivalent of its entire hardware inventory and the majority of its software inventory. But its data cannot be duplicated (at least not legally)!

Persistence—that is, lasting over time—comprises the fundamental underpinnings not merely of an organization's IT architecture, but of the organization's basic capability of functioning over time, carrying on as a "going concern." Persistent data exists independent from processing. Everything else can be viewed in relation to this superstructure *because* it is persistent, that is, long-lasting. One of the primary objectives of object orientation is *reusability of software*; but, due to this fundamental nature of the data product, effective reuse of data is arguably even more essential than reuse of software.

Many other established analysis and development approaches do indeed consider the data resource of a business independent of the functions to which it interfaces. The most widely known of these include

- The relational model (upon which all relational DBMSs are built)
- The Entity-Relationship approach
- The Information Engineering (IE) methodology

A number of side effects result from marginalizing the independent existence of the data resource, mostly to the detriment of precision of specifications.

- Lack of precision: ambiguity in defining specifications for data resources themselves
- Lack of precision: ambiguity in defining data interfaces, most notably
  - data-function interfaces
  - data-data interfaces, i.e., integrity rules

Because there is no recognition of data independent from function, there is consequently no recognition of a data-function interface. An interface is a boundary between two independent things, and if data and function are not independent, the notion of a boundary between them has no meaning.

But, as Ross Perot used to say, *listen here*: The most serious consequence of the marginalization of data resources is the *loss of data reusability*. Data-oriented analysis and design methods—currently out of fashion—stress the creation of a common, independent data resource, reusable by any and all sanctioned functionality. Data warehousing, the quintessence of data-oriented methods, is predicated on the optimization of data independence: "Here's the data—go ahead and use it as you see fit."

In conventional OO approaches, including the original UML, any part of the data resource of business, whether a logical entity or a relational table, is "just" a persistent class—a set of objects that for one reason or another happens to need to hang around for a while. An even more dogmatic OO position that has sometimes been taken is that persistent data is nothing but legacy—an artifact left over from an earlier historical epoch. Conventional OO, in subsuming data within function in pursuit of its prime objective, *software reuse*, actually tends to promote a disparate data resource, fragmented among multiple function-oriented classes.

Why would any organization deliberately avoid opportunities to maximize the usability of one of its most valuable resources? Real-world experience teaches otherwise. OO and UML are evolving and adapting. They must do so, because e-commerce systems, like the vast majority of other business systems, are accountable for treating the corporate data asset in a responsible manner.

The Function-Data Interface: Where's the CRUD?

For any data entity, there are just four basic methods, or data-function interfaces:

1. Create
2. Retrieve
3. Update
4. Delete

New synonyms may arise—instantiate, consume, emit, destroy, etc., etc.—for whatever reason, but in essence there is nothing any more complex than these four methods. Any and all other functions that interface with the data resource do so through one or more of these methods.

Venerable modeling tools, such as data-flow diagrams and CRUD matrices (examples of which appear profusely in Chapter 3), have been successfully utilized within venerable methodologies such as IE and others. These tools serve to specifically elicit and document requirements for these data interfaces, and as deliverables, can be transformed into data access specifications in design.

Agreement across data and object specialists that there are *entity classes,* or persistent classes, that correlate exactly one-to-one with data model entities and normalized relations, and are identified and designated by the use of the same methodologies, will go far to get things moving. Precise specification of the data-function interface within the UML can then begin with accommodation of concepts such as these—that have been proven successful over many years of application and database development. See Figure 10–2.

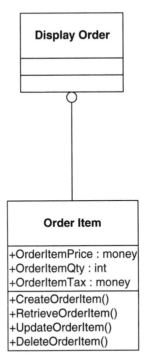

Figure 10–2
Example UML class model accommodating the CRUD concept.

The Data-Data Interface, or Data Rules

Conceptualized business rules, such as those discussed in Chapter 7, can be transformed directly into data integrity constraints. Data integrity constraints are data-data interfaces that limit the relationships allowed, either concurrently or successively, between various parts of the data resource (e.g., values, domains, attributes, relations). Types of data integrity constraints include

- Referential integrity constraints: primary-key/foreign-key relationships.
- Domain integrity constraints: allowed values for an attribute. The scope of a domain integrity constraint on an attribute can restrict any of the following:
  - only the variable itself
  - the variable *concurrently* with one or more other variables—i.e., the attribute's allowed values depend on the values of other attributes at the *same* time
  - the variable *over time*, either within itself or in relation to others—i.e.,

the attribute's allowed values depend on its own *preceding* value or the preceding value of other attributes.

• Entity integrity constraints: uniqueness of instances.

Object Constraint Language, or OCL, has been developed as a UML extension for specifying constraints. Not surprisingly, due to its OO lineage, the OCL specifies constraints within the province of function and software, rather than data.

Constraints, like data, are persistent by definition—they endure over time. Constraints also should be enforced consistently across, and be shareable by, all functions operating on data within their scope. It follows then that in whatever perspective they may appear, they should be related directly to the data that they regulate. Database stored procedures, for example, meet these criteria and are highly appropriate mechanisms for specifying and implementing data constraints.

Figure 10–3 graphically illustrates this concept.

Much thought is currently being devoted to the topic of rules and constraints. In addition to work on OCL by OO proponents, database and metadata specialists such as C.J. Date and Ron Ross continue to speak and write a great deal on the subject. (Date has gone so far as to propose that "rules are data.") If these efforts were to begin converging toward a single standard rather than to continue being approached from diverse positions, the results would be of much more benefit to information technology practitioners in general.

Figure 10–3
Where rules fit.

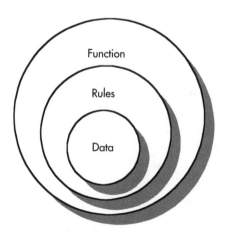

Resolution and Accommodation?

An overview of the positioning of the UML and the Java platform within a data architecture is presented in Table 10.2. The lightly-shaded areas indicate those data-related areas of the UML where the most evolution and adaptation is required and is currently taking place.

In the world of e-commerce application development, resisting UML or Java is likely to be as successful as stepping in front of a moving bus. (In the words of Craig Mullins, "Resistance is futile.") Given the rapid proliferation of OO approaches, and the shortcomings of conventional OO in fully addressing the data resource and its interfaces, is there light at the end of the tunnel or not?

What UML originally unified were three approaches that were very similar in the first place, all being OO and software-focused. A more ambitious and participatory unification of best practices of multiple modeling approaches could result in a comprehensive framework for IT architecture. UML, because of its wide marketing, visibility, acceptance, and utilization, could indeed evolve into the foundation for such a comprehensive framework. Data architecture methods and deliverables are currently active areas for enhancement in the UML.

Persistent business data has been successfully analyzed, designed, and deployed on computers for several decades. Much progress has been made during that time on techniques to help assure that computer-stored data effectively meets the requirements of those who create and use the data. There is a significant body of accumulated and successfully tested knowledge and experience within the database field.

Entity-relationship modeling works. Declarative business-rule modeling works. And above all, the relational model works. What is not needed at this time is yet another way to skin the cat. What is needed is accommodation within both the "object camp" and the "relational camp" of the existing successful techniques of each.

IE was a hodgepodge of several different types of models. What made them work together as an integrated whole was a rigorous cross-reference. A one-size-fits-all extension of the syntax of one area of the IT architecture into all others will not, in and of itself, guarantee adequate expressiveness of the language, satisfactory holistic integrity across interfaces, or transformations and perspectives.

There is evidence that, faced with persistent (pun intended) challenges with effectively addressing persistence within a conventional object paradigm, the OO ship is indeed slowly turning.

Table 10.2 Java and UML in the Data Architecture

	Scoping/Analysis		Design			Development/Deployment	
	Realization Perspective "As-is" Deliverables	Conceptualization Transformation Tasks	Conceptualization Perspective Deliverables	Solution Transformation Tasks	Specification Perspective Deliverables	Implementation Transformation Tasks	Realization Perspective "To-be" Deliverables
Data							
Data-Human							
Data-Function			UML		UML / Java		Java
Data-Data							
Data-Software					Java		Java
Data-Hardware							

Data is infiltrating object-orientation. Can the "object-data divide" be crossed? Absolutely, through acknowledgement, acceptance, and cross-training between the "everything-is-an-object" camp and the "data-is-all-that-matters" camp. If Tiosa Group can do it, your company can also—to the benefit of the company, its employees, its customers, and its partners.

Tiosa Group: One Last Visit

Overheard in the Cafeteria

Overheard in the cafeteria at Tiosa Group corporate headquarters. A conversation between a Java development team leader (JD) from Gasomatic and a database administrator (DB) from Tiosa Financial.

JD: Wazzup, DB? Hey, I need some of your time on something. Dan just asked me to develop a recommendation about standardizing on entity bean EJBs for persistence-layer management. He said I should get your group involved, to get your angle on it too.

DB: Hold on a minute. Can you repeat that so I can write it down? We should standardize on what?

JD: Entity bean EJBs . . . for persistence-layer management.

DB: Okay, what's persistence-layer management?

JD: Database access, in other words.

DB   Oh, okay, now I'm definitely interested. What are . . . EJBs?

JD: Enterprise JavaBeans. They're Java server-side components that operate within containers.

DB: What's a container?

JD: It's a runtime environment that provides an operating system process for executing components, and interfaces to application-server services like transaction management, session management, connectivity, and security.

DB: Cool. What are components, then?

JD: Component is a pretty general term. Components can range in scope from small utility-type modules to pretty big business functions. In Java terms, a component is specifically a group of one or more classes that complies with

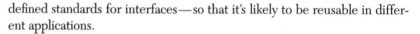

defined standards for interfaces—so that it's likely to be reusable in different applications.

DB: Got it . . . so . . . what's this entity bean thing? Is it like an entity in an entity-relationship model?

JD: Well, sort of, yeah. An entity bean is a JavaBean that's created specifically for managing persistent data, like in a database. And, well, since entity-relationship-model entities usually wind up as database tables . . . and . . . it would probably make sense to have an entity bean per table, then, yeah, the EJB would basically wrap up that entity along with its methods, er, functions.

DB: Oh, so you'd have all the create, retrieve, update, and delete functions grouped together in the methods in that entity bean, right?

JD: Now you're cookin'. Oops, gotta go . . . hey, can you email me with some times you could get together to prepare for this presentation for Dan? He wants something the middle of next week, so the sooner the better.

DB: Sure, soon as I get back to my desk. Sounds good.

In Dan's Conference Room

The next Wednesday, in CIO Dan's conference room, two diagrams (presented in Figure 10–4 and Figure 10–5) are under discussion.

JD: . . . and with this component/container/server model, different application-dependent business logic components share a common set of data access and integrity logic. DB will talk more about this in a minute.

So, we think we've put together something that we can take forward as development patterns for our e-business enablement initiative. A lot of it's dependent on Java 2 Enterprise Edition. Development tools and application servers are just now catching up on it, but we think it's going to be very viable in the long run, especially with the vendor backing it's getting. Now DB will talk in a little more detail about the software-data interface guidelines we're suggesting.

DB: Well, for persistence management . . . I mean, on the database side, we wanted to be sure to provide for maximum database performance, maximum integrity protection, and also present a highly reusable data resource for developers.

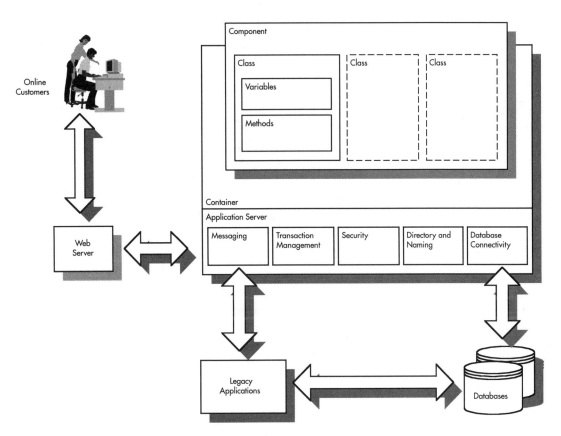

Figure 10–4
High-level e-commerce interfaces.

The direction we're recommending is presented on this more detailed slide [see Figure 10–5]. Keep in mind that JDBC, SQLJ, and Java stored procedures are relatively new technologies. Their availability and support by both database and application-server vendors is relatively young, but it's obvious that there's a lot of acceptance and momentum in their direction in both the vendor and user communities. Because of this, we feel that the technology will stabilize relatively quickly, minimizing the risk of pursuing this direction.

Along the same lines of risk mitigation, we feel that moving toward the implementation and management of our data integrity logic, or "business rules," in database stored procedures—and specifically Java stored procedures in the long run—will enhance both data access performance and data

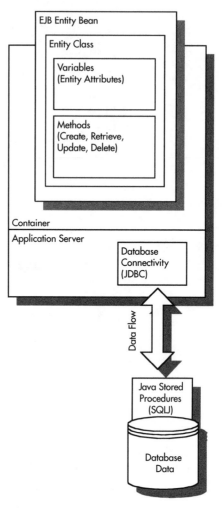

Figure 10-5
Suggested software-data interface detail.

resource quality. And as our e-commerce enablement efforts increase the exposure of our data assets to outside parties, this stored procedure layer will also help protect these assets from being deliberately or accidentally compromised.

JD: And if the stored procedures are developed in Java, we have fewer proprietary languages to support, and code portability is a much more viable option—making us less DBMS and operating system vendor-dependent over the long run.

Chapter 11

A Data E-Technologies Product Catalog

Lo! Men have become the tools of their tools.
—Henry David Thoreau

The intent of this chapter is to provide hints on a "shopping list" of software products that can be applied to make maximum use of a company's data resources when developing e-commerce capabilities such as those discussed in this book.

Developing a list such as this is perpetually fraught with difficulties. Products and vendors are constantly evolving. Software companies acquire other software companies and their products; product lines expand, transform, and are relabeled. In many cases, the act of categorizing complex, multifunction software product families is of necessity somewhat subjective. This is exacerbated by the considerable—and increasing—overlap between categories, especially

- Knowledge management (KM) and Enterprise Information Portals (EIP)
- Data mining, online analytical processing (OLAP), and business intelligence (BI)
- Enterprise application integration (EAI), application servers, and e-commerce servers
- Data mining and e-commerce servers (e.g., personalization)
- Database management systems (DBMSs) and just about everything else—including application servers, EAI, EIPs, OLAP, data mining, BI, and in the future, business rules engines

But, given these caveats, it is hoped the listings and their annotations in the tables of this chapter will provide a snapshot—accurate as of the date of writing—of these categories and markets and where the products and companies fall within them.

The selections are not intended to be exhaustive of each category, a futile goal at best, but rather to be representative and indicative of the classifications under which they appear. Many categories include both market leaders and trendsetters.

Some elaboration (meta-data) on the table column heads are as follows.

Company:	The corporate name of the maker of the software. Larger companies such as IBM and Microsoft may appear several times, under multiple classifications. This landscape is also quite liable to change, given the rapid pace of acquisition and consolidation among software vendors.
Company URL:	The "home page" of the software manufacturer. Pages with information on specific products can be moved over time, but are usually navigable by starting at the home page. If not, the vendor definitely has a problem with its data-human interface.
Product:	The name of the specific software product or product line, offered by the company, that is most representative of the category. In those cases where a company offers a line of products based on a designated common technology or server, this common product is listed.
Angle:	In the movie *White Christmas*, Bing Crosby's character at one point offers the observation that "everybody has an angle." Any company in a highly competitive market such as software has to have at least one angle—a characteristic that differentiates its product(s) from those of its competitors. This column attempts to identify some memorable, high-level means for you to differentiate between products within the same classification.
Info Links:	No sense in reinventing the wheel: Use this section as your portal to extended information on the listed products—Web-based and/or print. URLs point to either an independent review of the product or to informative and objective detailed information from the vendor, in cases where objective sources are difficult or impossible to find. Please note that Web pages may have been moved or deleted since this listing was compiled.

Web Analytics

The collection and presentation of data about interactions between users and Web sites is often designated as Web analytics. Products that specialize in these functions (see Table 11.1) generally collect this data through one or both of two different technical methods:

- By monitoring network traffic, also known as *packet sniffing*, or capturing data "on the wire"—reading the actual TCP/IP messages, or packets, passed between Web browsers and servers.
- By capturing data from the log files produced by Web servers.

A good (although biased) paper contrasting these two methods, "Log File Analysis vs. Packet Sniffing," is available at the WebTrends site.

The functionality provided by these products was presented in Chapter 4.

Business Intelligence

Many of these vendors' product lines (see Table 11.2) began as multipurpose, or traditional, enterprise-level query and reporting tools, and, in order to remain competitive, have branched out into other functional areas, including portals, OLAP, analytic applications, and Web analysis. Basic query and reporting functions were presented in Chapter 4.

Online Analytical Processing (OLAP)

The products in Table 11.3 represent various technological approaches to OLAP, including relational OLAP (ROLAP), specialized multidimensional databases (MOLAP), and hybrid (HOLAP) solutions that offer some of both ROLAP and MOLAP.

A very good source for information on OLAP products is "The OLAP Report" at *www.olapreport.com*.

These functions were presented in Chapter 4.

Table 11.1 Web Analytics Software

Company	Company URL	Product	Angle	Info Links
Accrue Software, Inc.	www.accrue.com	Insight	Insight is the original flagship reporting product. Accrue now offers a range of Web analytic products, including multi-dimensional analytics and data mining.	www.informationweek.com/756/accrue.htm www.internetwk.com/story/INW19990407S0006
Macromedia	www.macromedia.com	Aria Enterprise	Monitors network traffic. Bundled with ObjectStore object database (from eXcelon Corp.).	www.nufusion.com/reviews/1122rev.html?nf
NetGenesis Corp.	www.netgenesis.com	net.Analysis	Can monitor network traffic and also read Web-server logs. Uses third-party database such as Oracle or SQL Server.	www.nufusion.com/reviews/1122rev.html?nf
WebTrends Corp.	www.webtrends.com	WebTrends Log Analyzer	Reads Web-server logs. Uses third-party database such as Oracle or SQL Server.	webdevelopersjournal.com/software/webtrends_vs_hitlist.html www.nufusion.com/reviews/0712rev2.html

Table 11.2 Business Intelligence Software

Company	Company URL	Product	Angle	Info Links
Actuate Corp.	*www.actuate.com*	e.Reporting Suite	A relative newcomer, Actuate staked out its niche by focusing directly on using "Intranets" for delivery of business intelligence.	*www.zdnet.com/intweek/stories/ news/0,4164,2643799,00.html* *www.dmreview.com/master .cfm?NavID=198&EdID=1092*
Brio Technology, Inc.	*www.brio.com*	Brio.Enterprise	Brio began as a provider of query and reporting products, but it has branched out into several additional functional areas, including portals, OLAP, and Web analysis.	*www.dmreview.com/master .cfm?NavID=198&EdID=118* *www.intelligententerprise .com/db_area/archives/1999/ 990903/inthefield.shtml*
Business Objects SA	*www.businessobjects .com*	BusinessObjects 2000	A high-end, mature, and multi-functioned product line, including meta-data management and OLAP front-end functions.	*www.dmreview.com/master .cfm?NavID=198&EdID=2382* *www.intelligententerprise.com/ 000120/inthefield.shtml* *www.intelligententerprise.com/ 000605/news.shtml*
Cognos, Inc.	*www.cognos.com*	Impromptu	Impromptu is part of a large integrated product line, including OLAP and data mining software.	*www.intelligententerprise .com/db_area/archives/1998/ 9810/prod2.shtml* *www.dmreview.com/master .cfm?NavID=198&EdID=139*
Crystal Decisions	*www.crystaldecisions .com*	Crystal Reports	A veteran collection of reporting products ranging from low-cost to expensive. Crystal Reports provides the imbedded reporting functionality in several other products.	*www.dmreview.com/master .cfm?NavID=198&EdID=140*

Table 11.3 OLAP Software

Company	Company URL	Product	Angle	Info Links
Cognos, Inc.	*www.cognos.com*	PowerPlay	PowerPlay is integrated with Impromptu. It can also be used in conjunction with Microsoft Analysis Services.	*www.dmreview.com/master .cfm?NavID=198&EdID=1381*
Hyperion Solutions Corp.	*www.hyperion.com*	Essbase	The OLAP database market leader. Hyperion offers a number of financial applications, many of which utilize Essbase.	*www.intelligententerprise.com/ db_area/archives/1999/991611/ inthefield.shtml*
IBM	*www.ibm.com*	DB2 OLAP Server	Integrates Hyperion's Essbase with DB2.	*www.informationweek.com/ shared/printArticle?article =infoweek/779/prfraud .htm&pub=iwk*
Microsoft Corp.	*www.microsoft.com*	Analysis Services	What was formerly known as OLAP Services is now, in SQL Server 2000, part of Analysis Services. Provides MOLAP, ROLAP, and HOLAP technology.	*www.dmreview.com/master .cfm?NavID=198&EdID=1798* *Microsoft OLAP Solutions*, Thompsen et al., Wiley, 2000
Microstrategy, Inc.	*www.microstrategy .com*	MicroStrategy 7	The ROLAP pioneer. Has developed into a large multifunction analytical product line.	*www.intelligententerprise.com/ db_area/archives/1999/992004/ inthefield.shtml*
Oracle Corp.	*www.oracle.com*	Oracle Express	Oracle acquired Express from OLAP pioneer IRI.	*www.intelligententerprise.com/ a_appframe.shtml*

Turnkey Data Marts

E.piphany and Broadbase (Table 11.4) are turnkey, back-to-front data mart products that provide a foundation of ETL (extract-transform-load), multi-dimensional analysis and data mining functions. Both also offer a number of analytical applications, including several customer relationship management (CRM) functions. They utilize third-party relational database such as Oracle or SQL Server for ROLAP storage.

A good overview of turnkey decision-support systems can be found at *www.dmreview.com/master.cfm?NavID=198&EdID=355.*

Data Mining

A clear trend in this category (Table 11.5) is the embedding of data mining functionality—and in many instances, data mining products themselves—in other products, most notably in analytic product lines and even e-commerce servers. In some cases, analytic product vendors (i.e., E.piphany) have gone so far as to acquire data-mining product vendors (i.e., RightPoint).

Data mining functions were presented in Chapter 4.

Enterprise Information Portals

Enterprise Information Portals (Table 11.6) is a very dynamic software market segment. EIP functionality was presented in Chapter 4.

Specialized Database Products: Main-memory, XML, and Federated DBMS

This category (Table 11.7) is a mixed bag, with some very interesting ongoing developments. Vendors are constantly repackaging and repositioning their products. These technologies were discussed in Chapter 5.

Table 11.4 Turnkey Data Mart Software

Company	Company URL	Product	Angle	Info Links
Broadbase Software, Inc.	www.broadbase.com	Broadbase EPM	Several specialized analytical applications such as profitability analysis can be added on. "Shrink-wrapped" ETL mappings to several source applications such as BroadVision are available.	www.dmreview.com/master.cfm? NavID=198&EdID=376 www.dmreview.com/master.cfm? NavID=71&EdID=1127
E.piphany, Inc.	www.epiphany.com	E.5 System	CRM functions such as campaign management can be added on.	businessweek.com/1999/99_30/ b3639033.htm www.dmreview.com/master .cfm?NavID=198&EdID=2401

Table 11.5 Data Mining Software

Company	Company URL	Product	Angle	Info Links
IBM	*www.ibm.com*	Intelligent Miner	A powerful, full-functioned, standalone data mining tool geared toward technical users with a statistical background.	*www.dmreview.com/master .cfm?NavID=198&EdID=805*
Microsoft Corp.	*www.microsoft.com*	Analysis Services	A component of the SQL Server 2000 database product. Data mining functions are expressed as SQL extensions and mining models as database structures.	*Microsoft Analysis Solutions,* Thompsen et al, Wiley *Data Mining With Microsoft SQL Server 2000,* Pierre Boutquiin, Sams, 2001 *Data Mining with Microsoft(r) SQL Server 2000 Technical Reference,* Claude Seidman, Microsoft Press, 2001
Oracle Corp.	*www.oracle.com*	Oracle Data Mining (Darwin)	Oracle purchased pioneer data-mining software Darwin from Thinking Machines Corp. in 1999.	*www.dmreview.com/master _sponsor.cfm?NavID=71&EdID =1473* *www.dmreview.com/master .cfm?NavID=55&EdID=202*
SAS Institute, Inc.	*www.sas.com*	Enterprise Miner	When it comes to analytic applications, SAS hardly needs an angle. They have been around forever, have a good reputation, and have a huge product line.	*www.dmreview.com/master .cfm?NavID=198&EdID=1592*
SPSS, Inc.	*www.spss.com*	Clementine	SPSS is the perennial SAS competitor in statistical software. SPSS purchased ISL, Ltd., the original developer of Clementine, in 1998. Clementine was launched in 1994 as the first enterprise-strength, data-mining system aimed at business users.	*www.intelligententerprise .com/000717/feat2.shtml/*

Table 11.6 EIP Software

Company	Company URL	Product	Angle	Info Links
AlphaBlox Corp.	www.alphablox.com	AlphaBlox	AlphaBlox is a Web- and Java-based environment for developing composite analytic applications. Input data may be accessed from multiple sources and delivered in multiple formats.	www.infoworld.com/articles/hn/xml/00/ 03/06/000306hntech.xml www.dw-institute.com/ whatworks10/cs/cs16/cs16.html
Microsoft Corp.	www.microsoft.com	Digital Dashboard Resource Kit	Digital Dashboard is more a set of interfaces and concepts to facilitate the use of Microsoft products to construct portal applications than it is an actual product. The products include Outlook, Exchange, and Internet Explorer. A fundamental concept is that of "Web Parts"—Web-based interface components.	exchange.devx.com/upload/free/ features/exchange/2000/02feb00/br0100/ br0100.asp
Plumtree Software, Inc.	www.plumtree.com	Plumtree Corporate Portal	With the "Massively Parallel Portal Engine," Plumtree targets businesses with thousands of portal users.	www.zdnet.com/eweek/stories/ general/0,11011,2651597,00.html www.infoworld.com/articles/hn/xml/00/ 09/29/000929hnplumtree.xml
Sequoia Software	www.sequoiasoftware.com	XPS	XPS is an XML-based (Sequoia calls it "XML-pure") portal development environment.	biz.yahoo.com/bw/001012/md_ sequoia.html
Hummingbird	www.hummingbird.com	Hummingbird EIP	Hummingbird has an extensive line of portal-related products, including content management, knowledge management, and ETL.	www.dmreview.com/master .cfm?NavID=198&EdID=1617
IBM	www-4.ibm.com/ software/data/eip/	IBM Enterprise Information Portal	IBM establishes a unique position within the portal market by exploiting versions of several of its own products, including DB2 UDB, Lotus Domino, Content Manager, DataGuide, WebSphere, and MQSeries, within the IBM EIP offering.	www.wallstreetandtech.com/ story/supp/WST20000907S0017

Table 11.7 Specialized Database Software

Company	Company URL	Product	Angle	Info Links
Angara	www.angara.com	Angara Reporter Angara Converter	Formerly a standalone main-memory DBMS, Angara is now the underlying technology for a marketing ASP (application service provider) service.	www.altavista.com/cgi-bin/query?pg=r&m=4&i=OPsCdn4&m=18&u=zdnet.com/ecommerce/stories/main/0%2C10475%2C2625256%2C00.html
Cohera Corp.	www.cohera.com	E-Catalog System	Cohera was founded by venerable database guru Michael Stonebraker. An example of the e-business software vendor morphing phenomenon, Cohera began as a federated DBMS product. Now the FDBMS is the basis of the E-Catalog System.	www.intelligententerprise.com/db_area/archives/1999/992004/editpage.shtml www.dmreview.com/master.cfm?NavID=19&EdID=1555
eXcelon Corp.	www.exceloncorp.com	Javlin	Another example of the e-business software vendor morphing phenomenon, Object DBMS ObjectStore morphed into XML DBMS eXcelon, which then morphed into the Javlin EJB data server.	www.exceloncorp.com/products/white_papers/javlin.pdf
Software AG	www.softwareag.com/tamino	Tamino	Tamino is a native XML database, optimized for storing XML documents.	www.nufusion.com/news/2000/0119softagxml.html
TimesTen Performance Software, Inc.	www.timesten.com	TimesTen	TimesTen is the most visible (if not the only) remaining standalone main-memory database vendor.	www.intelligententerprise.com/db_area/archives/1999/990903/products.shtml

Virtual Data Warehousing

The growth in the quantities of data to be analyzed inexorably continues—and accelerates. The need for up-to-the-minute analytical data increases—last week's, or even last night's, data is no longer timely enough. And summarized data is less and less satisfactory—the level of detail required inexorably increases. In more and more cases, conventional data warehousing—that is, replicating data into a single physical database—will not provide a total solution. When data needs to be accessed in real-time from multiple sources, a "virtual" data warehouse (see Table 11.8) should be seriously considered. These technologies were discussed in Chapter 5.

Data Enrichment

Many vendors in this market (see Table 11.9) offer comprehensive suites of products, including address validation, name matching and data-quality profiling. These functions were presented in Chapter 7.

Customer Data Vendors

These vendors (see Table 11.10) compile and maintain data for resale on individuals, families, and businesses across the U.S. Commercial data providers were discussed in Chapters 6 and 10.

Product Data Vendors

These vendors (see Table 11.11) compile and maintain data on both commodity and specialized products for primarily retail businesses. Data such as product identifiers (e.g., UPC and bar codes), product specifications (sizes, weights), and graphics such as photographs are available. Commercial data providers were discussed in Chapters 6 and 10.

Table 11.8 Virtual Data Warehousing Software

Company	Company URL	Product	Angle	Info Links
Cerebellum Software	*www.cerebellumsoft .com*	IDI Server	A Java-based virtual data warehousing development environment, also expanding into portal products.	*www.dmreview.com/master .cfm?NavID=198&EdID=2383*
Information Builders	*www.ibi.com*	EDA Data Access Services	EDA, introduced during the client-server heyday in 1991, is the god-father of virtual data warehousing.	*www.dmreview.com/master .cfm?NavID=198&EdID=2633*
nQuire Soft-ware, Inc.	*www.nquire.com*	nQuire Suite	A relative newcomer to the world of virtual data warehousing.	*www.intelligententerprise.com/ 010101/strategic.shtml*
IBM	*www.ibm.com*	Data Joiner	A mature, pioneering data-integration product. A component of the IBM Visual Warehouse.	*www.dmreview.com/master .cfm?NavID=198&EdID=233*

Table 11.9 Data Enrichment Software

Company	Company URL	Product	Angle	Info Links
Evoke Software	www.evokesoftware .com	Axio	A multifunction product line, including data source profiling and business-rule detection from source code.	www.intelligententerprise.com/ 000626/inthefield.shtml
Innovative Systems, Inc.	www.innovative systems.net	Innovative-Find, Innovative-Match	Components of a mature, multifunction product set including real-time and batch name and address matching and householding. Many customers in the financial industry. Also provides customer-matching and address-validation services.	www.dmreview.commaster .cfm?NavID=198&EdID=1779
Harte Hanks Data Technologies	www.trilliumsoft.com	Trillium Software System	Consists of sequential components Converter, Parser, Geocoder, and Matcher. Trillium also provides training and consulting services.	www.informationweek.com/ 800/trillium.htm
Vality Technology, Inc.	www.vality.com	INTEGRITY Data Re-Engineering Environment	A large family of products. Vality also offers training and consulting services.	www.dmreview.com/master .cfm?NavID=198&EdID=846

Table 11.10 Customer Data Software

Company	Company URL	Product	Angle	Info Links
Acxiom Corp.	www.acxiom.com	InfoBase	Acxiom offers a suite of analytic and CRM products built on InfoBase.	www.dmreview.com/master .cfm?NavID=198&EdID=1188
Claritas, Inc.	www.claritas.com	Datamart on America	Claritas originated the PRIZM cluster concept, which defines every neighborhood in the U.S. in terms of 62 demographically and behaviorally distinct clusters, such as "Kids and Cul de Sacs," "Pools and Patios."	news.cnet.com/news/ 0-1005-200-2832619.html
Experian Information Solutions, Inc.	www.experian.com	INSOURCE	Experian offers a large range of products, organized for management of clients' customer lifecycles. The foundation of the product line is the INSOURCE database, created in 1996 through the partnership between Experian and Metromail.	www.dmreview.com/master .cfm?NavID=198&EdID=1743

Table 11.11 Product Data Software

Company	Company URL	Product	Angle	Info Links
1-800-Database Ltd.	www .1-800-database.com	1-800-DATABASE	Provides data and images on hundreds of thousands of products to more than 5,000 manufacturers, retailers, distributors, and marketing agencies.	mercantec.com/press/1999/1101DB.html
QRS Corp.	www.qrs.com	QRS Product Catalog	Part of an extensive line of products and services. The QRS Product Catalog database, in existence since 1988, includes over 75 million UPCs and associated product data loaded.	http://www.qrsi.com/news/press_room/00_01_18_bluemartini.asp

Payment Processing and Tax Data Vendors

These types of products (see Table 11.12) are critical links in allowing funds to flow correctly within e-commerce solutions. Payment-processing functions are typically both real-time (e.g., charge card authorizations) and asynchronous (e.g., moving the money after the transaction is originated) services. Tax calculations also need to be real-time, and the underlying data is much more likely to be hosted locally than at a service provider. Commercial data providers were discussed in Chapters 6 and 10.

Extract, Transform, and Load

ETL (see Table 11.13) comprises those traditional, batch-oriented, asynchronous data replication and organization processes that are not likely to disappear very soon. This is generally a mature product marketplace. ETL was discussed in Chapter 6.

Knowledge Management

KM is another very dynamic software market (see Table 11.14) with much overlap with Enterprise Information Portals. Functions provided by these products were presented in Chapter 6.

Application Servers

Application servers (Table 11.15) are a core platform for e-commerce data and software integration. These technologies were discussed in Chapter 10.

Table 11.12 Payment Processing and Tax Data Software

Company	Company URL	Product	Angle	Info Links
CyberCash, Inc.	*www.cybercash.com*	WebAuthorize	Integrated with Microsoft Site Server, Commerce Edition, and SAP R/3 e-commerce enterprise application.	*www.infoworld.com/articles/ tc/xml/00/11/13/ 001113tcgateways.xml*
CyberSource Corp.	*www.cybersource .com*	CyberSource Internet Commerce Suite™	Services are remotely accessed in real-time via the CyberSource Commerce Component.	*www.infoworld.com/articles/ tc/xml/00/11/13/ 001113tcgateways.xml*
Taxware International, Inc.	*www.taxware.com*	SALES/USE Tax System	Includes data on all taxing jurisdictions in the U.S. and Canada. Kept current with monthly updates. Uses a Product Taxability Matrix to maintain taxable status on detailed product sets.	*www.taxware.com/znewinfo/ articles/infowk.htm*

Table 11.13 ETL Software

Company	Company URL	Product	Angle	Info Links
BMC Software, Inc.	www.bmc.com	Enterprise Data Propagation (EDP)	BMC's EDP products focus on high-performance capture and movement of large volumes of dynamic data sources within an IBM mainframe environment.	www.gartnerweb.com/public/axl/reprints/bmc/00074666.html www.dmreview.com/master_sponsor.cfm?NavID=55&EdID=1448
Data Junction Corp.	www.datajunction.com	Data Junction	Low-cost, mature product set.	www.dmreview.com/master.cfm?NavID=198&EdID=2395
Evolutionary Technologies International, Inc.	www.eti.com	ETI*Extract	An ETL pioneer with a large installed base.	http://www.dmreview.com/master.cfm?NavID=198&EdID=2404
IBM	www.ibm.com	Visual Warehouse	A flexible toolkit for data warehouse construction. Includes basic components such as DataGuide and administration functions, as well as complementary components such as DB2 OLAP, ETI*Extract, and Vality Integrity.	ftp://ftp.software.ibm.com/ps/products/visualwarehouse/info/vw52/INSTALL.PDF
Informatica Corp.	www.informatica.com	PowerMart	If there is an "800-pound gorilla" in ETL, Informatica is it. The vendor has consistently enhanced and expanded its product set and has a very large customer base.	www.intelligententerprise.com/db_area/archives/1999/993003/products.shtml
Informix Corp.	www.ardent.com	Ardent DataStage, DataStage XE/390	Ardent is a relatively recent acquisition of Informix. XE/390 is mainframe (MVS)-focused.	www.dmreview.com/master.cfm?NavID=198&EdID=2419
Microsoft Corp.	www.microsoft.com	SQL Server Data Transformation Services	Bundled with SQL Server. Low cost-of-ownership solution. Can be used with other DBMSs as source and target. Transform logic is coded in VBScript or JavaScript.	msdn.microsoft.com/library/default.asp?URL=/library/techart/dts_overview.htm
Oracle Corp.	www.oracle.com	Oracle Warehouse Builder	Result of the acquisition of established ETL vendor Carleton Corp. by Oracle in 1999.	www.dmreview.com/master.cfm?NavID=198&EdID=2433

Table 11.14 Knowledge Management Software

Company	Company URL	Product	Angle	Info Links
Autonomy Corp.	*www.autonomy.com*	Autonomy Server	Autonomy's product line is built on its Dynamic Reasoning Engine™, which uses pattern matching, statistical, and data mining (i.e., neural network) technologies to identify and classify concepts in groups of documents.	*www.intelligententerprise.com/ db_area/archives/1999/992112/ feat1.shtml* *www.intelligententerprise.com/ 001205/decision.shtml*
Semio Corp.	*www.semio.com*	Semio Taxonomy	Semio holds patents in its core computational semiotics, or linguistics processing, technology (hence the company's name).	*http://www.intelligentkm.com/ feature/010101feat1.shtml*
Verity, Inc.	*www.verity.com*	Verity Intelligent Classifier	The Intelligent Classifier is the core component of the Verity product line. It supports what Verity calls a "hybrid approach"— a combination of human-controlled and automatic classification processes.	*http://www.dmreview.com/ master.cfm?NavID=198&EdID =2656*

Table 11.15 Application Server Software

Company	Company URL	Product	Angle	Info Links
Art Technology Group, Inc.	www.atg.com	ATG Dynamo Application Server	Dynamo implements the full Java 2 Enterprise Edition (J2EE) infrastructure, and Wireless Access Protocol (WAP).	www.planetit.com/techcenters/docs/ enterprise_apps_systems-data _management/product_review/ PIT20001227S0018 www.atg.com/customers/ case_studies/case_main.html
BEA Systems, Inc.	www.beasys.com	WebLogic	WebLogic utilizes TUXEDO (another acquisition of BEA), a mature middleware product, for data integration.	www.intelligententerprise.com/ 010101/dozen/infrastructure .shtml serverwatch.internet.com/ reviews/app-weblogic.html
IBM	www.ibm.com	WebSphere	Available in Standard, Advanced, and Enterprise editions. Advanced Edition adds EJB; Enterprise Edition adds EJB and CORBA support. Integrated with VisualAge for Java.	serverwatch.internet.com/reviews/ app-websphere.html#whatsnew

B2C E-Commerce Servers

This category consists of software suites that enable online retail sites (see Table 11.16). Must-have functions include order management, product catalog presentation, and personalization. E-commerce servers were discussed in Chapter 10.

B2B E-Commerce Servers

B2B e-commerce server vendors (see Table 11.17) have also been fertile ground for extension into data-integration technologies. A prime example is the acquisition of Active Software (an EAI vendor) by WebLogic. A critical function in all B2B servers is translating between languages, such as EDI and XML, and between dialects within languages. E-commerce servers were discussed in Chapter 10.

Middleware and Enterprise Application Integration

Products in this category (see Table 11.18) range from messaging middleware to full-functioned EAI. These technologies were presented in Chapter 6.

Relational DBMS

Relational DBMSs continue to be the workhorses of e-commerce. The major vendors listed in Table 11.19 have continued to add functionality to their products, such as messaging, OLAP, and data warehousing. New developments in relational DBMSs were discussed in Chapters 5 and 7.

Table 11.16 B2C E-Commerce Server Software

Company	Company URL	Product	Angle	Info Links
Blue Martini Software	*www.bluemartini.com*	Customer Interaction System	The Customer Interaction System is the Swiss Army knife of B2C servers. In addition to basic customer-interaction capabilities, it also includes data warehousing, data mining, and call center modules. Built on top of BEA WebLogic.	*www.intelligententerprise.com/ 000626/e_business.shtml*
BroadVision, Inc.	*www.broadvision.com*	One-to-One Enterprise	BroadVision is the B2C front-runner.	*www.informationweek.com/802/ vision.htm*

Table 11.17 B2B E-Commerce Server Software

Company	Company URL	Product	Angle	Info Links
Microsoft Corp.	*www.microsoft .com*	BizTalk Server	Built on SQL Server and Windows 2000, includes workflow functionality, XML document management, business-event logging, and reporting.	*http://www.xmlmag.com/ upload/free/features/xml/2000/ 05win00/bt0005/bt0005.asp*
eXcelon Corp.	*www.exceloncorp .com*	B2B Integration Server	eXcelon also provides consulting services in conjunction with their products.	*www.ies.aust.com/~ieinfo/ ten09.htm#_XML_FOR_B2B_1*
WebMethods	*www.webmethods .com*	WebMethods B2B	WebMethods acquired integration (EAI) vendor Active Software.	

Table 11.18 Middleware and EAI Software

Company	Company URL	Product	Angle	Info Links
CrossWorlds Software, Inc.	*www.crossworlds.com*	CrossWorlds	A full-functioned EAI product family with a hub-and-spoke architecture, built on top of IBM MQSeries.	*www.eaijournal.com/PDF/Crossworlds.pdf*
IBM	*www.ibm.com*	MQSeries	The most mature messaging middleware product.	*www.eaijournal.com/PDF/MQ%20Transaction%20Analysis%20-%20Tseng.pdf* *www.intelligenteai.com/feature/12/feat1.shtml*
Iona Technologies	*www.iona.com*	Orbix 2000	A CORBA-based object broker.	*www.eaijournal.com/news/article.asp?article=368*
Mercator Software, Inc.	*www.mercator.com*	Mercator Enterprise Broker	Full-functioned EAI solution that can run over a number of messaging products, including MQSeries and MSMQ.	*www.intelligenteai.com/feature/12/feat1.shtml* *www.informationweek.com/780/mercator.htm*
Microsoft Corp.	*www.microsoft.com*	Microsoft Message Queueing (MSMQ)	Messaging middleware for Microsoft-centric solutions.	*www.microsoft.com/msmq/features.htm*

Table 11.19 Relational DBMS Software

Company	Company URL	Product	Angle	Info Links
IBM	*www.ibm.com*	DB2	The only real relational database alternative for mainframes, and giving Oracle a run for its money on UNIX. Keeping up with features including multimedia, data warehousing, and data mining.	*www.intelligententerprise.com/000929/feat1.shtml*
Microsoft Corp.	*www.microsoft.com*	SQL Server 2000	Never has so much database-related software been offered to so many for such a low cost. One large differentiator of SQL Server is that so much software comes with it—most notably Data Transformation Services and Analysis Services. Buy a DBMS, get ETL, OLAP, and data mining thrown in too. On the downside—surprise!—SQL Server runs on Windows operating systems only.	*www.dmreview.com/master.cfm?NavID=198&EdID=698*
Oracle Corp.	*www.oracle.com*	Oracle 9i	Continues to leapfrog with IBM DB2 in expanding its scope—now includes messaging, data warehousing, and an application server. Licensing and pricing policies continue to be a source of contention with customers.	*www.intelligententerprise.com/000929/feat1.shtml*

Java and Object-Oriented Development

Software design and development functions provided by the products listed in Table 11.20 were presented in Chapter 10.

XML Development

XML development products (Table 11.21) can be used to create, map, and manage XML document formats and transformations. XML was discussed in Chapter 6.

Meta-data Management

The market in software products for meta-data management (Table 11.22), or "Repository with a capital R," has largely stagnated since 1999. This is a combination of market fragmentation (many ETL and reporting tools have their own meta-data facilities) and lack of strong direction from the larger players. Meta-data issues were presented in Chapters 4 and 7.

Database Administration Tools

DBMS products typically do not attempt to provide complete support for administration of the large, dynamic databases typical of today's e-commerce environments. Products such as those listed in Table 11.23 provide functions of this type, including change management, performance management and tuning, service level management, and recovery management.

Table 11.20 Java and Object-Oriented Development Software

Company	Company URL	Product	Angle	Info Links
Rational Software Corp.	*www.rational.com*	Rose 2000	Rational is on the leading edge of OO and UML development.	*www.sdmagazine.com/articles/ 2000/0004/0004h/0004h.htm*
Thought, Inc.	*www.thoughtinc.com*	CocoBase Enterprise O/R	A relative newcomer. Java-to-Relational mapping product that automatically generates EJB Entity Beans.	*www.sys-con.com/java/index2 .html* *www.thoughtinc.com/ MappingConcepts.pdf*
IBM	*www.ibm.com*	Visual Age for Java	An integrated development environment (IDE) for Java applications.	*www.sys-con.com/java/index2 .html*
WebGain	*www.webgain.com*	TOPLink	A Java-to-Relational mapping product that automatically generates EJB Entity Beans.	*www.sys-con.com/java/index2 .html* *www.bea.com/events/ EMEAConference/2000/ presentations/applications/ Mike_Norman.ppt*

Table 11.21 XML Development Software

Company	Company URL	Product	Angle	Info Links
Altova, Inc.	www.xmlspy.com	XML Spy 3.5	A reasonably priced integrated development environment (IDE) for XML. Includes editing and validation functions for XML Schema and XSL. Large and growing customer base.	www.sdmagazine.com/articles/ 2001/0102/0102d/0102d.htm
Data Junction Corp.	www.datajunction.com	XML Junction	Low cost-of-ownership solution for creating XML documents from other data formats. Built on the mature Data Junction product technology.	www.infoworld.com/articles/ ec/xml/00/04/24/ 000424ecjunction.xml www.wallstreetandtech.com/ story/supp/WST20000907S0016
eXcelon Corp.	www.exceloncorp.com	Stylus	A WYSIWYG editor for XSL stylesheets.	www.sys-con.com/xml/archives/ 0106/liptak/index.html
Microsoft Corp.	www.microsoft.com	BizTalk Editor, BizTalk Mapper	These are components of BizTalk Server. The Editor is used to define message layouts; the Mapper is used to define mappings and translations between source and target layouts—similar to an ETL tool.	www.intelligententerprise.com/ 000818feat1.shtml

Table 11.22 Meta-data Management Software

Company	Company URL	Product	Angle	Info Links
Computer Associates International, Inc.	*www.ca.com*	Platinum Repository	Platinum Repository is the most mature and widely used stand-alone meta-data product—evidenced by the retention of the name. CA acquired Platinum in 1999 and unfortunately has done little with this product since.	*www.dmreview.com/master .cfm?NavID=198&EdID=98*
IBM	*www.ibm.com*	DataGuide	DataGuide is part of the IBM Visual Warehouse product family. Quite reasonably priced, it provides a very good (although labor-intensive to set up) interface for juxtaposing meta-data and access to data sources.	*www.dbmsmag.com/9708d16 .html*
Microsoft Corporation	*www.microsoft.com*	Meta Data Services	Formerly the Microsoft Repository, this software is bundled with SQL Server. Due to identity problems, a developer (rather than business user) focus, and a severe lack of usable input and output interfaces, it is not living up to its potential.	*www.microsoft.com/sql/ productinfo/meta-data.htm*
Allen Systems Group, Inc.	*www.asg.com*	ASG-Rochade	Rochade was the pioneer client-server meta-data repository product, with a broad range of scanners for transforming various meta-data sources. It was acquired by Allen Systems Group as a result of its acquisition of ViaSoft.	*www.dmreview.com/master .cfm?NavID=198&EdID=2280*

Table 11.23 Database Administration Software

Company	Company URL	Product	Angle	Info Links
BMC Software, Inc.	www.bmc.com	MAINVIEW for DB2	BMC's PATROL family of products offers a wide range of data- and systems-management products across a number of diverse platforms. Its MAINVIEW for DB2 provides real-time and historical performance data from multiple DB2 systems in one display.	www.bmc.com/rs-bin/RightSite/getcontent/bmcdoc.pdf?dmw_objectid=0900320180 2a0607&dmw_format=pdf
Computer Associates, Inc.	www.ca.com	ManageIT	ManageIT combines the Platinum ProVision suite of products with CA's agent technology.	www.ca.com/analyst/meta_manageit.pdf
Precise Software	www.precisesoft.com	Precise/SQL	Precise/SQL is a graphical monitoring and performance-management product for Oracle environments.	www.dmreview.com/master.cfm?NavID=198&EdID=1028
Quest Software, Inc.	www.quest.com	Toad	The unfortunately-named Toad is a standard and reasonably-priced toolset widely used by Oracle DBAs and developers.	www.quest.com/case_studies/verifone_study.asp

Appendix

HOW TO READ A
DATA MODEL DIAGRAM

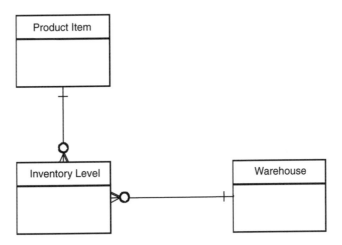

Figure A–1
A typical data model diagram.

Figure A–1 illustrates a standard data model diagram. This particular diagram includes:

Three *entities*—things about which a business needs to keep data—represented as labeled boxes.

Two *relationships* among the three entities—represented as lines between the entities.

Relationship lines are interpreted as follows:

The three-line "crows feet" indicate "many," a single line indicates "one."

The circle indicates "may have," the short line crossing indicates "must have."

Therefore, according to the diagram:

A Product Item *may have one or more* Inventory Levels.

An Inventory Level *must relate to one* Product Item.

A Warehouse *may have one or more* Inventory Levels.

An Inventory Level *must relate to one* Warehouse.

BIBLIOGRAPHY AND RECOMMENDED READING

Alhir, Sinan Si, *UML in a Nutshell*. O'Reilly and Associates, 1998.

Berry, Michael J. A, and Linoff, Gordon, *Data Mining Techniques for Marketing, Sales and Customer Support*. John Wiley & Sons, 1997.

Boar, Bernard H., *The Art of Strategic Planning for Information Technology, Second Edition*. John Wiley & Sons, 2000.

Brackett, Michael H., *Data Sharing Using a Common Data Architecture*. John Wiley & Sons, 1994.

Brooks, Frederick P. Jr., The Mythical Man-Month: Essays on Software Engineering, Second Edition, Addison-Wesley, 1995.

Christner, Bart, *MESPIN DESIGN 101*. Media Specifications Institute, manuscript, 2001.

Connelly, Robert; McNeill, Robin; Mosimann, Roland, *The Multidimensional Manager*. Cognos Inc.

Date, C. J., *What Not How The Business Rules Approach to Application Development*. Addison-Wesley, 2000.

Dobbs, John, "Competition's New Battleground: The Integrated Value Chain," Cambridge Technology Partners, 1999.

English, Larry, *Improving Data Warehouse and Business Information Quality: Methods for Reducing Costs and Increasing Profits*. John Wiley & Sons, 1999.

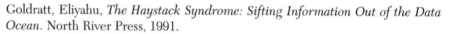

Goldratt, Eliyahu, *The Haystack Syndrome: Sifting Information Out of the Data Ocean*. North River Press, 1991.

Haynes, Ted, *The Electronic Commerce Dictionary: The Definitive Terms for Doing Business on the Information Superhighway*. Robleda Co., 1995.

Inmon, William H., *Building the Data Warehouse, Second Edition*. John Wiley & Sons, 1996.

Kalikota, Ravi and Whinston, Andrew B., *Frontiers of Electronic Commerce*. Addison-Wesley, 1996.

Kaplan, Robert S. and Norton, David P., *The Balanced Scorecard: Translating Strategy into Action*. Harvard Business School Press, 1996.

Kimball, Ralph and Merz, Richard, *The Data Webhouse Toolkit*. John Wiley & Sons, 2000.

Linthicum, David S., *Enterprise Application Integration*. Addison-Wesley, 1999.

Mullins, Craig, *DB2 Developer's Guide*, 4th ed. SAMS, 2000.

Object Management Group, *OMG Unified Modeling Language Specification*.

Perrone, Paul and Chaganti, Venkata S.R.K.R., *Building Java Enterprise Systems with J2EE*. Sams, 2000

Porter, Michael E., *Competitive Advantage: Creating and Sustaining Superior Performance*. Free Press, 1998.

Ross, Ronald G., *Business Rule Concepts*. Business Rule Solutions, Inc., 1998.

Schuldt, Ron, *The Universal Data Element Framework (UDEF). www.udef.com*.

Scully, Arthur B. and Woods, W. William A., *B2B Exchanges: The Killer Application in the Business-to-Business Internet Revolution*. ISI Publications Limited, 2000.

Seiner, Robert (Editor and Publisher), *The Data Administration Newsletter (TDAN). www.tdan.com*.

Simon, Alan, *Data Warehousing for Dummies*. Hungry Minds Inc., 1997.

The Middleware Company, *The Technical Benefits of EJB and J2EE Technologies over COM+ and Windows DNA*.

Tipler, Frank J., *The Physics of Immortality: Modern Cosmology, God and the Resurrection of the Dead*. Anchor Bible, 1995.

Zachman, John A. and Sowa, J. F., "Extending and Formalizing the Framework for Information Systems Architecture." IBM Systems Journal, vol. 31, no. 3, 1992.

INDEX

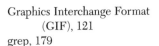

Index

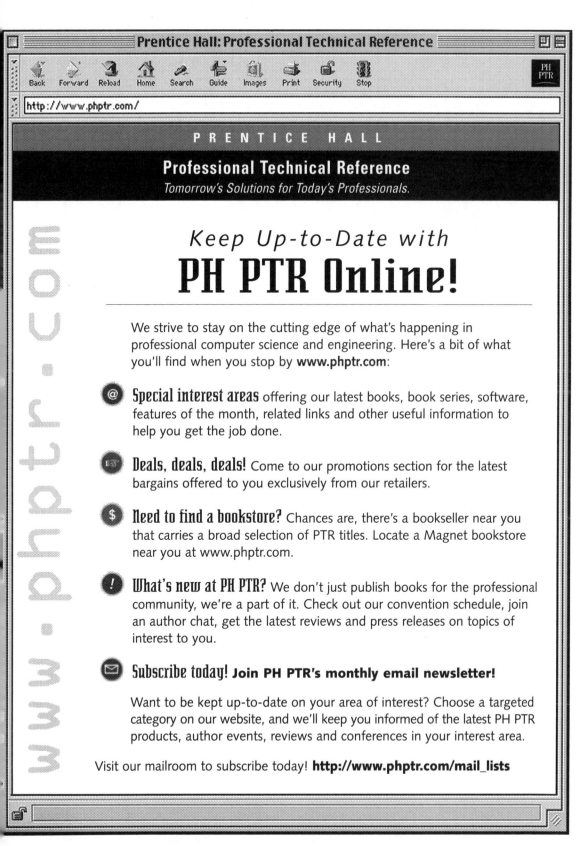

Prentice Hall: Professional Technical Reference

http://www.phptr.com/

PRENTICE HALL

Professional Technical Reference
Tomorrow's Solutions for Today's Professionals.

Keep Up-to-Date with
PH PTR Online!

We strive to stay on the cutting edge of what's happening in professional computer science and engineering. Here's a bit of what you'll find when you stop by **www.phptr.com**:

Special interest areas offering our latest books, book series, software, features of the month, related links and other useful information to help you get the job done.

Deals, deals, deals! Come to our promotions section for the latest bargains offered to you exclusively from our retailers.

Need to find a bookstore? Chances are, there's a bookseller near you that carries a broad selection of PTR titles. Locate a Magnet bookstore near you at www.phptr.com.

What's new at PH PTR? We don't just publish books for the professional community, we're a part of it. Check out our convention schedule, join an author chat, get the latest reviews and press releases on topics of interest to you.

Subscribe today! Join PH PTR's monthly email newsletter!

Want to be kept up-to-date on your area of interest? Choose a targeted category on our website, and we'll keep you informed of the latest PH PTR products, author events, reviews and conferences in your interest area.

Visit our mailroom to subscribe today! **http://www.phptr.com/mail_lists**

www.phptr.com

ibliothè ques | Library Netw
Univ ity

InformIT

Solutions from experts you know and trust.

| Articles | Free Library | eBooks | Expert Q & A | Training | Career Center | Downloads | MyInformIT |

Login   Register   About InformIT

Topics

Operating Systems
Web Development
Programming
Networking
Certification
and more...

www.informit.com

✓ Free, in-depth articles and supplements

✓ Master the skills you need, when you need them

✓ Choose from industry leading books, ebooks, and training products

✓ Get answers when you need them - from live experts or InformIT's comprehensive library

✓ Achieve industry certification and advance your career

Expert Access

Free Content

Visit *InformIT* today and get great content from PH PTR

Prentice Hall and InformIT are trademarks of Pearson plc /
Copyright © 2000 Pearson